Property Div

Property is more diverse than is usu
of property diversity, this book exp
placed human landscapes. In acknowl
us, the book highlights the paucity of
tions of property as defined by priv
universalizing model, the book analy
produces critical blind spots in modern p
offers a re-conceptualization of property th
of our rich and diverse relationships with la
real property types (private, public and co
standings of both interest and ownersh
substantiates an overarching theory of propert
ies from numerous jurisdictions, including
Australia, and the UK, its analysis of property
indeed other – than a place-less abstraction prov
bution to the contemporary law and theory of pro

John Page is a Senior Lecturer in Property La
University, Australia.

Property Diversity and its Implications

John Page

Routledge
Taylor & Francis Group
a GlassHouse Book

First published 2017
by Routledge
2 Park Square, Milton Park, Abingdon, Oxon, OX14 4RN

and by Routledge
711 Third Avenue, New York, NY 10017

a GlassHouse book

Routledge is an imprint of the Taylor & Francis Group, an informa business

British Library Cataloguing in Publication Data
A catalogue record for this book is available from the British Library

Library of Congress Cataloging-in-Publication Data
Names: Page, John (Law teacher)
Title: Property diversity and its implications / John Page.
Description: Abingdon, Oxon ; New York, NY : Routledge, 2016. | Based on author's thesis (doctoral - University of Queensland, 2014) issued under title: The implications of property diversity. | Includes bibliographical references and index.
Identifiers: LCCN 2016005767| ISBN 9781138193543 (hbk) | ISBN 9781315639307 (ebk)
Subjects: LCSH: Property—Philosophy.
Classification: LCC K720 .P34 2016 | DDC 333.3—dc23
LC record available at http://lccn.loc.gov/2016005767

ISBN: 978-1-138-19354-3 (hbk)
ISBN: 978-1-315-63930-7 (ebk)

Typeset in Baskerville by
by FiSH Books Ltd, Enfield

Contents

List of figures and tables

Figures

Table

Acknowledgements

Writing this book has been a labour of love. It has been a long, deeply satisfying journey to reach the diverse 'forest' lurking amongst the propertied 'trees'.

My first thanks go to Dr Ann Brower, who opened my eyes to property's potential in a tramper's hut, high above Lake Tekapo in New Zealand's remote, serenely beautiful backcountry. My second thanks go to Professor Ross Grantham, whose patience, wisdom and scholarly friendship proved great counsel over 5 plus years. My third thanks extend to Professors Margaret Davies and Eric Freyfogle, my thesis examiners, whose enthusiastic words of encouragement propelled me to this point. My final thanks, of course, go to my dear family, Myeka, Nicholas and Henry, who have shared the fun, adventures and laughs along the way.

An earlier version of Chapter 2 was published in *Modern Studies in Property Law* (7th edition 2013, Hart Publishing, Oxford).

Any errors and omissions are entirely my own.

John Page
Lismore, New South Wales, Australia
January, 2016

Introduction

Lawyers and non-lawyers alike derive great comfort in the much-vaunted stability of property in land. It is a dependable institution, often dull, sometimes arcane. Without giving it too much thought, we tend to respond to property in conventional, unreflective ways. We assume with property that 'what we see is what we get' (Rose 1994, p.297).

However, this unimaginative way of looking at property in land may be but a half-truth of a little-scrutinized dialectic. Perhaps, property is a lot more diverse than the orthodoxy supposes? This question forms the core premise of this book, the elaboration of an alternative description of property in land I call *property diversity*. This book argues that the descriptive truth of property, its grounded reality, is far more heterogeneous than we are conditioned to recognize. What we have got with property in land is what 'we have talked ourselves into seeing' (ibid.), a monotone where rights are private and its implications are universalizing. Contrary to this descriptively inadequate model, human landscapes are 'intensely propertied places' (Blomley 2004, p.xvi) where a plethora of rights, uses and claims overlap, compete and co-exist amidst inter-connective mosaics of private, public and common interests in land. These 'interests' are themselves equally diverse, ancient as well as novel, common law and statutory, shared and exclusive. And to complete the mosaic, our 'ownerships' are likewise pluralistic, ranging from strictly enforceable right through to vague concepts of belonging, illusory at law, yet routinely acted upon. In its rich, networked totality, this imaginative, open-ended 'seeing' of property in land comprises *property diversity*.

This book's early inspiration came from American property scholar Carol Rose, and her under-regarded notion of 'seeing' property in land, a phenomenon especially observable in places of great natural beauty, 'imperious landscapes' where property 'hits you in the eye' (Rose 1994). Rose describes seeing property in diverse forms, as pictures, metaphors, narratives or illusions. For her, the fence, well-trodden path, keep out sign, bundle of sticks, or folkloric tales of scarcity, are convenient ways of 'seeing' property, easily recognizable images that enable us to relate to the places in which we live. Canadian legal geographer Nicholas Blomley is another seminal influence. Blomley uses a neighbourhood in his home city of Vancouver, British Colombia, to 'map' the unreliability of the private ownership model to represent the lived experiences of its inhabitants.

Critically, to begin to 'see' property in the expansive and imaginative ways that Rose envisages, or Blomley endeavours to 'map', reveals certain self-evident truths about property in land. This enhanced visibility renders itself incrementally to the patient observer, a re-imagination that ultimately offers an alternative account of property in land. As a reconceptualization, it provides a more contextual explanation, a description of property patterns at a level of detail and accuracy that the 'existing' private ownership model can only begin to sketch out.

The book has a number of objectives. First, it seeks to explain why a narrow private ownership model of property prevails, such that 'property' and 'private property' are for most purposes synonymous. Both dominant and domineering, this singular liberal view stresses the primacy of individualism, the power of exclusion and the values of commodity. If represented geographically, this paradigm depicts only the boundaries of private parcels, the arbitrary de-contextualized lines that pre-figure the extent of an owner's right to exclude. Second, it argues that this perspective is an inadequate and incomplete description of property in land, canvassing the richness of the public and common estates, and the under-regarded social and communitarian nuances of private property (Alexander 2014). Third, and centrally, it describes a theory of property diversity in land, an articulation more representative of Hanoch Dagan's 'lived experiences' of property (Dagan 2011). Fourth, it considers in turn the countervailing implications of property monism and diversity for certain blind spots in modern property discourse, the proprietorial place of community, and the generation of obligation as an incident of land ownership. The book suggests that a simplistically private view of property in land yields normatively undesirable outcomes. However, it is not its intent to make the normative argument that we ought not to 'see' property in land through this hegemonic view. Instead, its focus is to identify these descriptive failings, to offer up an alternative vision, and to explore a number of implications of a reconceived diverse property mosaic.

Property diversity is described in detail in Chapter 4. But given its amorphous nature, and the book's incremental structure, it is desirable in this Introduction to offer a brief, overarching description of the concept. Property diversity *sees* the fullest range of property patterns in human landscapes, a higher altitude perspective that yields an unfamiliar vantage of a familiar subject. Importantly, it places the orthodox private right in proportionate context, amongst other less seen and less familiar property forms. Property diversity is the aggregate of a plurality of *types*, *interests* and *ownerships*. Characteristically, it is *contextual*, *multivalent*, *use*-premised and *eclectic*, amongst other attributes. Our many and varied relationships with land define its scope and form its content.

Type refers to the full panoply of existing private, public and common interests in land, and the many hybrid variants that arise in response to context or exigency. *Interests* comprise the vast array of 'estates' we hold in land: corporeal, incorporeal, common law, statutory, customary or *sui generis*. *Ownership* describes the vested interests we claim over land, the full gamut of propriety ranging from enforceable right under Joseph Singer's 'castle' view (2006), to qualified forms of private ownership tempered by norms of social-obligation (Alexander 2009), 'ownerships' based on public and common title, and beyond right, to vague concepts of belonging.

Contextual qualities of diverse property make the *res* the central object of the landed relationship. It defies the ubiquity of the bundle metaphor, where any stick can be substituted for another. John Lovett cites the Land Reform (Scotland) Act 2003 (LRSA) as an innovative exemplar of a property regime that *contextualizes* a new property right, the 'responsible right of access', to particular place. The LRSA overcomes an 'imaginative paralysis … about what is possible in property law design' (Lovett 2010, p.742).[1] Much like real property's 'extraordinary return to the land'[2] (Farran 2013), working examples of re-physicalized and diverse property dilutes the hegemonic paradigm. Context also de-emphasizes the importance of arbitrary boundary lines. Analogous to Larissa Katz's 'agenda-setting' (Katz 2008), diverse property prioritizes an owner's *use* of their land, not its bounded dominion. When exercised in ways that are reasonable and proportionate, *use* enlivens the potential of other owners to enjoy co-existing, contemporaneous rights in the same land.

The LRSA also actualizes a property regime that incorporates *multiple values*, another key characteristic of diverse property. That public rights of responsible access can be accommodated with an owner's privacy and security of residential use, demonstrates that competing values need not be mutually exclusive. And finally, the *eclecticism* of diverse property, perhaps an inevitable corollary of context, is another defining attribute. Escaping the closed list of 'what is property' in land requires an awareness of the 'otherness' in real property, and a willingness to consider the proprietorial attributes of erstwhile marginal interests (van der Walt 2010).

The book is structured in two parts. Part I argues that the hegemonic depiction of property in land is inaccurate and incomplete. In so arguing, Part I seeks to clear a theoretical space for a different conceptualization, the diverse property mosaic. In Chapter 1, private property is shown to be an adaptable institution (Dagan 2011), more qualified than its absolutist rhetoric suggests. The chapter challenges private property's exclusion thesis,[3] arguing that the right to exclude is inherently contingent, and as such capacious of other co-existing interests in land. In Chapter 2, public property is described not as a passive *res* awaiting capture, but an under-regarded estate with its own tenets and rationales, a comedy where 'the more the merrier' diffuses ownership and fosters propriety in the pursuit of an egalitarian, well-ordered society (Rose 1986). In Chapter 3, common property is seen to be different again, a halfway house, where an outside private shell conceals an inside communitarian collective. Common property manifests in unlikely, but everyday places – sporting clubs, community associations, company title units, and so on – its obviousness and under-estimated strengths giving lie to the overstated tragedy of the commons.

Part I adopts an accepted but not universal typology of property interests in land: *private, common* and *public.* What distinguishes one form of property from another is – to borrow a bundle analogy – 'how the quality and content of the bundle of rights varies in practice, and who holds the sticks' (Barnes 2009, p.11). With private property, the 'who' question is fairly straightforward. Jeremy Waldron describes this as the 'single organizing idea' of private property that a 'certain specified person is able to determine how a specified resource is to be used' (Waldron 1991, pp.59–60).

While private property is relatively uncontested,[4] there is far greater misapprehension, about the meaning, extent, and even identity of the common and public estates. Michael Brill (2002) says that common property provides for a 'community life', while public property provides for a 'public life'. Common property is not public property; it refers to use rights vested in community members who derive their propertied relationship with land through membership of that community. Outsiders are trespassers on common lands. By contrast, the 'who' in public property is less clear. Chapter 2 posits that ultimately the 'who' is the diffused 'unorganized public'.

Having cleared some theoretical space, Part II then proceeds to fill it with the exponential notion of property diversity, and (at least) several of its implications. In Chapter 4, the mosaic is particularized and deconstructed; its underlying principles, unifying themes and constituent elements canvassed in separate turn. Chapter 5 next locates property diversity, in the literature of sustainable communities, and the lived practice of three *in situ* case studies. These studies note a serendipitous coincidence between sustainable, so-called 'livable' communities, and their diverse patterns of property. The chapter does not argue that property diversity is a cause of such livability, but it does observe its otherwise unremarked presence. The chapter ends in an ambitious attempt to depict property diversity in pictorial form. Chapter 6 then examines the routine failure of the private ownership model to generate obligation alongside right as an incident of land ownership. By contrast, property diversity in Chapter 7 offers a paradigm where obligation is both theoretically feasible and normatively desirable, where stewardship is less likely to remain the law's 'awkward little secret' (Sax 1984). Chapter 8 concludes with an analysis of our underdeveloped proprietorial relationship with community, a consequence of a polarizing liberal paradigm that views community as a suspicious intermediary between the welfare-maximizing individual and the regulatory state. Again, it offers an alternative view, one where community has a resonance that helps to fill Joseph Sax's 'blank legal space'. Describing property in land in ways that connect people to context, rather than as abstract rights between persons about things, makes notions of community and obligation more feasible within a diverse property discourse.

Throughout this book, the word 'property' is liberally used. But in restricting itself to real property (and not for example personalty or intellectual property), the term refers only to our many propertied relationships with *land*. Its remit is broad and expansive. As foreshadowed, it encapsulates not only formal rights enforced by the state, but also uses, practices and claims observed or enforced through custom, norm or other unlikely sources outside property's 'central logic' (van der Walt 2010). Its open-ended approach to propertied interests in land is the antithesis of Wesley Hohfeld's precise taxonomy. To restrict its meanings to a closed list is to subvert a key purpose of this book, to notice van der Walt's margins, and the diversity inherent therein. To cite the Australian High Court, property is 'not a monolithic notion of standard content and invariable intensity [but] the most comprehensive of all the terms which can be used ... indicative and descriptive ... of all or any of the very many different kinds of relationship between a person and a subject matter.'[5]

This book is also deliberate in its canvassing of property diversity within the Anglo-American common law tradition. In so doing, it consciously sidelines other property traditions; in particular, native title property rights of First Nation peoples and civilian property doctrine. It does so reluctantly, but pragmatically, conceding that this elaboration of common law property diversity is in itself, paradoxically narrow. Yet, to do justice to such a vast sweep of global property is to embark on a lifetime's compendium, not a single monograph. Their valuable lessons are for another day, and perhaps other books.

As an eloquent advocate of the private right to exclude, Henry Smith is an unlikely ally to enrol in support of common law property diversity. However. Smith's observations of property as 'the law of things' are insightful and cogent. Smith writes, '[t]he first step toward understanding private law is to try not to take things for granted and to be as attentive to how things are *not* as to how things are' (2012, p.1692). This book agrees with, and seeks to enact Smith's observations. It does not take property in land for granted. It does not unthinkingly assume that 'what we see is what we get.' In large part, its attentive focus is on 'how things are not'. In unwittingly following Smith's prescriptions, its ambition is to take an imaginative step toward a better understanding of the vast and rich diversity of property in land.

Notes

1 Lovett cites extensive public education for both access takers and landowners as overcoming law and economics analyses that deride contextual property as imposing unfeasibly high information processing costs.
2 This describes the recent resurgence in places like the UK, Australia and the USA of community gardens, urban farms, community forests, guerilla gardening, and so on.
3 Private property is generally 'characterized by rights of exclusion ... while that which is characterized by rights of inclusion are termed public or common property' (Hamilton and Bankes 2010, p.26).
4 Uncertainty lies on the fringes, for example government ownership of an office building may be the practical equivalent of private ownership, but generally the 'owner answer' is clear.
5 *Yanner v. Eaton* (1999) 201 CLR 351.

References

Alexander, G 2009, 'The Social-Obligation Norm in American Property Law', *Cornell Law Rev.*, vol. 94, 745–819.

Alexander, G 2014, 'Property's Ends: The Publicness of Private Law Values', *Iowa Law Rev.*, vol. 99, 1257–96.

Barnes, R 2009, *Property Rights and Natural Resources*, Hart Publishing, Oxford.

Blomley, N 2004, *Unsettling the City: Urban Land and the Politics of Property*, Routledge, New York.

Brill, M 2002, 'Problems with Mistaking Community Life for Public Life', *Places*, vol. 14, no. 2, 48–55.

Dagan, H 2011, *Property, Values and Institutions*, Oxford University Press, New York.

Farran, S 2013, 'Earth Under the Nails: The Extraordinary Return to the Land', in N Hopkins (ed.), *Modern Studies in Property Law*, Hart Publishing, Oxford.

Hamilton, J W and Bankes, N 2010, 'Different Views of the Cathedral: The Literature on Property Law Theory', in A McHarg, B Barton, A Bradbrook and L Godden (eds), *Property and the Law in Energy and Natural Resources*, Oxford University Press, Oxford.

Katz, L 2008, 'Exclusion and Exclusivity in Property Law', *Univ. Toronto Law J.*, vol. 58, 275–315.

Lovett, J 2010, 'Progressive Property in Action: The Land Reform (Scotland) Act 2003', *Nebraska Law Rev.*, vol. 89, 739–820.

Rose, C M 1986, 'The Comedy of the Commons: Custom, Commerce, and Inherently Public Property', *Univ. Chicago Law Rev.*, vol. 53, no. 3, 711–81.

Rose, C M 1994, 'Seeing Property', in *Property and Persuasion Essays on the History, Theory, And Rhetoric of Ownership*, Westview Press, Boulder CO.

Sax, J 1984, 'The Rights of Communities: A Blank Space in American Law', presented Natural Resources Law Center, University of Colorado, School of Law, 11 July 11.

Singer, J 2006, 'The Ownership Society and Takings of Property: Castles, Investments, and Just Obligations', *Harv. Envtl. L. Rev.*, vol. 30, 309–38.

Smith, H 2012, 'Property as the Law of Things', *Harvard Law Rev.*, vol. 125, 1691–726.

Waldron, J 1991, *The Right to Private Property*, Oxford University Press, New York.
van der Walt, A J 2010, 'The Marginality of Property', in G Alexander and E Penalver (eds), *Property and Community*, Oxford University Press, New York.

Part I

The diverse private, public and common estates

Chapter 1

Private property and the domineering right to exclude

1.1 Introduction

Private property has been the dominant (and domineering) form of property in land since the eighteenth century. It has successfully marginalized and discredited alternative forms of property, such that today we see property through a myopic prism of private property rights. Hence, for most people, the terms 'property' and 'private property' are synonymous and interchangeable. This chapter challenges this narrow and incomplete description of modern private property that has conflated its reach and concealed its nuance. The chapter's aim is to better depict the private estate, and in so doing, clear sufficient space for property diversity.

The all-consuming edifice of private property, William Blackstone's famous 'sole and despotic dominion' and its hallmark right to exclude, is a structure less absolute than its persuasive rhetoric exhorts.[1] Private property was never unqualified or unfettered in its reach; public and communal rights and restraints have long defined the ambit of private rights. Likewise, the divide between public and private is (and was) porous, private rights exist in public property and public rights in private. For all its apparent and substantive dominance, a dual paradox lies at the heart of private property. First, the absoluteness of private rights, manifested in the right to exclude, is reliant on a flawed assumption that the public-private dichotomy is distinct and inviolate. This misassumption accentuates the propensity of private property rights to conflate, in the process distorting their integrity and obfuscating the coherency of private property's rationales. Second, the flawed public–private divide itself is premised on an historic interpretation of private property frozen in time. The mantra that private property must be stable and certain does not equate to its immutability. Private property is a dynamic social institution, subject to historical, social and political pressures, one that is constantly, albeit incrementally, dynamic.

The *substance* of private property is the security it affords right holders in their exclusive use and enjoyment of their rights. Yet the narrative or rhetoric of private property has diverged from this central organizing basis. Secure exclusivity of use has become exclusivity *simpliciter*, with the paramount right to exclude overshadowing the complexities and nuances of private property. Like private property itself, the right to exclude is not only singularly dominant, but domineering. This perversion has unduly distorted property discourse and fed a propensity for courts and legislatures to overstate the extent of private property rights. Private property is better understood as securing an exclusivity of use, coupled with a qualified freedom from interference, and not an arbitrary exclusivity of possession. Such a descriptive re-emphasis does not diminish the essence of private property, its security of title. However, it does enable the theoretical oxygen for other potentially co-existing property rights, uses and claims, as well as duties or obligations, to subsist. By seeing private property in such a light, we begin to see it in a pluralistic, diverse context.

In this chapter, the history of private property is analysed as it pertains to so-called 'settler societies', particularly the United States, Australia and New Zealand, beginning in section 2 with the seminal seventeenth- and eighteenth-century writings of William Blackstone and John Locke. Sections 3 and 4 then trace the shift from a pre-industrial to industrial society, and the implications and opportunities this presented to a burgeoning private estate freed from the inconvenient strictures of English property doctrine and energized by the bundle of rights metaphor. Sections 5 and 6 concentrate on the often-overlooked dynamism of private property, and the complexities that arise when stasis distorts key aspects of private property, exemplified by the public–private divide. Section 7 then considers the plausible yet descriptively flawed narrative of private property that has come to dominate, while section 8 distils the qualitative attributes of private property that form the core of its revised description. The chapter concludes by re-examining the rationales and justifications of the critical right to exclude in light of this re-defined paradigm.

1.2 Blackstone, Locke and historical origins

In charting the rise of private property and its hallmark right to exclude, it is convenient but not contrived to commence in 1765 with the *Commentaries* of William Blackstone. Blackstone wrote his *Commentaries* at a crucial era as England vigorously expanded its colonial empire. Blackstone's timely summation of the great body of common law jurisprudence enabled this important, and transportable, compendium to reach far beyond English shores, as Anglo-settler societies extended across North America and the Pacific Rim (Banner 2007). Blackstone's thinking proved foundational to many newly establishing jurisdictions (Alschuler 1996). Indeed, his summaries of the law were noetic. This was particularly so for concepts of property as nascent societies struggled with the political and social imperatives of settling vast, 'empty' hinterlands, whether in pursuit of Manifest Destiny, or more mundane, practical policies of closer settlement.[2]

Blackstone captured a notion of property that conformed to the spirit of the times, an articulation that matched the zealous conquering of frontier.

In writing of property, Blackstone famously observed:

> There is nothing which so generally strikes the imagination, and engages the affections of mankind, as the right of property; or that sole and despotic dominion which one man claims and exercises over the external things of the world, in total exclusion of the right of any other individual in the universe.
>
> ('Of the rights of things, of property in general', Book II, Ch. 1, cited in Jones 1973, p.119)

Unsurprisingly, much emphasis was placed on Blackstone's 'sole and despotic' prescription to justify an absolutist, highly individualized and exclusive notion of property in settler societies. Moreover, his definition divorced property from the things of the external world. But as Carol Rose observes (1998b), Blackstone's definitive assertion (Rose calls it the 'Exclusivity Axiom') was immediately followed by his own doubts as to the origin of such seemingly unequivocal rights, what Rose terms Blackstone's 'Ownership Anxiety'.

> And yet there are very few, that will give themselves the trouble to consider the origin and foundation of this right. Pleased as we are with the possession, we seem afraid to look back to the means by which it was acquired, as if fearful of some defect in title ... We think it enough that our title is derived by the grant of the former proprietor ... not caring to reflect that (accurately and strictly speaking) there is no foundation in nature or in natural law, why a set of words upon parchment should convey the dominion of land; why the son should have a right to exclude his fellow creatures from a determinate spot of ground.

Rose argues that the problem is that not enough property jurists have read that *much* Blackstone. 'If those who quote Blackstone's definition read further, they might come to think that Blackstone posed his definition more as a metaphor than a literal description ... a point of departure' (Rose 1998b, p.602). Indeed, had scholars headlined the later line in the same chapter, 'so it is agreed ... that occupancy gave ... the original right to the permanent property in the substance of the earth itself; which excludes everyone else but the owner *from the use of it*' (emphasis added), then perhaps property rights may well have taken on more usufruct-like characteristics. Rose concludes that Blackstone's 'Exclusivity Axiom' is a metaphoric over-statement, a 'trope', that 'conceal[s] the interactive character of property and give[s] an inappropriately individualistic patina to this most sociable of human institutions' (Rose 1998b, p.632).

Yet, it is not just Blackstone's text that was problematic, it was also the context in which he wrote. As Eric Freyfogle notes, Blackstone had different ideas about 'dominion' derived from late-eighteenth century English agrarian society, than we may understand the term in a twenty-first century urban environment. Freyfogle argues 'dominion' to Blackstone meant 'the right to quiet enjoyment ... the right to halt any appreciable interference by a neighbor' (Freyfogle 2003, p.68). Pointedly this did not equate to the absolute right to exclude. Rather it contemplated contexts where multiple rights co-existed lawfully, where reasonable co-enjoyment was implied, but unreasonable interference with another's peaceful use and enjoyment was an actionable breach of 'dominion'. Rose likewise factors in context, positing that Blackstone was aware of how feudal and entailed limitations on estates, and the obligations of riparian and nuisance law, 'seriously' qualified the extent of an owner's dominion (Rose 1998b, p.603). Murray Raff (1998) cites the not-so-distant English Revolution as one reason why the power to exclude would have been foremost on Blackstone's mind – the power to exclude the Crown. Even Blackstone himself, the alleged absolutist, acknowledges waste and nuisance as a contextually legal limit on a private owner's dominion.

More significantly, Blackstone's 'context' was one where non-exclusive property rights subsisted and co-existed with private rights. While the enclosure movement had gained considerable momentum in the second half of the eighteenth century, common property rights were still widespread. The myopia that 'property' and 'private property' were synonymous and interchangeable terms had not taken hold, rather property existed in more diverse forms. But Blackstone's 'sole and despotic' refrain became private property's 'sound bite'. Like most sound bites, they sell perception, a message, not substance or nuance. This message, Rose's 'trope', proved too successful, thereby informing and distorting an absolutist exclusive notion of private property, to the detriment of its qualified nuance.

If William Blackstone articulated a key, albeit selective, mantra, John Locke provided the theoretical underpinning for private property in the crucial early phases of settler society. Indeed, Lockean notions of property continue to stress the primacy of individual dominion, and are often used to describe politically conservative approaches to private property rights. Locke wrote a century before Blackstone, but his themes of the inherent worth of individual labour struck an especial chord in republican America.

> The basic Lockean system of property as a license for unlimited individual accumulation via unilateral action has held a powerful place in the American pantheon of political thought since the Revolution.
>
> (Raymond 2003, p.45)

According to Locke, ownership of one's own body was the starting point to justify the private ownership of external things. When one mixed individual labour with things found in the common fund, or natural world, something of value was created. Morally the fruits of one's labour justified that 'thing' being owned by the person whose labour had created it. This transfer of ownership was good for both the individual and the collective whole, improving land adds value (by ten-fold in Locke's estimation), an apt political narrative. Some value owned by an individual is better than no value owned by the collective. Locke's labour theory corroborated the individual acquisition of private property transformed by 'sweat equity', and provided a powerful, albeit naïve, justification for private property. But Locke also recognized the qualifications to his theory of property, the oft-cited proviso that there remained 'enough and as good' land for others, and that there was to be no wasteful surplus in one's acquisition, no 'spoilage'. Absolutism, even at the frontier, was always tempered by limit and restraint.

The Lockean vision of an 'agrarian democracy of small, self-sufficient property owners' (Fairfax et al. 2005, p.16) proved more potent in its rhetoric than its reality, as settler societies continued to evolve. Its rhetoric of rugged individualism, however, has remained a resilient image for the institution of private property, and much like Blackstone's 'sole and despotic dominion' developed noetic qualities that continue to speak to simplistic absolutism rather than complex subtlety.

1.3 The expansion of private property in settler societies

Informed by Blackstonian and Lockean ideals, the subsequent expansion of private property in settler societies in the late eighteenth and early nineteenth centuries was driven in large part by two contemporaneous influences: the political imperative of government to encourage closer settlement, and the desire for secure and durable property rights on the part of the new settler. The political imperative was nation-building; fledgling colonies or republics such as Australia, New Zealand and the USA were encouraging their citizens or subjects to settle the so-called 'wastelands' in ways that corroborated Locke's labour theory. Rewarding working on the frontier with land on the frontier seemed an equitable and efficient means of achieving Manifest Destiny, particularly where unoccupied land was perceived as a liability or weak point in the new colony or nation (Bromley 2000). Because unoccupied land carried a negative value to the Crown or federal government, giving it away to those who would strengthen the nation geographically and economically made sense. In the latter regard, the Lockean view of ownership also intersected with the classical economic view of efficient use of resources.

The second half of the equation was a desire on the part of the waves of new settlers to *acquire* land. Legal historian John McLaren observes the unparalleled opportunities settler societies provided to new immigrants to secure more durable and clearer private property rights, particularly accentuated by recent experiences of dispossession from common lands. McLaren further observes a 'selective historical amnesia' when it came to the 'forgetfulness of customary rights in common to land which settlers or their recent ancestors had enjoyed under English or Scots law' (McLaren 2001, p.135). Opportunity and selective amnesia signalled a strong preference for private property and its attributes of security or fixity of tenure. Thus, governments promised homestead title, or fee simple selection rights under legislation such as the 1862 Robertson Land Act in New South Wales. Frequently the grants were a post-hoc validation of the status quo of possession.

Andrew Buck identifies this trend as an early manifestation of a distinctly Australian form of property law.[3] Australian property departed from its English parentage by its emphasis on a universal and egalitarian access to land. Buck considers such 'possessive egalitarianism' (Buck 2006, p.138), an equal right to acquire, as a defining feature of Australian property. More broadly, property in the settler context was a market commodity, not an incident of family privilege, power and sinecure. Such universality of access triggered an early land rush by 'squatters', who defied colonial authorities and ignored vain attempts to restrict settlement within the official boundaries. (Roberts 1924; Roberts 1935; King 1957; Burroughs 1967). Land settlement policies had to adapt quickly to meet this expansionary exigency, initially in the form of a *sui generis* private pastoral tenure (Reynolds and Dalziell 1996),[4] and finally, selection rights to freehold provided the settler improved their parcel. The vicissitudes of drought in New South Wales in the late 1840s forced many sheep men, known as 'Prophets', to leave for New Zealand, where runs were taken up in the foothills and eastern slopes of the South Island Alps, again with the exhortation to settle the empty interior. (Acland 1930; Jourdain 1925).[5] In the USA, westward-bound settlers ran roughshod over established property laws (favouring absentee land speculators) and created new property relations that suited their context.

> Echoing John Locke's discussions of property ... settlers frequently argued that 'possession was the best title' and that to obtain true ownership of the wilderness lands on the frontier, a putative owner 'must not only claim it, but annex his labor to it, and make it more fit for the use of man; till this be done it remains in the common stock, and anyone who needs to improve it for his support, has a right'.
>
> (Penalver and Katyal 2010, pp.55–56)

By 1862, the Homestead Act accommodated this factual reality by sanctioning the grant of 160 acres of private fee simple title to settlers who improved their holdings.

In this relatively narrow temporal window, the expanding institution of private property reflected its pre-industrial, agrarian context. Freyfogle saw this expression of private ownership as a peaceable exercise of dominion or *quiet enjoyment* of the land, a settled image where 'the right to remain undisturbed' and its corollary to not interfere with another's peaceful use, was at its core (Freyfogle 2003, p.56). This nuanced right did not require, nor demand absolute exclusion, rather the principle of *sic utere tuo ut alienum non laedas* (use your property in such a way so as to not disturb/harm others) restrained interferences with an owner's use and enjoyment rights. Ironically, and tragically, such 'settled' or 'protective' principles did not apply to the dispossessed indigene.[6]

1.4 The evolving bundle of rights and the right to exclude

Locke's idealized agrarian society was a transitory phase; the advent of the unstoppable capitalist, industrial age required a re-articulation of private property that stressed the primacy of individual exclusionary power and the right to exploit. The bundle of rights metaphor gathered significant momentum in the late nineteenth century, in the process transforming modern property to conform to the economic imperatives of the new age (Arnold 2002). The evolution of the bundle metaphor is described in the American context in the following terms:

> [I]n the nineteenth century … property evolved from a unilateral and exclusive power over a material item, to a more malleable and divisible set of specific rights. Prior to the Civil War, property in the United States was generally viewed in terms discussed by John Locke … After the Civil War, America's strong commitment to the Lockean view of ownership weakened, and our concept of property fragmented. The familiar 'bundle of sticks' metaphor emerged, allowing society to treat rights as easily severable.
>
> (Fairfax et al. 2005, p.16)

The term 'bundle of rights' is often attributed to John Lewis' treatise on the law of eminent domain, published in 1888 (Goldstein 1998, p.367). Stuart Banner's history of American property traces its first use to US Supreme Court Justice James Wilson in the late eighteenth century. The term was popularized in the 1830s by English law professor John Austin, who lectured that property 'was not a thing a person owned … [but] the assemblage of rights a person had over a thing' (Banner 2011, p.57)

Banner agrees that its use became mainstream by the 1880s, its 'definition had been repeated so often that American lawyers thought of property as a bundle of rights and no longer the thing itself' (p.58).[7]

The bundle envisages a series of divisible rights or sticks, including rights to use and enjoy, exploit, alienate, possess, and of course, exclude. The fee simple holder arguably enjoys the greatest bundle of rights known to the common law, while a life estate holder has fewer sticks, deprived for example of full rights of alienation. The bundle metaphor highlights the divisibility of property rights, that rights can be separated and re-constituted in a flexible variety of right bundles. The metaphor also highlights the relativity of property, and the potential for the simultaneous ownership of divergent interests in the one land by multiple owners: 'ownership is not one aggregate right; it is many distinct rights, and a landowner can possess few or many of them' (Freyfogle 2003, p.19). The metaphor suited the changing times because it enabled the right to intensively exploit. And inherent in the untrammelled right to exploit was a security of exclusive possession free from any interference. The absolute right to exclude captured the full value of private capital in land and was an incentive for its efficient and intensive development. What was once qualified became absolute, conveniently building on the simple, yet incomplete, narratives of Blackstone and Locke.

This shift was most evident in Anglo-American common law. For example, in *Pennsylvania Coal Co. v Sanderson* in 1886,[8] the Pennsylvania Supreme Court (in keeping with a broader trend in American property jurisprudence in the late nineteenth century) affirmed the primacy of the right to develop and exploit. 'In *Sanderson*, the pendulum had completed its swing ... from an agrarian property system that protected quiet enjoyment and enforced *sic utere tuo* ... to the industrial property side, freely permitting intensive land uses with only modest concern about resulting harms' (Freyfogle 2003, p.73). Private property was by this point firmly entrenched as a market commodity, a series of divisible and exploitable sticks, where values of personhood or community were obsolete. Integral to the maximal intensive use of land was freedom from all types of interferences, substantial or peripheral, guaranteed by the private stick to exclude, a new core right 'to halt physical invasions of ... spaces – the right to exclude. This was the legal right that industries valued the most, because it allowed them to keep people off their lands.' (ibid., p.56)

The separable bundle also reinforced the *abstract* nature of private property rights. In the early twentieth century, scholar Wesley Hohfeld claimed there was no such thing as a legal right between a person and a thing, but merely between persons. In landmark articles in 1913 and 1917, Hohfeld argued that property rights were 'multi-tal', a series of identical personal rights enforceable against a large indefinite mass of individuals. The Hohfeldian analysis successfully removed legal relations from the physical facts, such that 'land is not property, but the subject of property' (Hohfeld 1913, p.22).

Its abstract utility meant that the right to exclude became the signature right amongst the other bundle rights. The US Supreme Court described it as 'one of the most essential sticks'[9] or 'one of the most treasured strands in an owner's bundle of property rights.'[10] In 1954, Felix Cohen provided a simple formula for private property and its dominant right to exclude.

> [T]hat is property to which the following label can be attached:
> To the world: Keep off X unless you have my permission, which I may grant or withhold.
> Signed: Private citizen
> Endorsed: The state.
>
> (Cohen 1954, p.374)

In this tradition, Thomas Merrill calls the right to exclude a 'gatekeeper right', a 'necessary and sufficient condition of identifying the existence of property '(Merrill 1998, p.731) Merrill castigates property realists who seek to downgrade the significance of the right to exclude.'[G]ive someone the right to exclude others from a valued resource ... and you give them property. Deny someone the exclusion right and they do not have property.' (ibid., p.730)

Yet by the beginning of the twenty-first century, disquiet over its unqualified pre-eminence increased, particularly when it impeded innocuous public access expectations. Jerry Anderson's comparative study of public access rights in England and the United States, criticized the US Supreme Court for 'canonizing' this right, its placement of the exclude stick at the 'top of the woodpile' without regard to context, community values, or norms.

> Rather than simply accept the right to exclude as a given, courts should carefully consider the interests it serves and determine whether, in some circumstances, it may be possible to accommodate greater public access without damaging the private owner's interests.
>
> (Anderson 2007, p.377)

Anderson criticizes the arbitrariness of the right to exclude, and its monopoly of the spatial spectrum of use without regard to the theoretical or practical consideration that other use(s) may peaceably co-exist. Anderson contrasts ancient English traditions about access to the countryside, with less entrenched American social and cultural values where primacy is placed on a landowner's private right to exclude.

Anderson's comparative study of public access to private countryside highlights that private property is a social institution, that its limits are defined and set by societal expectations and norms that vary from jurisdiction to jurisdiction and over time. In England, traditions of open access to the countryside (Anderson 2007, p.412), combined with a simmering class outrage unabated from the enclosure period (Sprankling 2006, pp.90–93), came to a long-delayed head with the enactment of the Countryside and Rights of Way Act in 2000. This legislation clarified uncertainties and ambiguities surrounding public access rights to private lands, in the process, shifting 'sticks' from the private owner to the public, and limiting the former's right to exclude without compensation (Anderson 2007, p.378). In Scotland, later 'right to roam' legislation swung the pendulum even further in favour of public rights (Lovett 2010). By contrast, in the USA, and analogously Australia and New Zealand, the historical emphasis focused on the role of private property as a secure and developable commodity, such that any experiments with property rights other than private have been transient (Freyfogle 2003, pp.23–24), or peripheral (Page 2009). The consequence in such jurisdictions, where the social and cultural context is less favourable, is that public access rights are weak and vulnerable.

However, a lack of legal formality is not to say that social pressures and norms in settler societies cannot exert inroads into a dominant right to exclude. Changed social attitudes to racial discrimination collided with the canonized right to exclude, in the US common law of public accommodations. Joseph Singer compared public accommodations laws across numerous US states, in particular the rights of business owners to exclude customers on the basis of race. Singer's comparative analysis provoked generic observations about the right to exclude in private property jurisprudence.

> What can public accommodations law teach us about private property? It suggests ... that all rights – even the basic right to exclude – are limited by the rights of others and by social interests.
>
> (Singer 1995, p.1450)

Moreover, in terms of the sticks found in a standard bundle, Singer does not assume that the right to exclude is an automatic given. Not all sticks necessarily 'get along with each other all the time.' (ibid., p.1452) Interestingly, Singer argues that where a fee simple owner invokes the state's aid in enforcing trespass laws, the private owner's interests inextricably overlap, becoming in the process 'imbricated' with those of the state (ibid., p.1451). This blending of private and public dilutes the absolutism of the right to exclude with the legitimate interests of the state. More broadly, Singer concentrates on the overlooked sociability of private property, its need to be understood as both contingent on, and shaped by the contours of social relationships (ibid., p.1462).

Richard Barnes likewise draws the nexus between property as a social institution, 'an institution that is responsive to the needs of society', and the limits of private property. Like Singer, Barnes does not automatically accept the right to exclude as paramount in terms of its absolute priority over other interests.

> Although strong private rights may dominate many areas of property discourse, the prioritisation of private rights is not a logical requirement of property per se, but a product of the social context in which property rights have evolved ... To narrowly construe property in 'terms of raw exclusory power' is to locate property in the hands of the past, not the present.
>
> (Barnes 2009, pp.25–26)

Eric Freyfogle takes an historical rather than a normative perspective on this issue. 'To understand private property fully ... we need to gain a sense of the path that private property has followed to get to where it is today' (Freyfogle 2007, p.28).[11] Freyfogle cites early public rights to unenclosed woodlands in New England, grazing rights on rangelands and customary hunting and fishing rights, together the 'lost right to roam', to argue that exclusion has always been qualified. Freyfogle believes the onus should shift from exclusion to shared use, but concedes that his arguments are unlikely to take root while lawmakers 'cannot imagine and do not remember a different [pre-industrial] legal world' (Freyfogle 2003, p.60).

Sections 2, 3 and 4 illustrated that private property rights are not immutably fixed. Change is constant, but it is slow, and appears imperceptible. The apparent inability to remember or imagine Freyfogle's different legal world is symptomatic of a wider institutional malaise, that the private estate is not sufficiently cognizant of the dynamic of change. This is exemplified by the tenacity of the obsolete private–public divide. Dynamism, stasis, and the public–private divide, and their collective impacts on how we define private property in land, are canvassed in sections 5 and 6.

1.5 The dynamism of private property

As a social institution, private property conforms to social, political and economic pressures. A multitude of scholars affirm its dynamism (Waring 2013). Hanoch Dagan writes of the dynamic public dimensions of private property (Dagan 2013). Joseph Sax describes property as 'continuously adjust[ing] to reflect new economic and social structures' (Sax 1992, p.1446). Jerry Anderson says property's balance is 'always tentative, subject to constant re-evaluation and trade-offs' (Anderson 2007, pp.376–77).

Yet the mantra that private property rights must be secure, certain and stable[12] feeds a widely held counter view that private property rights are fixed and inviolate. The difficulty lies in understanding that stability can encompass change – indeed, the latter enhances it. 'The very nature of a property regime demands that property be stable only relatively, not absolutely' (Rose 2000, p.14). Relative stability means principled evolution, the ongoing development of property principles and doctrines within coherent parameters, not *ad hoc* or unpredictable declarations of individualized justice (Dagan 2011, p.43). By contrast, absolute stability means no change at all, an ossified stasis that is an anathema to the incremental common law, the bedrock of property law.

In coping with relative stability, and the relative certainty it enables, the challenge for the law is to remain simultaneously principled and contemporary. To borrow a Carol Rose aphorism that 'property is persuasion', the 'persuasion' needed to ground new or evolving property rights must be consistent with principles and precedent. As English Law Lord Millett observes:[13]

> Property rights are determined by fixed rules and settled principles. They are not discretionary. They do not depend upon ideas of what is 'fair, just and reasonable.' Such concepts, which in reality mask decisions of legal policy, have no place in the law of property.

In the absence of principled balance, it is open to exploit Rose's aphorism, and the discourse of property generally, such that in a perverse reversal, persuasion becomes property.

Property also retires 'obscure, neglected or outmoded' property sticks, and crafts novel 'off the rack' property rights to respond to societal demands (Rose 1999, p.211). Andrew Buck identifies the mid nineteenth century as an innovative period for Australian land law, when English rights unsuited to local conditions, for example primogeniture or the fee tail, were abolished, and new property regimes such as Torrens title were enacted (Buck 2006). In the early twenty-first century, the propertization of carbon offsets poses similar dilemmas; are ancient rights, like the profit-à-prendre, capable of adaptation, or are *sui generis* statutory rights more coherent (Hepburn 2009)?

Private property in land maintains its relevance by being dynamic. Where its descriptions become stagnant or outmoded, its inaptness risks its integrity (Dagan 2011). The private–public divide, and its universalization of property rights as 'private', is a standout example of problematic, definitional stasis.

1.6 The public–private divide

The public–private divide views property rights as private individualized rights diminished or restricted by public regulation. The dichotomy is relatively simple; the right to develop or exploit land is a natural private right, an incident of owning land. Public restraints on that private right are not an incident of the private right, but an overarching regulation or impediment sourced from a detached public realm.

The consequence of the public–private divide is that property is exclusively within the private realm, and a matter for the private law. Public interests in property constitute a restriction or encumbrance on the private right, imposed from the other side of the divide. Public interests in property are therefore not 'property rights', since 'rights' belong only in the private realm. Conceptually the dichotomy emphasises simplicity over complexity, and a pale duality over a rich plurality. Property is either private, or it is not. And the concept that private, public or common rights may subsist simultaneously in a given parcel is the antithesis of this clean dichotomy.

The origins of the public–private divide stem from the late nineteenth century, rising in tandem with the bundle of rights metaphor, and the urban–industrial intensification of land use.

> By late century evolving legal thought had come to portray American life as separated into two spheres: a private sphere and a public, governmental sphere. Private property was placed in the private category ... Regulation, by contrast was a public governmental act.
>
> (Freyfogle 2003, p.80)

The quarantining of property into the private realm set the scene for later conflicts over the ostensible loss of private property rights as environmental and planning regulation encroached into the private owner's bundle of rights. Private ownership became a form of allodial or absolute ownership, fed by the noeticism of the 'sole and despotic dominion' mantra, and a context where rights were purely private (Freyfogle 2007, pp.20–4).

In particular, the divide reinforced the ideology that property was solely concerned with the promotion of personal economic welfare and the protection of individual privacy. Land was no longer a part of an inclusive compact rooted in context or community; rather, private rights were an exclusive, autonomous abstract, freed from communitarian sentiments and obligations (Freyfogle 2003, p.81). The public–private divide also proved the catalyst for the 'curious' modern myopia that 'property' and 'private property' are one and the same, even where alternatives to private property are patently 'ubiquitous, if unremarked' (Rose 1998a, p.132). Rose cites economic and social reasons for this contemporary unwillingness to see property other than private property.

Hanoch Dagan is critical of the polarities of the public–private divide. The private law of property 'cannot and should not have its own inner intelligibility' (Dagan 2013, p.270). Rather, it is a series of related 'institutions' with varying 'public dimensions', dependent on public factors such as social context, human relationships and the nature of the propertied resource. In Dagan's account, private property rests on a pluralist view of society (ibid., p.262) and correspondence to its grounded truth. In terms of the right to exclude, Dagan identifies three public values that qualify the right; autonomy, personhood and community.

> None of these values sanctions an absolute right to exclude; furthermore, to varying degrees, they even positively require curbing such a right and recognising the right to entry of non-owners.
>
> (Dagan 2013, p.284)

Autonomy arises where non-owners or marginalized groups enjoy limited rights of entry; a qualification that serves their independence and sustains human dignity. Equally, a qualified right to enter may be constitutive of a non-owner, a furtherance of *personhood*, particularly where the owner's property is merely fungible. Last, Dagan says that qualified rights to enter serve public values of *community*, by creating 'institutional infrastructure' that fosters co-operation and the attainment of human flourishing (ibid., pp.285–6).

The public–private divide is a late-nineteenth century construct, an artifice detached from both present and past. For centuries, private freehold estates have been subject to wide restrictions that collectively represented an amorphous public interest in land. Feudal or Crown obligations were the hallmark of the doctrines of tenure and estates. The fee socage tenure that prevailed after the Tenures Abolition Act 1660 remained an estate of uncertain duration, capable of reversion to the Crown through escheat. Natural rights of support, air and light modified landowner's rights since time immemorial, while common law doctrines of prescription and adverse possession acknowledge the relativity of a landowner's title, and the supervening interests of third parties in private property. Since the seventeenth century, the vesting of future interests in land has been subservient to the public interest in freedom of alienation, enforced by the rule against perpetuities. Private property in the common law tenurial tradition has rarely been absolute. Arguably it is less so now, as land use and environmental regulatory laws intersect with property with increasing frequency and sophistication.

In the twenty-first century, the notion of a pure private–public dichotomy is even less defensible. Joseph Sax (1982) says it was dated decades earlier in the 1970s, when high-profile cases such as *Penn Central* legitimized the subsistence of public rights in private property without the former constituting the taking of a private right.[14] Rather, such cases exemplify that the private–public divide is porous (Brower et al. 2009), and that any former distinctiveness, real or perceived, is blurred. Private property rights are burdened with public restraints and public interests proliferate (Babcok and Feurer 1977), while public and private rights co-mingle in public lands (Brower et al. 2009). We have moved from perceptions of transparent dichotomies, to realities of translucent blends. This progression has not passed unobserved. Margaret Davies states that 'the distinction between public and private ... is not a bright line' (Davies 2007, p.11). Kevin and Susan Gray see public and private operating, 'not dichotomously, but continuously across a spectrum in which adjacent connotations shade easily into one another' (Gray and Gray 1999, p.11). Amnon Lehavi describes modern property as a 'conscious jigsaw puzzle [where] ... the boundaries between the public and private realms are not clear-cut nor hermetic ... the two spheres are sophisticatedly intertwined' (Lehavi 2008, p.1991).

Yet despite these and other like observations, the common law has not 'internalised' these deeper understandings of property (Gray and Gray 1999, p.13), and remains locked in what Lehavi calls its 'Blackacre Paradigm' (Lehavi 2013, p.6). This paradigmatic tension is highlighted when public rights of access intersect with the right to exclude. Security of private use invariably requires freedom from interference, but a blanket position is not always apt, it depends on exigency, geography, history and culture. The importance of context is exemplified, on the one hand, by rights to countryside access in England or Scotland,[15] and the supremacy of New Zealand high country 'trespass rights' on the other (Brower and Page 2012). The risk of having an absolutist, arbitrary starting point when defining private property is that it ignores such social context and disregards the different types of property to which it may relate. Kevin and Susan Gray describe this 'prerogative' of property as 'both total and totalitarian' in its unidirectional tendencies (Gray and Gray 1999, p.15).

1.7 The plausible narrative of private property

The tenacity of the public–private divide and the primacy of the right to exclude has entrenched a plausible, yet narrow narrative of private property that airbrushes away inconvenient truths. In the seventeenth and eighteenth centuries, Locke and Blackstone recognized the significance of qualification and context. In the twenty-first century, limitations on the right to exclude have increased in number and scope, as statute expands its reach. But as Freyfogle instinctively surmises, the force of this curiously detached narrative is likely to endure while ever lawmakers cannot imagine and do not remember a different, diverse legal world.

Absolute, arbitrary and capricious exclusion has also proved enduring because it is part of a generally positive story about private property. Rose's normative view of property is strongly influenced by her earlier career as a professor of English literature. Her disciplinary background makes it clear that 'property needs a tale, a story, a post-hoc explanation ... [one] that fills the gap in the classical theory, that makes property "plausible"'. In Rose's estimation, Locke and Blackstone are both excellent storytellers who have crafted a plausible narrative of modern private property (Rose 1990, p.52).

In settler societies, much of this narrative stems from a formative nation-building era, when the settlement of empty hinterlands was a political imperative. Thus, possession is the origin of property, landowners should not sleep on their rights, the law rewards the productive use of land, and so forth. All tend to justify questionable title, to assuage Blackstone's self-doubt or 'ownership anxiety,' and serve to make the arbitrary exclusiveness of private property plausible as the key to a wider story.

However, what if the dominant narratives of private property were those of Blackstone's self-deprecation rather than despotic dominion? How different would our understandings of private property be? There are no definitive answers to such rhetorical questions. However, the continuing felicity of private property's plausible narrative can be examined from an alternative perspective, by ascertaining the strengths of a pluralistic private property, and re-evaluating the rationales for the modern right to exclude in such a diverse context. Sections 8 and 9 address each of these tasks in turn.

1.8 Attributes and propensities of private property in land

If we are to escape an all-consuming, exclusionary view of private property in land, *exclusivity* must be seen in the context of the institution's other co-existing yet under-regarded characteristics. This section identifies *security of use, clarity* and *durability*, as well as a redefined *exclusivity*, as critical attributes of private interests in land. The quality of *dynamism*, already traversed in section 5, could likewise be added to this list.

There is no unanimity about the precise content of private property rights. Tony Honore describes 11 'incidents' of property ownership:

> the right to possess, the right to use, the right to manage, the right to the income of a thing, the right to the capital, the right to security, the rights or incidences of transmissibility and absence of term, the prohibition of harmful use, liability to execution, and the incident of residuarity.
>
> (Honore 1961, p.113)

Anthony Scott (2008) discerns fewer: six 'characteristics' of exclusivity, duration, flexibility, quality of title, transferability, and divisibility. Curiously, neither Honore nor Scott identifies the right to exclude.

This omission is perverse given that the right to exclude has become the defining incident of modern private property, a process Richard Barnes describes as a 'thinning out' of private rights, a hierarchical ordering where excludability is at the top of the qualitative 'woodpile'. Thomas Merrill and Henry Smith (2007, p.1850) say that exclusivity, in particular the presence or not of the right to exclude is private property's *sina qua non.* What other presently existing, yet under-regarded rationales could explain the 'propertiness' of a private thing, such that we can digress from this definitional closed loop?

It is submitted that the quality of private rights turns on a plurality of characteristics: the *security* and *exclusivity* they offer their individual holder, and their more generic *clarity* and *durability.* The latter attributes of clarity and durability remain the same desired qualities that nineteenth-century settlers sought in response to the equivocal and vulnerable common rights they left behind in their metropolis, a phenomenon that continues to inform the narrative of private property in settler societies.

In terms of *security,* private property delivers the benefits of secured and assured title. Secure title provides the holder with the requisite self-confidence to invest in the right over the long term. Assurance of title is the institutional guarantee the state provides private property.

> Assurance of property rights refers to institutional support for systems of creation and enforcement of property rights. Assurance of property rights differs from the security of property rights in that assurance refers to the general political and legal environment in which those rights exist. In contrast security ... refers to characteristics of specific rights. Secure rights are those which the owner is not in danger of losing.
>
> (Fuchs 2003, pp.67–8)

Consider the core private rights. The right to possess is a secure right, assuredly enforced by remedies premised on interferences with possession, and a common law conception of property that is one of possession not ownership (Green and Randall 2009, pp.80–1). The right to use and enjoy is likewise secure, there is no compulsion to share private use rights, individual use is certain, and is capable of whole or part transfer to others. The right to exclude, as previously discussed, is 'absolute, arbitrary and capricious', and as a result of such excess, is excessively secure. Rights can be *secure* (in the sense that the right is not in danger of loss) without the added requirement of untrammelled freedom from interference. By shifting the focus from exclusive dominion to secure use, security of title remains unaffected. Of course, there are circumstances where security of title is best guaranteed through exclusion, but not automatically so. Equally, there are 'large slabs' of property law that would cease to exist if exclusion was private property's sole organizing principle (Dagan 2006, pp.85–6). As Dagan later surmises, property rights depend on social context, human relationships, and the nature of the resource itself, not its purported exclusivity (Dagan 2011).

Thus, *exclusivity* is a conundrum. Exclusivity has been largely construed through the private–public prism of raw exclusory power, and an extreme interpretation of exclusion. Larissa Katz says that 'proponents of the boundary approach trad[e] on an ambiguity in the meaning of "exclusive"' (Katz 2008, p.277). She argues that exclusivity is a subtle concept, encompassing not only the power to exclude others from 'the object of the right', but also an owner's 'special position to set the agenda about the use of a resource', an *exclusive* privilege that others do not share (ibid., p.278).

Anthony Scott likewise illustrates its nuances, describing exclusivity as a freedom from interference in the valid exercise of the right, not necessarily a right to keep all others out. Such interferences may come from adjoining landowners, through spill over problems, or governments, by regulation.

> [R]ight holders need exclusivity to be independent – to free themselves from losses and costs ... Exclusivity has two distinct meanings; freedom from interference with having to share a resource with others ... and freedom from government regulation that restricts the ways he can use the resource in order to promote the public good.
> (Scott 2008, p.6)

The freedom from having to share a resource with others is patently achieved by the raw exclusory power of an arbitrary right to exclude. But equally it is achievable through a secure and exclusive right to use, Katz's 'special position' reserved to the holder and therefore free from neighbourly interference in the exercise of its use. This latter interpretation is consistent with Freyfogle's qualified right of freedom from interference, rather than an absolute right to exclude. It is also consistent with a view of private property as regulating access to, and the exclusive use of, scarce resources. Private property's attribute of *exclusivity* feeds the propensity for private rights to overwhelm or dominate property discourse generally, but it is the slanted interpretation of 'exclusion' to equate to 'raw exclusory power' that triggers this inherent propensity to conflate.

If the strengths of private property rights lie in their clarity, durability, security and exclusivity (howsoever the latter is construed), then private property's propensity to dominate wider property discourse is its inherent institutional flaw. This encroachment is well illustrated in the context of private rights in public resources.

> Private rights in public resources have a propensity to encroach into the public domain, and privatize residual rights and interests lacking

legal certainty or definition. The corollary of this tendency is the suppression of any latent public rights in the public resource.

(Page 2009, p.403)

The tendency for private rights to fill and expand the vacuum of legal uncertainty reduces the chances for a mosaic of private and non-private rights to co-exist simultaneously in a multiple use context. Its conflation arises from a convergence of influences traversed to date in this chapter, the settler narratives of private property, the private–public divide, and the pre-eminence of raw exclusory power in defining exclusivity. This propensity to conflate flourishes when the scope and ambit of property rights, non-private and private, are weak or ill defined.[16]

1.9 Modern justifications of the right to exclude

In a pluralistic understanding of private property, the right to exclude must be justified by reasons other than its own self-assertion. The *economic* rationale for the right to exclude is a logical starting point. It is logical because the right to exclude originally rose to prominence as private property adjusted to an expanding industrial economy, re-configuring itself into the familiar bundle of rights. Freedom from any interference, substantial or peripheral, secured the maximum economic advantage for the landowner, rather than the less assertive right to quiet enjoyment. However, the pursuit of untrammelled economic expansion is no longer an overriding imperative. Indeed, there are parallels between the fading economic justifications of the right to exclude and the antiquated rationales for the private–public divide. In the early twenty-first century, environmental concerns occasionally trump the 'good' of economic growth. The need to imbue property with an environmental ethic (Rose 1994a) is an equally desired and expanding public good. Moreover, secure rights of use and enjoyment are now equally effective in delivering the economic 'goods' of prosperity or growth, suggesting that the late-nineteenth century monopoly that exclusion once enjoyed is less plausible.

There is also a *moral* justification for the right to exclude. Thomas Merrill and Henry Smith argue that 'morally grounded exclusion rights [subsist] at the core of property' (Merrill and Smith 2007, p.1852). Enforceable property rules require widespread respect and support, and as such they must be 'grounded in robust moral notions that are easy to communicate and shared by the relevant members of the population' (ibid., p.1855). The importance of protecting possession against unwarranted intrusion, the priority accorded to those first in time, and the protection of property itself as a moral good, are proffered as moral justifications for the right to exclude. In support of the latter, the authors cite scenarios such as intentional trespass, bad faith adverse possession and takings for economic development[17] as examples of moral outrage engendered by 'taking from the innocent and distributional injustice' (ibid., p.1880). Likewise, Shramkrishna Balganesh justifies the right to exclude by the moral norm of inviolability. He describes the right as 'a normative device, which derives from the norm of resource inviolability ... the right to exclude operates as an analytic tool, which seeks to transplant the norm of inviolability from morality to law.' Importantly, the right is seen as 'the correlative of the duty to keep away from a resource over which the norm applies' (Balganesh 2008, p.600). The example of cars parked and locked on the street is used to illustrate the norm; we keep away from locked vehicles because we adhere to a societal norm respecting the inviolability of someone else's resource. Yet conversely, Dagan describes the morality of exclusion as 'normatively disappointing' (Dagan 2011, p.44), an account that fails to reflect the reality of an owner's social responsibilities, or a non-owner's limited rights of entry.

Morality, like private property, is dynamic; it is not frozen in time. Public sentiment frequently shifts in its judgment of what is morally deserving of protection, and what is inviolate. To adopt a well-used example, the taking of 'innocent' public access rights could become Merrill and Smith's contemporary 'moral outrage'. If so, 'distributional injustice' may turn on its axis and the morality tales of unwarranted intrusion or inviolability may fall away when privileged private interests collide with legitimate public ones. In such cases, the morality of inclusion, not exclusion, could deliver the public good desired.

Another powerful justification for the right to exclude is that it is the *origin* of property rights; all other rights are derived or sourced from the right to exclude. Thomas Merrill explains it as one of logical primacy, such that other property attributes can be derived from the right to exclude 'with relatively minor clarifications.' (Merrill 1998, p.740) Merrill also stresses that the process does not work in reverse, that the right to exclude cannot be derived where other property attributes are the starting point. Others see this first primacy stemming from an evolutionary origin (Loncarich 2014).

However, this argument is not universally logical. There are important property rights where the right to exclude is peripheral to the right's subsistence. Easements are non-possessory incorporeal rights that permit the use of another's resource in a sanctioned way. The right to exclude is not the basis of an easement right; rather it is its antithesis. Nor is the right to use and enjoy particularly grounded on exclusion, use rights exist in common property where the right is shared by the many. Carol Rose also sees it differently, famously arguing that the *right to possess* is the first status origin of property (Rose 1985). Moreover, possession and exclusion are also not always inextricably linked. Rather the notion of possession of land in the Anglo common law tradition, dominated by the combined effects of the doctrines of estates and tenure, is a nuanced, technical one. Mark Wonnacott clarifies that the term 'possession' of land is used in a number of ways, but the proper or technical meaning describes an abstract relationship between a person and a corporeal estate. '[P]ossession in this sense describes a relationship between a person and a corporeal estate in land (a fee simple, a lease ...) rather than the relationship between a person and any physical feature of the land' (Wonnacott 2006, p.2). Like its once dominant economic rationale, exclusion does not enjoy uncontested monopoly privilege as the universal origin of all property rights.

Conversely, there are reasons why the right to exclude should be qualified. The history of property, and the private estate's *dynamism* suggest that an exclusivist, land as commodity version of private property is merely a present iteration, not a timeless, fixed one. Indeed, the high-water mark in its current form may have already passed. Historical precedents suggest that private property takes many forms, like Freyfogle's 'settled agrarian' model, where private, public or common rights co-existed with a private owner's more qualified right to quiet enjoyment, and 'the rights of one landowner are necessarily constrained by the rights of neighbours, [the] right to quiet enjoyment, [the] right to remain undisturbed' (Freyfogle 2003, pp.16–7). Freyfogle posits that this era may return in an environmentally informed future, a 'modern, ecologically informed variant of the agrarian property regime of the late 18th century' (ibid., p.94). This view of property sees a heightened place for private use, '[p]erhaps we need to apply more broadly the idea that all of nature remains in a sense in public hands, with private owners receiving only prescribed rights to use' (Freyfogle 2007, p.141). Such ideas are anathema to dominion-centric notions of exclusive possession.

Similarly, long-established doctrines that protect the interests of third parties, as well as the widespread intervention of statute, also erode absolute exclusive possession. The doctrine of prescription, relying on practises going back to time immemorial, creates new third party property rights 'where a court finds long, open and uninterrupted use' of another's private land (Butt 2010, p.470). Legislatures also find little compunction in diminishing the right to exclude if it is convenient for the purposes of erecting a dividing fence, sanctioning an encroachment or trimming overhanging branches from trees.[18] Such limitations on the right to exclude, whether sourced from ancient common law doctrine, or recent legislation, corroborate the more general thesis that other private, public or communal rights or sticks may exist in a parcel of private property. Sax describes this as 'qualified private ownership' where 'the rights of each user can only be defined with reference to the claims of other users' (Sax 1971, p.154).

Another way of seeing qualified private ownership is through a water-based paradigm. For example, Freyfogle exhorts us to embrace the potential of water, to 'cast aside all of our reassuring, but ultimately confining, notions about what it means to own private property'. In this alternate paradigm, property rights escape from their landed restraints, transforming into 'interconnected and relative' use entitlements (Freyfogle 1988, p.1530).

The 'plausible' narrative of despotic dominion is not the only narrative of private property. There are many alternative, incommensurable accounts and rationales that affirm private property as a pluralistic institution. As Dagan observes, 'the pluralism of private property reflects the heterogeneity of [its] real-life manifestations.' (Dagan 2011, p.xii) Ultimately, the ambit of the modern right to exclude is 'justified only when it contributes to the common good...If property is legitimate only when it promotes the common good, and if ideas about the common good shift, then the rules of ownership ought to shift along with them' (Freyfogle 2007, pp.20, 26).

1.10 Conclusion

This chapter argues that private property affects how we see property in land because of its disproportionate emphasis on an absolute, arbitrary right to exclude, leading to a modern myopia that 'property' and 'private property' is synonymous. We have been seduced by the noetic writings of Blackstone and Locke and the pedagogical elegance of the bundle of rights, in the process overlooking or forgetting that private property is a social institution moulded and informed by change and context. We have also overlooked the relatively recent history of private property, and ignored the evidence that the public–private divide is more a graded spectrum of degree than an undivided dichotomy.

Private property is critical in so many respects; it serves the public good by providing secure title that enables certainty and stability in property, and its efficient exploitation forms the basis of economic prosperity. Its narratives reward the productive use of land. But the security of title and economic prosperity that it engenders do not necessarily rest on an arbitrary right to exclude. The justifications for an unqualified right to exclude are not beyond critique. The extent to which the all-consuming right can be modified to allow a more nuanced freedom from interference permits the theoretical oxygen for other rights (private, public or common) to subsist and co-exist. In many cases, the net practical effect may be the same, particularly in densely populated cities. However, by articulating a revised private property that acknowledges that property is relative, and supersedes an obsolete public–private divide, the possibility to see property across human landscapes in all its forms is enhanced, substituting singular use for multiple uses, and critically, private uniformity for property diversity.

Notes

1 Rose argues that property is 'persuasion', those who yell loudly and consistently get their message heard (Rose 1994b).
2 The US Homestead Act 1862 limited fee grants to new settlers of often unviable parcels of 160 acres, the objective to promote closer settlement.
3 Seen in unique property rights like crop liens or pastoral leases.
4 Imperial Waste Lands Occupation Act 1846 and Order in Council March 1847.
5 These settlers had 'unlimited faith in the squatting system and a great contempt for freehold' (Acland 1930, p.2).
6 The irony lost on new settlers was that the dispossession of indigenous land-holders mirrored in historical terms the dispossession arising from the efficient enclosure of common 'waste lands' into productive private lands (Buck 2006, pp.14–30).
7 'Even the dullest individual knows and understands that his property in anything is a bundle of rights' (Banner 2011, p.58).
8 113 Pa. 126 6 A 453 (1886)
9 *Kaiser Aetna v. United States* 444 US 164, 177; *Dolan v. City of Tigard* 512 US 374, 384 (1994); *Nollan v. California Coastal Commission* 483 US 825, 831 (1987); 'The right to exclude others is perhaps the quintessential property right'. *Nixon v. United States* 978 F.2d 1269, 1286 (D.C. Cir. 1992).
10 *Loretto v. Teleprompter Manhattan CATV Corp.*, 458 US 419, 435.
11 Freyfogle was more direct in a personal conversation with the author in April 2013, when he stated that we are 'clueless if we do not understand property history'.
12 *National Bank Ltd v. Ainsworth* [1965] AC 1175.
13 *Foskett v. McKeown* [2000] 1 AC 112, 127 per Lord Millett.
14 *Penn Central Transportation Co. v. New York City*, 438 US 104 (1978).
15 Countryside and Rights of Way Act 2000 (UK); The Land Reform (Scotland) Act 2003.
16 Conflation can be seen in the New Zealand high country, where a private right of pasturage in Crown pastoral tenure lacked an explicit right to exclude, and the public right of access was weak and diffuse. The private right ultimately expanded into a quasi-freehold estate, eliminating any residual public interests in the land (Brower and Page 2012). Only the public sidewalk is seen as the counter-example to this conflation propensity (Blomley 2011).
17 Merrill and Smith cite the controversy over *Kelo v. City of New London* 125 S. Ct. 2655 (2005) as being based on basic moral intuitions (2007).
18 Access orders can be made by courts, effectively qualifying the private owner's right to exclude, see for example Access to Neighbouring Land Act 2000 (NSW).

References

Acland, L 1930, *The Early Canterbury Runs*, Whitcomb & Tombs, Christchurch.

Alschuler, A 1996, 'Rediscovering Blackstone', *U. Pa. L. Rev.*, vol. 145, 1–55.

Anderson, J 2007, 'Britain's Right to Roam: Redefining the Landowner's Bundle of Sticks', *Georgetown International Environmental Law Rev.*, vol. 19, 375–435.

Arnold, C A 2002, 'The Reconstitution of Property: Property as a Web of Interests', *Harvard Environmental Law Rev.*, vol. 26, 281–364.

Babcock, R and Feurer, D 1977, 'Land as a Commodity Affected with a Public Interest', *Wash. L. Rev.*, vol. 52, 289–334.

Balganesh, S 2008, 'Demystifying the Right to Exclude: Of Property, Inviolability, and Automatic Injunctions', *Harvard Journal of Law & Public Policy*, vol. 31, 593–661.

Banner, S 2007, *Possessing the Pacific: Land, Settlers, and Indigenous People from Australia to Alaska*, Harvard University Press, Cambridge, MA.

Banner, S 2011, *American Property, A History of Who, Why and What We Own*, Harvard University Press, Cambridge, MA.

Barnes, R 2009, *Property Rights and Natural Resources*, Hart Publishing, Oxford.

Blomley, N 2011, *Rights of Passage: Sidewalks and the Regulation of Public Flow*, Routledge, Abingdon.

Bromley, D 2000, 'Private Property and the Public Interest: Land in the American Idea', in W G Robbins and J C Foster (eds), *Land in the American West: Private Claims and the Common Good*, University of Washington Press, Seattle, WA.

Brower, A and Page, J 2012, 'When the Law is Silent: Trespassers W…: Law and Power in Implied Property Rights', *The Environmental Law Reporter: News and Analysis*, vol. 42, no.3, 10 242–10 259.

Brower, A, Page. J D, Kennedy, A L and Martin, P 2009, 'The Cowboy, the Southern Man, and the Man from Snowy River: The Symbolic Politics of Property in Australia, the United States and New Zealand', (2009) 21(3) *Georgetown International Environmental Law Review*, vol. 21 no. 3, 455–493.

Buck, A 2006, *The Making of Australian Property Law*, Federation Press, Sydney.

Burroughs, P 1967, *Britain and Australia 1831-1855 A Study in Imperial Relations and Crown lands Administration*, Oxford University Press, Oxford.

Butt P 2010, *Land Law*, The Law Book Co., Sydney.

Cohen, F 1954, 'Dialogue on Private Property', *Rutgers Law Rev.* vol. 9, no. 2, 357–387.

Dagan, H 2006, 'Property and the Public Domain' *Yale Journal of Law and the Humanities*, vol. 18, 84–93.

Dagan, H 2011, *Property, Values and Institutions*, Oxford University Press, New York.

Dagan, H 2013, 'The Public Dimension of Private Property', *Kings Law Journal*, vol. 24, 260–288.

Davies, M 2007, *Property Meanings, Histories, Theories*, Routledge, Abingdon.

Fairfax, S, Gwin, L, King, M A, Raymond, L and Watt, L 2005, *Buying Nature: The Limits of Land Acquisition as a Conservation Strategy, 1780–2004*, MIT Press, Cambridge, MA.

Freyfogle, E 1988, 'Context and Accommodation in Modern Property Law', *Stanford L. Rev.*, vol. 41, 1529–1556.

Freyfogle, E 2003, *The Land We Share: Private Property and the Common Good*, Island Press, Washington, DC.

Freyfogle, E 2007, *On Private Property: Finding Common Ground on the Ownership of Land*, Beacon Press, Boston.

Fuchs, D 2003, *An Institutional Basis for Environmental Stewardship: The Structure and Quality of Property Rights*, Kluwer Academic, Dordrecht.

Goldstein, R 1998, 'Green Wood in the Bundle of Sticks: Fitting Environmental Ethics and Ecology into Real Property Law', *B.C. Envtl. Aff. L. Rev.*, vol. 25, 347–430.

Gray, K and Gray, S 1998, 'The Idea of Property' in S Bright and J Dewar (eds), *Land Law Themes and Perspectives*, Oxford University Press, New York.

Gray, K and Gray, S 1999, 'Private Property and Public Propriety' in J McLean (ed.), *Property and the Constitution*, Hart Publishing, Oxford.

Sarah Green, S and Randall, J 2009, *The Tort of Conversion*, Hart Publishing, Oxford.

Hamilton, J W and Bankes, N 2010, 'Different Views of the Cathedral: The Literature on Property Law Theory', in A. McHarg et al. (eds), *Property and the Law in Energy and Natural Resources*, Oxford University Press, Oxford.

Hepburn, S 2009, 'Carbon Rights as New Property: The Benefits of Statutory Verification', *Sydney Law Review*, vol. 31 no. 2 239–271.

Hohfield, W 1913, 'Some Fundamental Legal Conceptions as Applied in Legal Reasoning', *Yale Law Journal*, vol. 23, 16–59.

Honore, AM 1961, 'Ownership' in AG Guest (ed.), *Oxford Essays in Jurisprudence*, Oxford University Press, Oxford.

Jones, G (ed.) 1973, *The Sovereignty of the Law: Selections from Blackstone's Commentaries on the Laws of England*, Macmillan, London.

Jourdain, W 1925, *Land Legislation and Settlement in New Zealand*, Government Printer, Wellington.

Katz, L 2008, 'Exclusion and Exclusivity in Property Law' *Univ. Toronto Law J.*, vol. 58, 275–315.

King, C J 1957, *An Outline of Closer Settlement in NSW*, Dept. of Agriculture, Sydney NSW.

Lehavi, A 2008, 'The Property Puzzle', *Georgetown Law Rev.*, vol. 96, 1987–2028.

Lehavi, A 2013, *The Construction of Property: Norms, Institutions, Challenges*, Cambridge University Press, Cambridge.

Loncarich, K 2014, 'Nature's Law: The Evolutionary Origin of Property Rights' *Pace Law Rev.*, vol. 35, 580–642.

Lovett, J 2010, 'Progressive Property in Action: The Land Reform (Scotland) Act 2003' *Nebraska Law Rev.*, vol. 89, 739–820.

McLaren, J 2001, 'The Canadian Doukhobors and the Land Question: Religious Communalists in a Fee Simple World' in A Buck and J McLaren (eds), *Land and Freedom: Law Property Rights and the British Diaspora*, Ashgate, Farnham.

Merrill, T W 1998, 'Property and the Right to Exclude', *Nebraska Law Rev.*, vol. 77, 730–755.

Merrill, T W and Smith, H E 2007, 'The Morality of Property', *William & Mary Law Rev.* vol. 48, 1849–1895.

Page, J 2009, 'Grazing Rights and Public Lands in New Zealand and the western United States: A Comparative Perspective', *Natural Resources Journal*, vol. 49, 403–432.

Penalver, E and Katyal, S 2010, *Property Outlaws: How Squatters, Pirates, and Protestors Improve the Law of Ownership*, Yale University Press, New Haven, CT.

Raff, M 1998, 'Environmental Obligations and the Western Liberal Property Concept', *Melb. Univ. Law Rev.*, vol. 22, 657–692.

Raymond, L 2003, *Private Rights in Public Resources*, Resources for the Future, Washington, DC.

Reynolds, H and Dalziell, J 1996, 'Aborigines and Pastoral Leases: Imperial and Colonial Policy 1826-1855', *UNSW Law Journal*, vol. 19, 315–377.

Roberts, S 1924, *History of Australian Land Settlement 1788-1920* (1924), Macmillan & Melbourne University Press, Melbourne.

Roberts, S 1935, *The Squatting Age in Australia,* Melbourne University Press, Melbourne.

Rose, C M 1985, 'Possession as the Origin of Property', *Univ. Chicago Law Rev.,* vol. 52, no. 1, 73–88.

Rose, C M 1990, 'Property as Storytelling: Perspectives from Game Theory, Narrative Theory, Feminist Theory', *Yale Journal of Law & the Humanities,* vol. 2, 37–57.

Rose, C M 1994a, 'Given-ness and Gift: Property and the Quest for Environmental Ethics', *Envtl. Law,* vol. 24, 1–31.

Rose, C M 1994b, 'Seeing Property' in *Property and Persuasion Essays on the History, Theory, And Rhetoric of Ownership,* Westview Press, Boulder, CO.

Rose, C M 1998a, 'The Several Futures of Property: Of Cyberspace and Folk Tales, Emission Trades and Ecosystems', *Minn. L. Rev.,* vol. 83, 129–182.

Rose, C M 1998b, 'Canons of Property Talk, or Blackstone's Anxiety', *Yale L.J.,* vol. 108, 601–632.

Rose, C M 1999, 'What Government Can do for Property (and Vice Versa)' in W Samuels and N Mercuro (eds), *The Fundamental Interrelationships between Government and Property,* Routledge, Stanford, CT.

Rose, C M 2000, 'Property and Expropriation: Themes and Variations in American Law', *Utah Law Review,* vol. 25, 1–41.

Rose, C M 2006, 'The Moral Subject of Property', *Wm. & Mary L. Rev.,* vol. 48, 1897–1926.

Sax, J 1971, 'Takings, Private Property and Public Rights', *Yale L.J.,* vol. 81, 149–186.

Sax, J 1982, 'Some Thoughts on the Decline of Private Property, *Wash. L. Rev.,* vol. 58, 481–496.

Sax, J 1992, 'Property Rights and the Economy of Nature: Understanding *Lucas v. South Carolina Coastal Council*', *Stan. L. Rev.,* vol. 45, 1433–55.

Scott, A 2008, *The Evolution of Resource Property Rights,* Oxford University Press, Oxford.

Singer, J 1995, 'No Right to Exclude: Public Accommodations and Private Property', *Nw. U.L. Rev.,* vol. 90, 1283–1481.

Sprankling, J, Coletta, R and Mirow, M C (eds) 2006, *Global Issues in Property Law,* West Academic Publishing, St. Paul, MN.

Waring, E 2013, 'Private-Private Takings and the Stability of Property' *Kings Law Journal* vol. 24, 237–259.

White, C 2008, 'Conservation in the Age of Consequences' *Nat. Resources J.,* vol. 48, 1–13.

Wonnacott, M 2006, *Possession of Land,* Cambridge University Press, Cambridge.

Chapter 2

Towards an understanding of public property

2.1 Introduction

Public property in land is remarkable for its unremarked ubiquity, obvious to identification, yet oblivious to coherent understanding (Rose 1998b). While richly embroidering human landscapes, we remain pauperized by the public estate's theoretical under development.[1] As American scholars Jon Souder and Sally Fairfax observe, '[t]he flourishing literature concerning property ... is little reflected in the debate surrounding US public resources. Discussions of public lands – our national parks, forests, wildlife refuges, and grazing districts – has been surprisingly unconcerned with theories of property, access and ownership' (Souder and Fairfax 2000, p.89). Leigh Raymond concurs, noting the surprising absence of property rights from the public lands 'conversation' (Raymond 2003b, p.315). This chapter agrees. It argues that public property in land exists, but that it is under recognized (and indeed often unseen) because of the dominance of the private paradigm. This chapter sets out to reveal the extent of the public estate in our midst, and in that process to legitimize and thereby normalize the already existing place of public real property in a diverse property mosaic.

Section 2 commences with a brief definition of public property in land. Section 3 then reviews the spectrum of public property type, from corporeal to incorporeal, then beyond to custom and illusion. Section 4 aims to identify public property's proprietorship. The conundrum of 'who owns public property' and in what capacity, are vexing, inexact issues. Section 5 scrutinizes *inclusion,* its elusive, unconsummated relationship with access, analogies to use and enjoyment, and how it facilitates property as propriety. Section 6 concludes with a call for greater sophistication in public property discourse.

As Fairfax and Raymond intimate, scrutiny and analysis of public property in land is overdue. To myopically overlook the public estate is to consign its values and meanings to the periphery. Conversely, to better 'see' (Rose 1994) the diversity of public property in land is to dispel the corrosive implication that it is at one extreme, an oxymoron (Rose 1986), or at the other, a perverse variant of private ownership (Merrill 1998; Gray and Gray 1999b).[2] To better understand public property is to make clearer sense of what is ours.

2.2 Defining public property

Public property is frequently defined by what it is not; property that is *not* private property, a residual and counter-contextual explanation (Brower 2008). Common property is arguably better understood. (Dagan and Heller 2000; Ostrom 1990) The public estate suffers the paradoxical risk that it is non-property, a passive *res* awaiting capture.[3] As Margaret Davies argues, 'within the liberal context, the private nature of property is naturalised and universalised, as though other forms are somehow less ethically defensible' (Davies 2007, p.13). Centuries of marginalization of non-private property, dating from the enclosure period (Rose 2003, p.91) have obscured public property; it's seeing dispersed and drowned out by private rhetoric.

To define public property is to jettison the familiar private paradigms of exclusion and alienability. By necessity, it is to embrace that property is 'not a monolithic notion of standard content and invariable intensity [but] the most comprehensive of all the terms which can be used … indicative and descriptive … of all or any of the very many different kinds of relationship between a person and a subject matter.'[4] For narrative purposes, public property is defined as the sum of 'interests [in land] in which the individual concerned has no greater claim than any other member of the public,'[5] collective rights, enjoyed by individuals in common with others, and measured by their public sum.

This chapter expands on this preliminary definition by identifying three indicators of public property in land: the diversity of its *type*; the conundrum of its *ownership*; and its right of *inclusion*. Each attribute amplifies further comprehension; type expands recognition; ownership exposes the fault line between property's collective and individual values, while inclusion represents the hope of a nascent touchstone right, presently ill formed and amorphous.

2.3 The spectrum of type

Public property in land takes a plethora of forms. This section seeks taxonomic order by adopting a blunt categorization familiar to property lawyers: corporeal versus incorporeal. Corporeal public property refers to tangible, identifiable lands. Incorporeal public property comprises non-possessory, intangible, less than fee interests in land. The study of type then diverges to examining the sources of public property beyond statute and the common law, those of custom, even the imaginings of illusion.

Traditionally seen as government-owned land, the spectral breadth of public property type demonstrates both a surprising diversity, and a refutation of any distinct public–private divide in property. Rather, public property occupies space across a broad continuum, where degrees of public-ness are relative, not absolute questions.

2.3.1 Corporeal public property

Public property is most recognizable in its corporeal form, typically alienated land held by the state or Crown, state agencies,[6] or public lands leased to long-term private right-holders.[7] Public land held by government agencies is primarily land dedicated or reserved for public purposes. Its usage depends on its public function: conservation; resource exploitation; education; transport; health; defence; public administration; recreation,[8] and so on. Then there are public lands with no present use; un-alienated Crown lands or non-allocated public domain lands that have not been dedicated, reserved, or otherwise dealt with. Interspersed is an inchoate miscellany, the like of permissive occupancies, travelling stock routes, or 'paper' roads, *ad hoc* interests that reflected periodic policy imperatives. To list the broad sweep of corporeal public property in land in any one jurisdiction is to embark on an exercise of miscellany, as Table 2.1 below illustrates.

The physical footprint of corporeal public property is impressive. In the USA, one-third of the continental landmass comprises federally owned public lands.[9] In three of the 11 western states, the percentage exceeds 50 per cent.[10] In Australia, Crown land amounts to fifty per cent of the landmass of the populous state of New South Wales. In more sparsely settled Western Australia, it is 93 per cent. State-owned conservation land alone constitutes one-third of New Zealand's area. Yet, despite its superlative acreage, public property lacks the legitimacy or normalcy of private property, a consequence of a binary liberal worldview that naturalizes the primacy of the private rights holder and views the state with deep suspicion (Frug 1980, Blomley 1994). Hence, its boundaries, physical and metaphorical, are perpetually tested, while collective values are seen as inferior to the individual values of private property. In the western USA, 'sagebrush rebellions' (Nelson 1995) or 'storms over the rangelands' (Hage 1989) are well-documented episodic revolts against the public property estate. Elsewhere, the unidirectional propensity of private rights to encroach into public space has been observed (Brower et al. 2009).

The sheer size of the corporeal public estate seemingly fails to address such existential or normative shortcomings. That it may take incorporeal form unlocks potentialities for new, non-reactive ways to see and understand public property in land.

Table 2.1 Corporeal public property in land in New South Wales

National parks estate
Principal Act: *National Parks and Wildlife Act 1974* (NSW)

National parks, section 30E National Parks and Wildlife Act 1974 (NSW)
Historic sites, section 30F
State conservation areas, section 30G
Regional parks, section 30H
Karst conservation reserves, section 30I
Nature reserves, section 30J
Aboriginal areas, section 30K
Wildlife refuges, section 68
Wild rivers, section 61
Marine parks, *Marine Parks Act 1997* (NSW)
Conservation agreements, Part 4 Division 12

Crown land estate
Principal Act: *Crown Land Act 1989* (NSW)

Crown lands available for lease, special lease, or licence, Part 4, Divs 3, 3A, & 4
Crown lands dedicated for public purposes, Part 5 Division 2
Crown reserves, Part 5 Division 3
State Parks, Part 5 Division 3
Crown reserve trusts, Part 5 Divisions 4 and 5
Enclosure permits, Part 4 Division 6
Crown public roads, (formed and unformed), *Roads Act 1993* (NSW)
Travelling stock reserves, *Rural Lands Protection Act 1998* (NSW)
Submerged lands, coastal harbours and river entrances, Section 172
Commons*, *Commons Management Act 1989* (NSW)

Residual Crown tenures:
Principal Act: *Crown Lands (Continued Tenures) Act 1989* (NSW)

Incomplete purchases
Perpetual leases
Term leases
Special leases
Permissive occupancies
Leases to the Commonwealth

Western lands pastoral estate
Principal Act: *Western Lands Act 1901* (NSW)

Pastoral holdings, Part 6 Division 2
Rural leases, Part 6 Division 2
Urban leases, Part 6 Division 3
Special purpose leases, Part 9E

Forestry estate
Principal Act: *Forestry Act 1916* (NSW)

State Forests, Part 3 Division 2
Timber reserves, Part 3 Division 2
Flora reserves, Part 3 Division 2

Note: * Commons are technically common property, not public property.

2.3.2 *Incorporeal public property*

Less recognizable is public property's manifestation as an array of incorporeal property rights. As less than fee interests, they comprise a panoply of covenants, easements, servitudes and *sui generis* statutory rights, held by the state, state agencies, the public at large, or private entities that act in the public interest. Incorporeal rights subsist over both private lands, as public rights encumbering private title, and corporeal public land.[11]

Conceptualized as abstract, non-possessory sticks within the bundle metaphor, incorporeal public rights are separate and divisible from the physical land itself. For example, the right of recreational access to private property is a use and enjoyment stick held by the general public. When enacted in England by the Countryside and Rights of Way Act 2000, the statutory right was described in bundle terms as a transfer or re-allocation of 'a valuable property right from private landowners to the public' (Anderson 2007, p.246).

Despite its abstract nature, incorporeal public property plays a surprisingly key role in contextualizing property right to place and connecting otherwise fragmented land parcels (Freyfogle 2007, pp.107–27).[12] Examples include scenic easements that preserve natural vistas (Cunningham 1968, Hutton 2000), public footpaths that link villages across privately owned farmland (Sydenham 2002), or conservation covenants that form wildlife corridors across private habitat. Re-inserting links between disparate property ownerships militates against Eric Freyfogle's 'tragedy of fragmentation', the private rights-dominated landscape where property holdings are island enclaves 'with no mechanisms to achieve landscape-scale goals' (Freyfogle 2007, p.35). Freyfogle prescribes as a remedy the reconceptualization of private property and a need to 'reassert the public's varied interests in private lands' (Freyfogle 2003, pp.177, 203).

The conservation easement exemplifies the connectivity potential of incorporeal public property. A statutory interest modelled on the common law easement (Mayo 2007, p.27), the US conservation easement is

> A nonpossessory interest of a holder of real property imposing limitations or affirmative obligations the purposes of which include retaining or protecting natural, scenic, or open space values of real property, assuring its availability for agricultural, forest, recreational or open-space use, protecting natural resources, maintaining air or water quality, or preserving the historical, architectural, archeological, or cultural aspects of real property.[13]

Conservation easements first appeared in the 1930s (Cunningham 1968, pp.181–83), but their use did not become widespread until 50 years later, when tax incentives encouraged the donation or sale of perpetual conservation easements to public agencies or land trusts (Brewer 2003, pp.148, 155). By the beginning of the twenty-first century, conservation easements were 'the fastest-growing method for protecting land' in the USA, preserving 1.2 million acres from development, at growth rates over the preceding decade of 377 per cent (Gustanski 2000, p.14). Many conservation easements vest in or benefit land trusts, 'non-profit organizations that preserve or enhance environmental amenities ... on private land' (Parker 2004). Landscape resources protected by conservation easements include open space, wetlands, forests, scenic views, recreation and trails, greenways, and coastlines (Gustanski 2000, p.21). The legal justification for conservation easements is said to be 'significant public benefit' (Brewer 2003, p.116; French 2006, p.2532). Often the public benefit is indirect, the provision of 'ecosystem services ... a nice view ... habitat for wildlife, [or] protected farmland' (Brewer 2003). Direct public 'goods' manifest as walking trails linking national parks, or trails using disused railway corridors. 'Some 78% of land trusts are reported as being involved in maintaining land for public access or recreational purposes' (Gustanski 2000, p.22).

In Australia, conservation agreements,[14] or positive covenants protecting environmental, cultural, heritage or natural resource values,[15] are analogous incorporeal public rights, the benefit vesting in the relevant land conservation agency. Such interests protect private or Crown leased land containing 'scenery, natural environments or natural phenomenon worthy of preservation.'[16] The American land trust is replicated by not-for-profit organizations such as the Nature Conservation Trust, where voluntary landowner agreements and revolving fund arrangements protect natural and cultural heritage and run with the land through registration.[17] In New Zealand, conservation or open space covenants, under statutes like the Queen Elizabeth the Second Natural Trust Act 1977, fulfil similar functions to protect ecological or landscape values (Donohue 2003; Ewing 2009).

The English public footpath is yet another example of incorporeal public property. It differs from the wider right to roam in that the footpath right is restricted to established pathways. The public footpath was the transport corridor of agrarian England. 130,000 miles of public footpath remain in England and Wales, as part of original enclosure orders, easements protected through prescription or dedication, or common rights (Anderson 2007, pp.380–83). The public right is resilient, private owners cannot obstruct a footpath's continued access, nor discourage its public use. If an affected landholder seeks to divert the pathway, a public path diversion order may be made, but only where the alternative is not 'substantially less convenient for the public in consequence of the diversion'.[18]

The public trust doctrine, the impression of public obligations on private and public lands, also fits the incorporeal tag (Sax 1969). Harrison Dunning describes the public trust in incorporeal terms as a 'public property right [that] manifests itself as an interest, like an easement, that burdens ownership of the resource' (Dunning 1988, p.520; also Eichenberg, Bothwell and Vaughn 2001, pp.247–48). Kevin Gray's 'regulatory property' is analogous, private property subject to an overriding public interest that effectively 'vests the property in the citizenry subject only to such privileges ... the state positively confers for the time being on the nominal 'owners' of the assets concerned' (Gray 2010b, p.245).

The significance of incorporeal public rights is threefold. First, they broaden our understanding of public property to encompass a diversity of rights beyond fee simple state ownership. Second, they highlight the anachronism of any distinct public–private divide. Conservation easements or public footpaths exemplify that public rights subsist on private lands, and condemn by their existence the notion of a distinct property duality as 'confusion elevated to principle' (Geisler 2000, p.79). Third, they demonstrate public property's potential to invigorate connections across human landscapes; to link property with place and context, and obviate the risks of countless 'tragedies of fragmentation'.

2.3.3 *Customary public property*

The sources of public property are not restricted to the mainstream. Property's commodification has masked its ancient alter ego, one with meaning for personhood, identity and community. Customary public property evidences faint but 'surprising connections' between 'informal usages and understandings' about public property, and their binding effect amongst 'those who practice and share them' (Bederman 1996, p.1375).

Custom is an awkward, seemingly anachronistic source of modern property law, particularly in settler societies lacking the social history from which idiosyncratic customary rules arose.[19] Nonetheless customary norms find ways to percolate into the margins of property discourse. Robert Ellickson's 'order without law' in Shasta County, California, observes the powerful, all-pervasive effect of custom in generating rights, including property rights, amongst tightly knit communities of ranchers (Ellickson 1991). He concludes that such informal rules arise 'through decentralized social processes, rather than from the law' (Ellickson 1991, p.139). Similarly, Gregory Duhl studies food cart owners at Temple University, and surmises that 'the ordering of lunch trucks and carts ... illustrates how, in the absence of private property ownership, communities adopt and follow customs and norms to create and order property rights' (Duhl 2006, p.207).

Carol Rose escapes territorial constraints to explore the wider relationship between custom and public property, noting that 'custom provides powerful insights into the nature of "inherently public property"' (Rose 1986, p.722). Rose posits that the effective management of public property arises 'through the medium of the customs and habits of a civilized citizenry' (ibid., p.774). Efficient, albeit informal governance of public resources by the customary public averts a tragedy of the commons, and instead enhances a sociable 'comedy of the commons', where the greater the use of public property, the greater the resource's social value is maximized, and the 'solidarity and fellow-feeling of the whole community' is reinforced. Thus, the more is the merrier (ibid., p.759). In such a vein, David Bederman writes of 'custom's bright and cheery demeanor' that permits public rights like 'rustic villagers to dance around the Maypole' or 'hardy fishermen to dry their nets on the shore as they have for time immemorial' (Bederman 1996, pp.1381–82). Like Rose, Daniel Nazer's study of surfer norms (Nazer 2004) also escapes the strictures of a localized community. Rather, the global surfing community was a 'large and heterogeneous' one that developed normative patterns of property over public surfing waves, with only minor geographical variations. Such norms require users to 'respect the rules and respect the locals'.[20]

The paradox of custom and property is 'how often custom wins' (Raymond 1997; Anderson and Hill 2004). Even in the courts, custom as the basis of a public right occasionally prevails (Ubhi and Denyer-Green 2004; Eagle 2010). In Oregon, the celebrated case of *State ex rel. Thornton v. Hay* [21] established a state-wide public easement over private dry sands on the basis of customary practice (Bender 1998).

2.3.4 Illusory public property

This discussion of type concludes with a foray into illusory public property. Rose argues that people even 'see' property as false claims, 'the imaginative construction of property ... where the law recognizes none' (1994, p.274). Much of her discussion centres on people claiming transient entitlements to public spaces as their imagined own, such as lunchtime 'rights' to park benches. Kevin Gray's study of the property norms of spatial order in queues is an analogous example (Gray 2010).

Arguably the modern shopping mall best typifies illusory public property, 'private space masquerading as a public space' (Kunstler 1993, pp.119–20). As 'open-access private properties' (Geisler 2000, p.75), or privately owned 'quasi-public property' (Gray and Gray 1999a), these hybrids foster illusory expectations of public rights of inclusion. The illusion is shattered when private owners enforce behaviour or dress codes, or restrain public assembly or political protest. In such circumstances, 'private proprietorial power [the right to exclude] intrudes into the public sphere' (Davies 2007, p.11). To social commentator Howard James Kunstler, 'the mall commercialized the public realm' (Kunstler 1993, pp.119–20). So impoverished is the public estate, we imagine it where it is not.

2.3.5 *Type and property diversity*

The diverse range of public property type is a reminder that public property is capable of being seen in the most likely, and unlikely of places. Incorporeal property in particular underscores that there is no bright line (Davies 2007, p.11), no distinct public–private divide. Rather public property can be found across a continuum, where 'notions of "public" and "private" operate, not dichotomously, but continuously ... in which adjacent connotations shade easily into one another,' and 'finely intercalated distinctions or gradations' (Gray and Gray 1999a, pp.11, 18) segue from state-owned public lands to customary public rights. In seeking to understand public property through the spectrum of type, it is the differing degrees of public-ness in land, rather than the formal technicality of individual type, that may prove the most instructive.

Importantly, a wider seeing of public property in land enlivens a pluralistic mosaic of property rights and uses. Public property contributes to the mosaic by adding different tiles, corporeal and incorporeal to the private monotony. The more we see a variety, and greater quantity, of different property types (Brower and Page 2011, p.305), the less conditioned we become to a self-imposed straitjacket where property and private property are synonymous.[22] Optimistically, property diversity has the potential for human landscapes to become less like a universalized Blackacre (Freyfogle 2003, p.110), and more representative of where we live (Garbutt 2011, pp.29–30).

Legal geographers emphasize that law, including property, is best understood by context, 'by reference to its place in and relationship to social, economic, political and ecological systems'. In so doing, they reject an idealized paradigm where the 'law's separateness ... [is] deaf to material, physical, spatial and cultural influences' (Holder and Harrison 2003, p.3). The law is 'world-ed', where context is not simply an inert setting, but 'inextricably implicated in *how* law happens' (Braverman et al. 2014, p.1). Edward Relph, a humanist geographer, argues 'an authentic attitude to context or place is important ... because from such a relation, authentic places emerge, places which ... sustain the earth and those dwelling on it' (Relph, cited in Garbutt 2011, pp.54–55). Property matters in the pursuit of a contextual authenticity, 'both symbolically and literally' (Jacobs 2010, p.6). Eric Freyfogle's bleak description of Champaign County, Illinois, where the public owns less than 1 per cent of the county 'setting aside roadways and the remnants of a now-abandoned [and contaminated] air force base' (Freyfogle 2011, p.271), is a depressing and literal vision of property uniformity. To Freyfogle, public lands are the 'remedy for private irresponsibility' (Freyfogle 2003, p.96). Kunstler's *The Geography of Nowhere* is an equally grim visage of the decline of the American public realm, the 'landscape tissue that ties together the thousands of pieces of private property that make up a town, a suburb, a state' (Kunstler 1993, p.27).

While largely a descriptive exercise, the spectrum of type subverts the inevitability of Kunstler's thesis, or the unremitting bleakness of Freyfogle's imagery. Its opportunities lie in expanding the definitional parameters of what is public property. Its significance lies in its consequence, a weakening of private ubiquity, and the optimistic consequences this may pose for re-physicalizing property rights to place. Its lesson is that there are viable alternatives to Champaign County-like uniformity. Seeing a wide diversity of public type may alter such restrictive path dependencies for the better.

2.4 The conundrum of ownership

Ownership is premised on the vesting of property rights in a recognizable entity in their capacity as owner (Waldron 1991), a 'right to have and to dispose of possession and enjoyment of the subject matter.'[23] In the case of public property, the ownership entity assumedly has a public status, the state, or an agency of the state (Rose 1986, p.719). But this assumption poses further questions; does the state or state agency own the land absolutely, or pursuant to some trust for and on behalf of its citizens? And what of private groups such as land trusts that hold stick rights in property that benefit the public? These questions suggest that like the public–private divide, the issue of ownership is likewise not a 'bright line' (Davies 2007).

Putative ownership by the public at large is a further muddying of the ownership waters. Rose argues that rights in 'inherently public property' are controlled neither by government agencies nor private entitles, but by society at large (Rose 1986, p.720). This owner is the 'unorganized', yet not disorganized, public. (ibid., p.722) In the USA, ownership of inherently public property by the 'unorganized public' is given effect by the doctrine of public trust. Originally concerned with core areas such as navigable waterways, the public trust has proven a 'resurgent concept' (Sax 1982, p.482), bringing within its ambit new forms of contestable 'inherently public property'[24] that recognize community or public values in diffuse resources (Rose 1998a). This in turn expands the types of property capable of ownership by an amorphous unorganized public.

Joseph Sax frames ownership from a values perspective, in the process identifying a fault line common to the cultural divide between property as a private commodity, and property's social or communitarian meanings. He states that '[t]he debate over ownership of the public lands is basically part of a much larger controversy over the legitimacy of collective versus individualistic values' (Sax 1984a, p.130). Courts tend to prefer individualistic values: '[t]he common law tradition is not entirely friendly to group rights' (Rose 2006, p.13). In Australia, the High Court held that members of the public generally do not acquire any proprietary estate or interest in public land. But its judgment was framed from the perspective of the private paradigm, where 'right ... does not in its context mean a public right; it means an individual right of a proprietary nature', and 'interest' mean 'interests held by persons in their individual capacity'.[25] Yet the court did touch on what public ownership may entail.

> It [the statute] does not embrace interests in which the individual concerned has no greater claim than any other member of the public. All members of the public have a right to pass freely along and across public highways but none have in their capacity as members of the public any estate or interest in such land. Likewise members of the public may be entitled pursuant to particular statutes to use specified areas of Crown lands for the purpose of recreation ... All members of the public may have the right to go upon such land [to] freely walk thereon ... and may resist attempts by the Crown or anyone else to eject them from such land.[26]

Ownership of public property must be seen in context, informed by property's collective values, where rights are measured in terms of their collective sum rather than individual entitlement. In section 4, three specific questions will be canvassed: must public property be owned by a discrete ownership entity; is public ownership an absolute concept; and is the better question one of state agency *management or control* rather than ownership?

2.4.1 Entity or no entity?

Unlike private property, the involvement of a distinct ownership entity may not be a theoretical necessity for public property (Waldron 1985). Rose's 'unorganized public' exemplifies that inherently public property may be owned by the collective public at large. The absence of an overarching entity does not facilitate anarchy, but rather the customs of a 'civilized citizenry' ensures good governance. The *prima facie* answer to this question suggests that there is no limitation on who owns public property. The state, a state agency, the public at large, even (in the case of conservation easements) private owners, may 'own' public interests in land.

Direct ownership by the state or a state agency is a paradigm framed within private property's individualistic values and rhetoric of exclusion. It also has perverse consequences. Richard Barnes observes that ownership of collective property by the 'individual' state is in effect a variation of private ownership that precludes it generating 'a specific normative meaning' (Barnes 2009, p.154). Margaret Davies agrees in part. In articulating a 'taxonomy of owners', she lists five possible classes of owner: private individuals, companies, governments, a limited community, or the public at large. Davies argues that individual and corporate ownerships are 'private', while 'government ownership of resources such as office buildings [is also] essentially private' (Davies 2007, pp.63–64). On the other hand, ownership by limited communities or the public at large is 'dispersed'. But government ownership of 'public infrastructure, and environmental resources such as parks and beaches on trust for the public' (ibid., p.64) are neither private nor public, an unsatisfactory lacuna that falls between the stools. Crawford Macpherson describes 'state property' as 'corporate private property', where a 'smaller body of persons authorized to command its citizens' exercise a corporate right to exclude (Macpherson 1999, pp.5–6). It is as if explicit ownership by a state or state agency taints public property's *publicness,* and relegates the ownership of key public places (such as Davies' parks and beaches) to an uncertain no-man's land.

By contrast, 'public domain goods' are in Davies' terms 'fundamental to a flourishing community; they provide us with the basic ability to move about, to undertake trade and commerce, to engage in recreation, to situate ourselves historically, culturally, or even spiritually, to communicate and express ourselves' (Davies 2007, pp.65–66). As Rose argues, they vest in an 'unorganized public'. Macpherson also writes of an 'unorganized public', a mass of individuals with individual rights in 'analogous common property'.[27] He argues that rights in such property are 'the most unadulterated kind of property', a right of each natural person not to be excluded from the property's use and benefit' (Macpherson 1999, p.6; Barnes 2009, p.154).

Ownership by the public at large, whether Rose's amorphous mass, or MacPherson's mass of individuals, may be preferable since it avoids unfavourable analogy with private ownership and sidesteps the implications of exclusion. And by invoking property's collective values, it may prove the sanguine catalyst for greater normative meaning for public property in land.[28]

2.4.2 *In trust for the public?*

References to public property in land frequently invoke the concept of trust. To borrow its terminology, the trust may be express (in the case of charitable trusts), or implied or resulting (where 'trust' is used in a non-technical sense). Private land trusts also conform to this paradigm, signifying that the public stick they hold over private land is impressed by obligations in favour of local communities, the wider public, or the public interest.[29]

Souder and Fairfax use the educational state land trust as a platform for advocating that 'trust principles ought to occupy a more prominent place in our understanding of publicly owned land than they do' (Souder and Fairfax 2000, p.89). Rather than some scholar's wishful thinking of 'wouldn't it be lovely', the authors argue that the state land trust, as 'arguably the oldest of all federal programs and ... the most durable national approach to public resource ownership' already provides an enduring template. Raising its profile presents an opportunity for a 'new but not untested route to thinking about public ownership' (ibid., p.90).

By contrast, the public trust doctrine enjoys a high profile, and is the subject of a rich literature. Its contemporary resurrection since the 1970s is attributed to Joseph Sax (1969), although its history can be traced to the *jus publicum* of Roman law, and the English common law before its reception in the United States (Sax 1969, pp.475–78; Higgins 2005, pp.183–84). Its origins lie in the nature of property in rivers, lakes and foreshores adjoining water bodies as inherently public property, or 'at least subject to a kind of inherent easement for certain public purposes' (Rose 1986, p.351). While private ownership of foreshores was possible, the incorporeal public property inherent to those lands (such as rights to navigable waters) was itself inalienable (Dunning 1988, p.516).

Its common law credentials were affirmed in the 'lodestar' (Sax 1969, pp.489–91) case of *Illinois Central Railroad Company v. Illinois*,[30] where the US Supreme Court upheld the State's repeal of a land grant comprising foreshores and submerged lands on the Chicago waterfront. The court held that these lands were public trust resources, such that the initial grant by the state to the railroad company was void. The doctrine was neglected until growing environmental awareness in the late 1960s re-awakened its potential, 'liberating it from its historical shackles' (Sax 1980), to protect public rights in a diverse range of public resources. These include access rights over the dry sands of beaches, or limits on the appropriation of water to serve public trust values.[31] Even 'property' in surfing waves has been linked to the public trust (Nazer 2004). This expansion has relied on a lateral interpretation of its founding shackles, a creative linking of new public resources with the common denominators of navigable waters or foreshores below the high water mark.[32] These newer forms of public trust property have been described as possessing a 'natural suitability for common use' and tendency towards 'scarcity' (Dunning 1988, p.523), or qualities essential for communication, travel and sociability (Rose 1986). Despite its critics, (for example, Jawetz 1982) the public trust is 'a recognition of important public property rights' (Dunning 1988, p.516) premised on the fragmentation of ownership between bare legal title and beneficial property subject to public trust. In the case of private lands, the grantee holds a naked fee subject to public trust rights (Stevens 1980). In the case of public lands, there is no merger that extinguishes the public trust.

Trust relationships in public property also arise through the gift or transfer of private land to public authorities for specified purposes,[33] as conditions of planning consent, or by operation of statute. For example, in New South Wales, the Crown reserve trust is a statutory creature under the Crown Lands Act.[34] The New Zealand Reserves Act establishes a similar regime. That Act applies to Crown land classified under section 16 according to its primary or principal purpose. Purposes include recreation, historic or scenic reserves. Title to reserves is vested under sections 26 and 26A, such that 'all land so vested shall be held in trust for the purpose or purposes for which the reserve is classified'. In a New Zealand High Court judgment dealing with conflicting private uses on Crown land, *Gibbs v. The New Plymouth District Council* section 26A was scrutinized,[35] the court concluding that 'the general public of New Zealand must be regarded as the beneficiaries. The concept is one of public ownership' ([16]–[17]). The Reserves Act 'confer[s] legal ownership ... in the Crown while making it clear that the land is held on trust for all New Zealanders' ([14]).

Nor is the language of trust necessarily restrained by a lack of an equitable or statutory basis for the beneficial relationship claimed. Narratives surrounding the public estate, particularly iconic public property, often describe such lands as being held in trust for, or on behalf of its citizens. This proprietorial claim is substantiated by broad-brush references to the nature of democratic governance, or the people's common legacy in important natural resources. On the fiftieth anniversary of the US National Park Act in 1966, National Geographic magazine quoted first parks director Stephen Mather claim that the park system belonged 'to everyone – now and always' (Grosvenor 1966, p.2). The landmark Report of the Public Land Law Review Commission in 1970, repeated this common legacy view, '[t]hese lands are a natural heritage and national asset that belong to us all' (Public Land Law Review Commission 1970, p.20).

An implied trust seemingly results from state ownership, accentuated where the lands are iconic, or under threat of loss (Philp 2008, p.44). While the nominal owner may be the state, its title is a threadbare one. The true beneficial owner, illusory or otherwise, is the people. Davies' description of 'parks and beaches being held in trust for the public' (Davies 2007, p.64) is a previously traversed exemplar of this narrative. Carol Rose speaks similarly of 'the public ... as a kind of beneficial owner of diffuse resource right' (Rose 1996, p.276), while legal historian Harry Scheiber talks of legislatures acting as trustee 'for the best interests of the public' with regard to certain types of public property (Scheiber 1984, p.223).

The concept of trust permeates public property, its doctrines, statutes and rhetoric. Its redolence suggests an inclination for public property to vest in the collective sum of us. But where does that leave the individualistic state or state agency?

2.4.3 Ownership or management rights?

Eric Freyfogle believes that the 'biggest difference between public and private lands has to do with management power over the land.' Yet again, there is no bright line, with 'decisions about public lands ... mostly made by public decision-makers, but not completely so [while] private involvement in public-lands is extensive' (Freyfogle 2003, p.93).

Freyfogle's emphasis on state management rather than ownership may be apt. Where the state is a bare trustee, its role is reduced to management of trust assets for the exclusive benefit of the true beneficial owners, who retain the bulk of the key bundle rights. The state's residual right is essentially a right to manage, and this right is constrained by trust obligations. Shorn of most of the hallmark property rights, it may be unrealistic to describe the state's dearth of bundle rights in public property as proprietorial.[36]

Indeed, from the state's perspective, is ownership *per se* the prime objective for its public property estate? As Sally Fairfax and her colleagues observe:

> Ownership does not ensure control. The relevant myth here suggests that if you own land, you can protect it. The reality … is that formal ownership frequently provides little control or resource protection at all. This is particularly true on federally owned land, despite federal ownership being commonly portrayed as the preferred tenure arrangement for conservation.
>
> (Fairfax et al. 2005, p.257)[37]

The state as bare owner may be better employed devoting its energies to the effective control of the public land it manages on behalf of its citizens. Good state management may reinforce the integrity of public property, and silence its critics (Brower at al. 2009).[38]

Ownership of public property is a vexed issue. Its inexactitude suggests that it is not the defining characteristic of public property that it should be. Who owns public property, and in what capacity, are complex questions lacking ready answers. Part of the struggle to respond may be attributed to a values paradigm of dominant individualism. Its end result leaves us less equipped to meaningfully understand the ownership of public property in land.

2.4.4 Ownership and diffusion

One clearer way to explain the conundrum of ownership is the idea of diffusion, Rose's 'the more the merrier' (Rose 1986). Simply, the more dispersed our sense of 'ownership', the more interested we become in its management and welfare. Diffusion rests on an instinctive imperative that citizens should conceive of public property as 'their own', no matter how 'thin' the ownership.

The disaggregation of property ownership amongst the public at large decentralizes property 'rights' and spreads relative degrees of ownership amongst a wide class of persons (Page 2011). Joseph Singer describes this dispersal as inherent in his 'nuisance' or 'citizen' model of property. 'The effect is to identify multiple persons who have legally protected interests in the same piece of property and therefore have something to say about how it is used' (Singer 2000, p.88). Singer further refines this view into a relational one where links to place became explicit, the 'environmental' or 'good neighbor' model, (Singer 2006 and 2010) where dispersed property rights are 'overlapping or imbricated' (Singer 2010, p.60), such that individual or collective acts have wider flow on effects to neighbours and the environment. Diffusion facilitates self-adjusting 'checks and balances' though the spreading of ownership across landscapes. 'These trans-boundary overlaps ... constrain an owner's ability to act unilaterally, while at the same time diffuse ownership to a wide range of owners with different vested interests in their ownerships' (Brower and Page 2012).

The exponential expansion of a class of (self) interested public owners has two effects, first it spreads the individual public's sense of ownership; second, intricate levels of overlap mean that everyone has a vested interest in the consequences of another's (adverse) acts over public property. One's sense of property in a public place thus elevates itself from ambiguity to a diffused sense of propriety, a concern for its welfare, and a willingness to get involved to protect it. That the law will act to protect public property rights (Rose 1986), sometimes at the behest of the state, but often at the instigation of informal community or representative groups, is a tangible outcome of the diffusion of ownership of public property in land.

Diffusion is deeply conceptual and problematic in practice. How can scattered public 'ownership' rights be regulated and enforced? What can prevent a motivated, self-interested few capturing the public estate to the detriment of an apathetic many? The American experience of the public trust suggests a role for the judiciary as guardians of the public interest in public property. This chapter does not purport to provide ready answers to such prosaic matters. Yet, fundamentally, developing a sense of public propriety requires paradigmatic change. Articulating what a right of inclusion may encompass is one step in beginning such an incremental shift.

2.5 The right to include

If exclusion is the hallmark right of modern private property, logically inclusion should be public property's inverse gatekeeper (Hamilton and Bankes 2010, pp.19, 26). As a guiding principle, what is meant by a right to include? Does its foil define it, such that it is a right *not* to exclude? (Mitchell 2008) Or does it have an independent, positive meaning, a right to *access* 'material resources' (Waldron 1991, p.31)?

Carol Rose warns that

> It is a serious mistake to think of property only in metaphors of exclusion, boundaries, and disengagement ... Human interactions make property into a thoroughly malleable institution, and one that adjusts to a vast variety of subjects.
>
> (Rose 1992, p.2420)

Rose's advice intimates that exclusion is a flawed place to start. Nor is Rose alone in observing that property is a 'thoroughly malleable institution' that moulds to context. (Singer 2000; Sax 1992, p.1446) To define inclusion by what it is not is counter-contextual and affirms that exclusion is the *sine qua non* of property. Inclusion deserves a stand-alone definition.

Language is one starting point. *Roget's Thesaurus* lists numerous synonyms for *inclusion,* including participation, membership, affiliation, eligibility, admission; terms that embody shared or common possession of space. The links between language and property are intimate and powerful; Rose describes them as central to her legal scholarship. Language is not only words in a thesaurus, but in a broader sense, a means of persuasive communication; in the case of property, its symbols, visual cues, or collective narratives. Rose proffers a number of images as the 'expressive endeavor' or 'symbolic presentation' of public property; streetscapes, parks, highways, and most evocatively, a fresco of a sociable street scene in medieval Siena, a good life where 'people stop to chat with one another and with the street vendors', engage in commerce, sit and laugh, and 'watch the other passers-by' (Rose 1990, p.18). The democratic sharing of a public space is an uncomplicated way to see public property, an image that captures the diverse language of inclusion. It is the antithesis of private property's expressive endeavour: the fence, gate, keep-out sign, and private world inside.

2.5.1 Inclusion and access

Access ought to be the epitome of inclusion. It lies at the heart of Rose's street scene. Yet the right of access is far from clear-cut. Some public lands are openly accessible; others have conditions attached to their intrusion (such as the payment of entrance fees in popular national parks), while in other cases, there is no access at all (military land, or dedicated wilderness, or wildlife preservation areas).[39] In the USA there is also a constitutional overlay affecting public property historically open to the public, the 'public forum.' '[I]n such places [parks, sidewalks, town squares] the government's ability to permissively restrict expressive conduct is very limited.'[40] Conversely '[p]ublicly owned or operated property does not become a "public forum" simply because members of the public are permitted to come and go at will'.[41] In Australia or New Zealand, no such constitutional implications impact on public access. In other cases, legislation may give an occupier of prescribed public lands the discretion to eject intruders provided a prior demand to leave is made, deeming the recalcitrant intruder a trespasser.[42] Such legislation places the emphasis on the right to exclude, at times confusing Barnes' 'needs of society as a whole' with the 'self-serving interest' of the particular occupier, public or private.[43] In sum, access as a proposition is a mélange of unqualified, qualified or denied entitlement (Waldron 1992, pp.297–98).

Even where access appears unfettered, externalities may practically restrict freedom of entry. A surrounding landholder may effectively capture the public lands by impeding the most feasible points of access. A consequence of effective capture is their *de facto* privatization. Private capture of public lands in New Zealand's iconic high country is the subject of separate academic scrutiny (Brower 2008; Page and Brower 2007). Equally, contested access through private land to beach and coastal foreshore attracts vocal, high-profile attention (Dyer 1972). In June 2010, *Stop the Beach Renourishment v. Florida Department of Environmental Protection*[44] was 'the [US Supreme Court's] case of the year for planners and land use practitioners' (Lucero 2010, p.3), a curious dispute about property rights, accretion and littoral access.[45]

Beaches are much-loved public places (Bederman 1996). Access to them engages the *many* as well as the *few* (Olson 1968) in both its practice and idea. Yet despite their revered status, a brief comparison of 'beach law' in the USA and New Zealand illustrates that access is far from being a uniform touchstone of the public estate and its inclusiveness.

Access to the wet sands of American beaches through privately owned dry sands is a 'perplexing' issue (Stevens 1980, p.230). Public rights are piecemeal (Bender 1998, p.914), limited by the low tide in some states, extending to the mean high tide mark in others, and in Texas protected by public rolling easements to the first vegetation line (Eichenberg, Bothwell and Vaughn. 2001; Peloso and Caldwell 2011, pp.57–58). Inconsistent applications of doctrines such as prescription or implied dedication yield unpredictable outcomes. In a handful of states, there has been a 'Lazarus-like' resurrection of beach access rights, which David Bederman ascribes to four models; nineteenth-century common law doctrine in New England, statutory codification of custom in Texas, judicial instrumentalism in Oregon and indigenous rights in Hawaii (Bederman 1996, pp.1379–408). Outside Bederman's 'four corners', the extension of the public trust to the dry sands has been most expansively achieved in New Jersey (Archer et al. 1994, pp.107–8). Elsewhere, the public trust has produced outcomes that are underwhelming (Archer et al. 1994, p.106; Higgins 2005, pp.183–84). In California, a famous beach culture has not equated to universal access rights over upland dry sands. While Californian courts have been active in expanding other categories of public trust property (Archer et al. 1994, p.23), sea-locked tidelands remain contested (Dyer 1968, p.578). The

Supreme Court's oft-cited decision in *Nollan v. California Coastal Commission*[46] held that a consent condition requiring owners of a beachside home to grant a public easement over their private beach, was a compensable taking of property. Nollan affirms that beachfront easement access is 'purchased by the landowner ... [it was never] a separate, state-owned legal interest' (Heller 1998 p.1220; Archer et al. 1994, pp.83 and 105). Rather, eminent domain, resumption with compensation, is the most appropriate means of securing public beach access. In contrast, uniform beach access rights in Oregon were achieved on the basis of a state-wide custom in *State ex rel. Thornton v. Hay* ('*Hay*').[47] Despite its critics (Duhl 2006, pp.216–17; Bederman 1996, p.1381), *Hay* delivered to 'Oregonians ... the unique privilege of beach access and recreation ... on Oregon's 362-mile coastline' (Bender 1998, p.913).

Steven Bender evaluates the bundle held by the Oregon littoral landholder post-*Hay*, and concludes that only the right to exclude is missing. *Hay* is an interesting exemplar of property plurality; Bender observing that side by side with the public right of access is the private right to prevent unreasonable public use. Accessing wet sands of American beaches is fraught with inconsistency. Entitlements vary widely, with rationales ranging from state custom (implemented by statute or common law), to divergent interpretations of the public trust.

In New Zealand, public confidence in access to the beach and coastal foreshore, once a given, has eroded since 2003. A 'perfect storm' (Grinlinton 2003, p.314) of indigenous Maori customary claim to the foreshore (the *Ngati Apa* case[48]), a government report identifying the incomplete nature of the Queen's Chain (The Land Access Ministerial Reference Group 2003), and the ongoing decline of traditional conventions about access to the outdoors,[49] contribute to heightened disquiet about public "no-go zones".[50] The Foreshore and Seabed Act 2004 (NZ) and its extinguishment of Maori customary title, failed to assuage underlying anxiety, seemingly confirming the view that the feared spectre of plurality of foreshore ownership was 'something of a red herring ... a comparatively minor aspect of a much bigger issue' (Boast 2005, p.6). Its repeal and replacement by the Marine and Coastal Area (Takutai Moana) Act 2011 (NZ), ushers in an untested regime for access to foreshores. Section 11 divests Crown ownership of the foreshore and seabed, and substitutes it with a new concept of a 'common marine and coastal area', land owned by no one. Critics describe this nomenclature as 'spin doctoring', one that does not change radical title in the New Zealand Crown (Grinlinton 2003, p.326). Public access to the 'common marine and coastal areas' is preserved under section 26(1), yet others charge that this is flawed; access is precluded where there are sacred Maori lands, section 26(2), and the Act is silent on customary owners imposing fees for access (Round 2011). A vocal campaign to restore Crown ownership of the foreshore and seabed is reactively driven by the fear of losing a New Zealand birthright and common heritage, the right of free access to the beach.[51]

The divergent US and New Zealand experiences are indicative of a wider malaise. The right of public access is an underdeveloped, incomplete discourse in the common law, no more so in the case of the much-loved beach. Its immaturity means that access is far from a default benchmark of public property rights. In speaking of coastal access in New Zealand, Richard Boast opines that the right is in need of 'serious consideration of what such a right may involve ... [and] how it should influence law and policy. [P]rincipled public discussion ... has been sadly absent' (Boast 2005, p.6).

The Countryside and Right of Way Act 2000 (UK) ('CRoW'), and its extension to coastal areas by the Marine and Coastal Access Act 2009 is a proactive intervention into the vagaries of public access. CRoW is idiosyncratically English, a long delayed, ideologically couched response to the loss of ancient access rights. Jerry Anderson compares public access rights in England and the USA, and concludes that different social histories, landowning patterns, geography, and cultural mores, lead to different attitudes to public access (Anderson 2007, pp.418–21). Anderson's observations of America share parallels with other settler societies, such as Australia and New Zealand.

CRoW balances competing interests – private landowner versus public access – its objective being the creation of a functional mosaic of property pluralism in the open countryside. The Act does not institutionalize unrestricted access; rather it imposes measured restraints that do not 'interfere unduly with the landowner's privacy or business' (Sydenham 2002, p.88). Hence 'excepted land' excluded from access includes cultivated land, or land within 20 metres of a dwelling.[52] Alternatively, conditions are imposed on public conduct, a breach of which leads to the loss of rights of access. These include not closing gates, lighting fires or disturbing persons engaged in lawful activity on the land. Such a policy-based approach justifies the denial of access in the wider public interest. CRoW is a template for accommodating public and private property interests in landscapes where recreational access is desired or feasible, albeit not an unflawed one (Mitchell 2008, p.356).

A more extensive statutory right of access has been enacted in Scotland, a 'responsible right of access' to land and inland waters. (Lovett 2010, p.776). The Scottish scheme exemplifies that a jurisdiction can practically create

> a property regime that to a considerable extent replaces the ex ante presumption in favor of the right to exclude ... with an equally robust, but rebuttable, ex ante presumption in favor of access.
>
> (Lovett 2010, pp.816–17)

Settler societies with social, political and historic contexts very different from Scotland or England are less likely to generate the demands for similar access entitlements over private lands.[53] Nonetheless, such jurisdictions show that what Lovett terms an 'imaginative re-design' of property law is possible, one that accommodates public inclusion and access alongside private rights that are seemingly antithetical.

2.5.2 Inclusion and use and enjoyment

In the absence of direct legislative intervention, access is an inadequate (or at least premature) indicator of inclusion. Inclusion must embrace wider meanings than physical ingress and egress. Can public property be used and enjoyed without physical access? As discussed, the incorporeal conservation easement serves a multitude of public goods. These include the provision of ecosystem services, viewsheds, open space or wildlife corridors. Inherent in each is an intangible and indirect public *enjoyment* absent access.

The right of use and enjoyment is described as hierarchically lower, 'less compelling' (Underkuffler 2003, p.25), than other significant property rights, in particular the right to exclude. Despite its importance, for example Tony Honore listed *use* as one of 11 critical incidents of ownership, 'surprisingly little is written about its content' (Douglas 2013, p.360). While the private right is dominated by the descriptor of active *use*, its public equivalent may have a different emphasis, one where physical use is ancillary to a primary enjoyment. Alternatively, the public right may be conjunctive, a right of use or enjoyment. Where physical access is permitted, the public right may encompass both limbs – use and enjoyment – but where other indirect public benefits ensue minus access, the right falls away to one of enjoyment *simpliciter*. The umbrella right of inclusion is analogous to a diffuse public enjoyment of land, in which individual members of the public derive a public good, but where individual enjoyment of that good is no greater than any other member's enjoyment. Pointedly, access is a non-essential component.

In *Stop the Beach Renourishment*, public and private littoral rights intersected. While academic attention focused on the case's implications for the judicial taking of private property, the US Supreme Court decision also had resonance for public property, and its inherent *enjoyment*. There the 'public property right' to 'place a sand buffer on publicly owned submerged land … to protect coastal property owners and the community as a whole' overrode any private right to future landward accretion. '[T]he (private) right to accretions was … subordinate to the State's right to fill' (Echeverria 2010). By contrast, in New South Wales, *Vaughan v. Byron Shire Council* similarly concerned a right to fill. But in *Vaughan*, the private landowner was demanding the right to renourish storm-damaged sea front, while the council asserted a public expectancy to future landward erosion, so-called 'planned retreat' against expected sea level rises arising from climate change. In Florida, an active public property right prevailed over a passive private right. In NSW, the reverse applied, a passive public right yielded to an active private right. While public *enjoyment* in erosion retreat is nuanced, public *enjoyment* in accretion seaward of beach renourishment is more identifiable. The *enjoyment* facilitates a wider public good, namely the immediate protection of coastal communities. Equally, reasons for denying a public enjoyment (in *Vaughan* the council's policy of planned retreat) should satisfy an overriding public good, for as Carol Rose explains '[a]ny encroachment on public rights has to be justified by an even greater benefit to the public's well-being' (Rose 1996, p.278). Beach renourishment cases suggest that the *enjoyment* of public property rights requires a weighing up of relative public goods, straightforward in some cases, finely balanced in others.

The public good is a malleable, circumstantial concept, periodically invoked to justify property in its various forms. Jeremy Waldron observes the paramountcy of a 'collective social interest' in defining collective property, where the 'problem of allocation ... is resolved by favoring the use which is most conducive to the collective social interest' (Waldron 1985, p.328). Richard Barnes concurs, '[t]he organizing idea of collective property is that the needs of society as a whole take precedence over those of individuals' (Barnes 2009, p.154). What overarching 'public good' explains public enjoyment? Why should the public enjoy a general right to be included? *Propriety* offers the beginnings of at least one answer to these questions.

2.5.3 *Inclusion and propriety*

To Gregory Alexander, the commodity view of property is only one half of the dialectic of modern property. The missing half, 'property as propriety', provides the 'material foundation for creating and maintaining the proper social order', a civic conception of a 'properly ordered society' (Alexander 1997, pp.2–3). Propriety enables the 'well-lived life' (Alexander 2009, p.763), in which individual interaction and reciprocity of social obligation within community constitutes 'human flourishing in a very deep sense' (ibid., p.761). Human flourishing speaks to property's marginalized personal and communitarian values.

> Flourishing is an unavoidably cooperative endeavor rather than an individual pursuit or purely personal project. Our ability to flourish requires certain basic material goods and a communal infrastructure ... However much we value our personal independence, it is quite literally impossible for a person to flourish without others.
>
> (Alexander and Penalver 2012, p.87)

Public property in land is an important component in the propitious, well-ordered community. It is the 'communal infrastructure', the physical and metaphorical common ground, where shared activities 'socialize, democratize and educate society' (Rose 1986, pp.779 and 781). Rose's evocative street market is testament to this. In its corporeal form, it provides space for egalitarian recreation (Laitos and Carr 1999). In its incorporeal form, it may minimize the tragic risk of fragmentation, (Freyfogle 2007, pp.9–24), or engender what Kevin Gray terms 'pedestrian democracy', a 'flourishing of the civil and ecological communities of which we humans are a part' (Gray 2010a, p.52), that heightens 'civic responsibilities and ... participation in an integrative society of equals' (ibid., p.54). By contrast, modern private property marginalizes propriety. Its commoditization leaves scant scope for alternative paradigms, the likes of stewardship or 'economies of nature' to take root (Sax 1992; Sax 2011, p.14). Its abstraction de-couples right from place, preferring anonymous cartographic space (Meine 2004; Blomley 2004 p.91), to the lived sociable experience of community.

Kunstler's study of the decline of America's cities highlights the importance of public property to properly ordered communities. Kunstler writes of growing up in a soulless suburbia whose 'motive force [was] the exaltation of privacy and the elimination of the public realm.' By contrast, summer camp visits to Lebanon, New Hampshire, with its 'town square, band shells, elm street trees, and various civic buildings of agreeable scale – the library, the town hall, the opera house' highlighted the lost dignity and consequence of public space (Kunstler 1993, p.13).

Public property forms a key part of 'organically whole communities.' Kunstler cites 'productive work, markets, cultural institutions, (and) different classes of people' (ibid., p.48) as critical to the social fabric. Public property informs to varying degrees many of these civil pre-requisites. Its facilitation of recreation, democratic values, and overarching sociability, even happiness, are factors that mould 'well-lived lives.' Each will be discussed in turn. Rather than a false dawn for public access, the right to include may be best understood as a right to a proper social order, a right to inclusive enjoyment of a well-ordered community.

The links between recreation and public lands are many, ranging from practical to ethereal, passive to active, and co-existing to competing.[54] There is near academic unanimity in the USA that recreation replaced commerce as public property's socializing *raison d'etre* by the second half of the twentieth century.[55] 'Dispersed recreation ... the opportunity to hunt, fish, hike, explore' (Nelson 1995, p.211) constitute new reasons to retain public lands. Sally Fairfax describes the American public estate 'riding into a different sunset' (Fairfax 1981), with once alternative ideas – relaxation, health, adventure, exploration, social, scenic and natural values, solitude and spiritual replenishment – becoming mainstream. Joseph Sax explores the spirituality of passive recreation, tracing the origins of the parks system to landscape architect Frederick Law Olmsted, and his 'contemplative visitor', the non-consumptive recreationist whose reflections on nature 'provide a chance to express distinctiveness and to explore our deeper longings' (Sax 1980a, p.42). Scott Lehmann similarly writes of the restorative qualities of public lands, places that 'take us out of ourselves ... release us from unrewarding preoccupations while at the same time engaging our interest and curiosity' (Lehmann 1995, p.170). Such observations are redolent of property's ancient role of identity.

Ideologically, public property reinforces democratic values (Singer 2009), a 'powerful symbolic affirmation of the egalitarian ideal in a largely private system' (Nelson 1995, p.213). David Bollier observes that 'access to open, uncontrolled public spaces is directly related to the vitality of democratic culture' (2014, p.58), citing the creation of new public squares in post-Franco Barcelona as one example. Likewise, Olmsted views the urban public park as 'particularly helpful for democratic values ... rich and poor would mingle ... and learn to treat each other as neighbors' (cited in Rose 1986). In New Zealand, an ethos of open access to land and natural resources, was manifested by indicators such as public rights to fish and game, and the convention of public access to the outdoors (Curry 2001).[56] Egalitarianism is a powerful sub-current that finds outlet and expression in public property.

Finally, public property fills a gap in the narrative of property ignored in a private commoditized paradigm, that of sociability (Graham 2010). Rose's 'comedy of the commons' has been previously traversed as an overarching rationale for public property. At its base is the need for public property to serve society by making us sociable.

Indeed, more than just being sociable, public property may make us happy. Charles Montgomery, exploring the intersection of urban design and the 'science of happiness', says that to make so-called 'happy cities', people require inclusion and 'some sort of equality' (Montgomery 2014, p.6). Not being excluded from city life is the function of public space, such that the humble sidewalk, park, or bike path is elevated to a 'psycho-spiritual realm' (ibid., p.7). 'Great public space is a kind of magical good. It never ceases to yield happiness. It's almost happiness itself' (ibid.). By contrast, the twentieth-century urban legacy – the rise of the automobile and the privatization of public space – saw common civic space 'disregarded and degraded' (ibid.). Its yield was unhappiness.

> Urban residents ... denied the opportunity to enjoy the city's simplest pleasures; walking on convivial streets, sitting around in public; talking; gazing at grass, water, falling leaves and other people.
>
> (ibid.)

Public property is critical to the social and communal fabric. It fills the void vacated by a commoditized private property, such that Alexander's theory is optimally *public* property as propriety. Rather than a false dawn for access, the right to include may be better understood as a universal entitlement to flourish in well-ordered communities, places symbolized by Rose's deeply expressive streetscape. Public property enables well-lived lives by acting as an 'entrance to community' (Penalver 2005), the vehicle through which public inclusion imposes and legitimizes the idea of public property rights in land.

2.6 Conclusion

While some advocates for public property may argue for its greater 'publicness',[57] it has been an objective of this chapter to highlight the little-regarded 'property' in the equation. In so doing, diverse interests in public land have been explored; vexed issues of ownership canvassed; and aspects of inclusion laid open to initial scrutiny.

Structure, sophistication and coherence should be our ambitions for public property in land, such that we see more clearly and better understand the vast public estate that exists in our midst.[58] If such a descriptive seeing becomes normalized, property in land will be enriched by the greater diversity that ensues, the addition of an undisputed and commensurately valued public tile in the mosaic.

Notes

1 'There is little written about public property ... except in contradistinction to private property' (Hamilton and Bankes 2010, pp.19–20).
2 Merrill dismisses public property as a variant of private property, the only difference being that a state agency holds the right to exclude 'stick' instead of a private holder (Merrill 1998).
3 Blomley describes public property as being 'bereft of property, a terra nullius' (Blomley 2008, p.321).
4 *Yanner v. Eaton* (1999) 201 CLR 351.
5 *Stow v. Mineral Holdings (Australia) Pty Ltd* (1977) 51 ALJR 672, 679.
6 For example, Part 5 Crown Lands Act 1989 (NSW).
7 State lands leased or licensed to pastoral right holders under various Land Acts in jurisdictions including NSW, Queensland or New Zealand. In the USA, a loose equivalent is the Taylor Grazing Act permit.
8 For example, the Bureau of Land Management and the US Forest Service administer 315 million acres of public grazing lands (Hess 1992, p.11).
9 *One Third of the Nation's Land: A Report to the President and to the Congress by the Public Land Law Review Commission*, (1970).
10 In Nevada it is 82%, Utah 64% and California 61% (Lehmann 1995, pp.4 and 22–23).
11 For example, Part 4A, sections 77A and 77B Crown Lands Act 1989 (NSW).
12 It is *surprising* because of the historical tendency of private property since enclosure to decouple property right from context (Graham 2010, p.66).

13 § 1(1) Uniform Conservation Easement Act.
14 § 69C(1)(a) National Parks and Wildlife Act 1974 (NSW).
15 § 77A Crown Lands Act 1989 (NSW); § 88D and § 88E Conveyancing Act 1919 (NSW).
16 § 69C(1)(a) National Parks and Wildlife Act 1974 (NSW); § 77A(1) Crown Lands Act 1989 (NSW).
17 §§ 30(1) and 37 Nature Conservation Trust Act 2001 (NSW).
18 § 119(6) Highways Act 1980 (UK) c. 66.
19 There is no universal agreement as to the meaning of the term custom (Loux, 1993).
20 In 2012, police were called to enforce surfer norms on crowded waves on Australia's Gold Coast, "Police begin surf rage patrols", available at: www.abc.net.au/local/stories/2012/01/19/3411501.htm
21 462 P.2d 671 (1969).
22 Macpherson identifies as a modern 'misusage' the identical treatment of property and *private* property (Macpherson 1999, p.2).
23 *Yanner v. Eaton* (1999) 201 CLR 351.
24 Squillace 1988; Rieser 1991; Archer et al. 1994, pp.22–30; Wilkinson 1980.
25 *Stow v. Mineral Holdings (Australia) Pty Ltd* (1977) 51 ALJR 672, at 679.
26 *Stow v. Mineral Holdings (Australia) Pty Ltd* (1977) 51 ALJR 672, at 679.
27 Macpherson uses the examples of 'public parks, city streets, highways', as property for 'common use' (Macpherson 1999, p.4).
28 Or ownership can become so diffused that it disappears altogether. Under the Te Urewera Act 2014 (NZ), ownership by the Crown of a former national park was revoked, and the land, Te Urewera, now simply owns itself; see Chapter 4.
29 Conservation trusts are 'clearly invested with the public interest' (Fairfax and Guenzler 2001, p.5).
30 146 US. 387 (1892).
31 *National Audubon Society v. Superior Court ('Mono Lake')* 33 Cal. 3d 419, 658 P.2d 3.
32 For example, in *Mono Lake,* the link was the potential navigability of waters in the lake. The substance was however concerned with preserving environmental flows from the lake.
33 In the Australian High Court in *Brisbane City Council v. Attorney-General (Qld)* [1978] 3 CLR 299, land transferred on the condition that it be preserved as a showground gave rise to a charitable trust that precluded its owner, the Brisbane City Council, from selling the land.
34 Crown reserve trusts are "[a] legal body which cares for a Crown reserve on behalf of the people of NSW.' www.lpma.nsw.gov.au/trusts/trusts2. See also Divisions 4 and 5, Part 5, Crown Lands Act 1989 (NSW).
35 *Gibbs v. The New Plymouth District Council* [2006] NZHC 231.
36 'In some cases ... property rights may contain so few traditional sticks in the bundle as to defy continued description by the term *property*' (Raymond 2003a, p.18).
37 A relatively recent example from Australia is the Victorian Government's ownership of its high country national parks. Its title did not prevent the Australian Federal Government enforcing a ban on private cattle grazing in alpine national parks (Karvelas 2011).
38 Again in the Victorian high country a criticism of national parks is their failure to manage fire risk. This in turn corroborates the argument for private cattle grazing rights in national parks to 'eat down' the fuel. Such perceptions in local communities diminish the wider integrity of public land holding.
39 For example, there is no public access to Codfish Island in New Zealand, home

to the Department of Conservation breeding program for the endangered flightless kakapo parrot.

40 *United States v. Grace*, 461 U.S. 171, 177 (1983).

41 *United States v. Grace*, 461 U.S. 171, 177 (1983).

42 Inclosed Lands Protection Land 1901 (NSW); Trespass Act 1980 (NZ).

43 In New Zealand, the Trespass Act 1980 (NZ) is described by its opponents as draconian: Proceedings of the Federated Mountain Clubs Backcountry Recreation 2000 Conference, *Ruling and Regulating or Freedom of the Hills*, St. Arnaud, Nelson Lakes, September 27–29, 1991.

44 130 S.Ct. 2592, June 17, 2010. It was held that building sand buffers to protect coastal communities was a 'public property right ... that had no effect whatsoever on any property rights held by coastal property owners under Florida law' (Echeverria 2010, p.4).

45 It is 'curious' because the petitioners were private landowners protesting about state efforts at sand buffering.

46 483 US 825 (1987).

47 462 .2d 671 (1969).

48 *Attorney-General v. Ngati Apa* [2003] 3 NZLR 461.

49 See, for example, Proceedings of the FMC Backcountry Recreation 2000 Conference, *Ruling and Regulating or Freedom of the Hills*, St. Arnaud, Nelson Lakes, September 27–29, 1991.

50 The front cover of *North and South* magazine in August 2008 pictures a beach and a strand of barbed wire, 'Your access to public places is under threat', *North and South*, August 2008.

51 A public advocacy group, The Coastal Coalition, leads the campaign; see www.nzcpr.com/CoastalCoalition.htm.

52 Schedule 1, CRoW. Landowners also have the right to exclude access for up to 28 days per year upon notice, section 22 CRoW.

53 Hostile reactions by adjoining landowners to the New Zealand Walking Access Act 2008 (NZ) watered down public access rights (Lovett 2010, p.817).

54 Recreation on public lands is treated as a natural resource as much as mining, forestry or grazing (Coggins et al. 2007).

55 'Following World War II, recreation demand boomed as the country's population became larger, richer, and more mobile' Herman D Ruth and Associates, 'Outdoor Recreation Use of the Public Lands', *Report prepared under contract with the Public Land Law Review Commission*, Berkeley, CA, 1969, Vol. I, [I-5].

56 The ethos and principles of the early Acclimatisation Societies (forerunners to the NZ Fish and Game Council) were to keep freshwater fisheries and wildlife game in the public estate, s. 23 Wildlife Act 1953 (NZ), s 26ZN Conservation Act 1987 (NZ).

57 Project for Public Spaces at www.pps.org.

58 In the western USA, there is widespread teaching of Public Land Law (Arnold 1916). In Australia and New Zealand, there is a dearth of public land literature. In NSW there has not been a book on public lands since 1973 (Lang 1973). In New Zealand it is 1967 (O'Keefe 1967).

References

The Land Access Ministerial Reference Group 2003, *Walking Access in the New Zealand Outdoors* (the Acland Report).

Alexander, G 1997, *Commodity and Propriety: Competing Visions of Property in American Thought 1776–1970*, University of Chicago Press, Chicago.

Alexander, G 2009, 'The Social-Obligation Norm in American Property Law', *Cornell Law Rev.*, vol. 94, 745–819.

Alexander, G and Penalver, E 2010, 'Introduction' in G. Alexander and E. Penalver (eds), *Property and Community*, Oxford University Press, New York.

Alexander, G and Penalver, E 2012, *An Introduction to Property Theory*, Cambridge University Press, New York.

Anderson, J 2007, 'Britain's Right to Roam: Redefining the Landowner's Bundle of Sticks', *Georgetown International Environmental Law Rev.*, vol. 19, 375–435.

Anderson, T and Hill, P 2004, *The Not So Wild, Wild West: Property Rights on the Frontier*, Stanford University Press, Stanford, CA.

Archer, J, Connors, D, Laurence, K and Bowen, R 1994, *The Public Trust Doctrine and the Management of America's Coasts*, University of Massachusetts Press, Amherst, MA.

Arnold, E 1916, 'The Study of Public Land Law in the Western Law Schools', *4 Cal. L. Rev.*, 316.

Barnes, R 2009, *Property Rights and Natural Resources*, Hart Publishing, Oxford.

Bederman, D 1996, 'The Curious Resurrection of Custom: Beach Access and Judicial Takings', *Columbia Law Review*, vol. 96, no.6, 1375–455.

Bender, S 1998, 'Castles in the Sand: Balancing Public Custom and Private Ownership Interests on Oregon Beaches', *Oregon Law Rev.*, vol. 77, 913–47.

Blomley, N 1994, *Law, Space, and the Geographies of Power*, The Guildford Press, New York.

Blomley, N 2004, *Unsettling the City: Urban Land and the Politics of Property*, Routledge, New York.

Blomley, N 2008, 'Enclosure, Common Right and the Property of the Poor', *Social and Legal Studies*, vol. 17, 311–31.

Boast, R 2005, *Foreshore and Seabed*, Lexis Nexis, Wellington.

Bollier, D 2014, *Think Like a Commoner: A Short Introduction to the Life of the Commons*, New Society Publishers, Gabriola, BC.

Braverman, I, Blomley, N, Delany, D and Kedar, A 2014, *The Expanding Spaces of Law: A Timely Legal Geography*, Stanford University Press, Stanford, CA.

Brewer, R 2003, *Conservancy: The Land Trust Movement in America*, University Press of New England, Hanover, NH.

Brower, A 2008, *Who Owns the High Country? The Controversial Story of Tenure Review in New Zealand*, Craig Potton Publishing, Nelson.

Brower, A and Page, J 2011, 'Property Rights Across Sustainable Landscapes: Competing Claims, Collapsing Dichotomies, and the Future of Property' in D Grinlinton and P Taylor (eds), *Property Rights and Sustainability: The Evolution of Property Rights to Meet Ecological Challenges*, Brill-Nijhoff, Leiden.

Brower, A and Page, J 2012, 'Does (Property) Diversity beget (Landscape) Sustainability?' in P Martin et al. (eds), *Environmental Governance and Sustainability*, Edward Elgar, Cheltenham.

Brower, A, Page. J D, Kennedy, A L and Martin, P 2009, 'The Cowboy, the Southern Man, and the Man from Snowy River: The Symbolic Politics of Property in Australia, the United States and New Zealand', *Georgetown International Environmental Law Review*, vol. 21 no. 3, 455–93.

Coggins, G, Wilkinson, C, Leshy, J and Fischman, R 2007, *Federal Public Land and Resources Law* (6th edn), Foundation Press, New York.

Cunningham, R 1968, 'Scenic Easements in the Highway Beautification Program', *Denv. L.J.*, vol. 45, 167–80.

Curry, N 2001, 'Rights of Access to Land for Outdoor Recreation in New Zealand: Dilemmas Concerning Justice and Equity', *Journal of Rural Studies*, vol. 17, 409–19.

Dagan, H and Heller, M 2000, 'The Liberal Commons', *Yale Law Journal*, vol. 110, 549–623.

Davies, M 2007, *Property Meanings, Histories, Theories*, Routledge, Abingdon.

Donohue, D 2003, 'The Law and Practice of Open Space Covenants' *NZJEL*, vol. 7, 119–68.

Douglas, S 2013, 'The Content of a Freehold: A 'Right to Use' Land', in N Hopkins (ed.), *Modern Studies in Property Law*, Hart Publishing, Oxford.

Duhl, G 2006, 'Property and Custom: Allocating Space in Public Spaces', *Temple L. Rev.*, vol. 79, 199–248.

Dunning, H 1988, 'The Public Trust: A Fundamental Doctrine of American Property Law', *Envtl. L.*, vol. 19, 515–25.

Dyer, D 1972, 'California Beach Access: The Mexican Law and the Public Trust', *Ecology L.Q.*, vol. 2, 571–611.

Eagle, S 2010, 'Unitary Law of State Takings', *Planning and Environmental Law*, vol. 62, no. 9, 5–7.

Echeverria, J 2010, 'Green Light for Beach Renourishment, Red Light for Judicial Takings', *Planning and Environmental Law*, vol. 62, no. 9, 3–5.

Eichenberg, T, Bothwell, S and Vaughn, D 2001, 'Climate Change and the Public Trust Doctrine: Using an Ancient Doctrine to Adapt to Rising Sea Levels in San Francisco Bay', *Golden Gate U. Envtl. L.J.*, vol. 3, 243.

Ellickson, R C 1991, *Order Without Law: How Neighbors Settle Disputes*, Harvard University Press, Cambridge, MA.

Ewing, K 2009, 'Conservation Covenants and Community Conservation Groups: Improving the Protection of Private Land', *NZJEL*, vol. 12, 316–37.

Fairfax, S and Guenzler, D 2001, *Conservation Trusts*, University Press of Kansas, Lawrence.

Fairfax, S 1981, 'Riding into a Different Sunset: The Sagebrush Rebellion', *Journal of Forestry*, vol. 79, no. 8, 516–82.

Fairfax, S, Gwin, L, King, M A, Raymond, L and Watt, L 2005, *Buying Nature: The Limits of Land Acquisition as a Conservation Strategy, 1780–2004*, MIT Press, Cambridge, MA.

French, S 2006, 'Perpetual Trusts, Conservation Servitudes, and the Problem of the Future', *Cardozo Law Rev.*, vol. 27, 2523–33.

Freyfogle, E 2003, *The Land We Share: Private Property and the Common Good*, Island Press, Washington, DC.

Freyfogle, E 2007, *Agrarianism and the Good Society: Land, Culture, Conflict and Hope*, University of Kentucky Press, Lexington.

Freyfogle, E, 2011, 'Private Rights in Nature: Two Paradigms', in P. Burdon (ed.) *Wild Law: The Philosophy of Earth Jurisprudence*, Wakefield Press, Kent Town, Australia.

Frug, G 1980, 'The City as a Legal Concept', *Harvard Law Rev.*, vol. 93, 1057–154.

Garbutt, R 2011, *The Locals: Identity, Place and Belonging in Australia and Beyond*, Peter Lang, Bern.

Geisler, C 2000, 'Property Pluralism', in C Geisler and G Daneker (eds), *Property and Values Alternatives to Public and Private Ownership*, Island Press, Washington, DC.

Graham, N 2010, *Lawscape: Property, Environment, Law*, Routledge, Abingdon.

Gray, K 2010a, 'Pedestrian Democracy and the Geography of Hope', *Journal of Human Rights and the Environment*, vol. 1, 45–65.

Gray, K 2010b, 'Regulatory Property and the Jurisprudence of Quasi-Public Trust', *Sydney Law Rev.*, vol. 32, 221–41.

Gray, K and Gray, S 1999a, 'Civil Rights, Civil Wrongs and Quasi-Public Space', *European Human Rights Law Review*, vol. 4, 46–102.

Gray, K and Gray, S 1999b, 'Private Property and Public Propriety' in J McLean (ed.), *Property and the Constitution*, Hart Publishing, Oxford.

Grinlinton, D 2003, 'Private Property Rights versus Public Access: The Foreshore and Seabed Debate', *NZ Journal Envtl. Law*, vol. 7, 313–41.

Grosvenor, M B 1966, 'Today and Tomorrow in Our National Parks', *National Geographic*, July, vol. 130(1), 1–46.

Gustanski, J 2000, 'Protecting the Land: Conservation Easements, Voluntary Actions, and Private Lands', in J Gustanski and R Squires (eds), *Protecting the Land: Conservation Easements Past, Present and Future*, Island Press, Washington, DC.

Hage, W 1989, *Storms Over Rangelands: Private Rights in Federal Lands*, Free Enterprise Press, Bellevue, Australia.

Hamilton, J W and Bankes, N 2010, 'Different Views of the Cathedral: The Literature on Property Law Theory', in A. McHarg et al. (eds), *Property and the Law in Energy and Natural Resources*, Oxford University Press, Oxford.

Heller, M. 1998, 'The Boundaries of Private Property', *Yale L.J.*, vol. 108, 1163–225.

Hess, K 1992, *Visions Upon the Land, Man and Nature on the Western Range*, Island Press, Washington, DC.

Higgins, M 2005, 'Public Access to the Shore: Public Rights and Private Property,' in D Whitelaw and G Visgilio (eds), *America's Changing Coasts: Private Rights and Public Trust*, Edward Elgar, Cheltenham.

Holder, J and Harrison, C 2003, 'Connecting Law and Geography' in J Holder and C Harrison (eds), *Law and Geography*, Oxford University Press, Oxford.

Hutton, W 2000, 'Conservation Easements in the Ninth Federal Circuit', in J Gustanski and R Squires (eds), *Protecting the Land: Conservation Easements Past, Present and Future*, Island Press, Washington, DC.

Jacobs, H 2010, 'Stop the Beach Renourishment: Is an Answer Blowin' in the Wind?', *Planning and Environmental Law*, vol. 62, no. 9, 7–9.

Jawetz, S 1982, 'The Public Trust Totem in Public Land Law: Ineffective – and Undesirable – Judicial Intervention', *Ecology L.Q.*, vol. 10, 455–85.

Karvelas, P 2011, 'Commonwealth Overrides Victoria on Issue of Grazing in Alpine Park', *The Australian*, March 18.

Kuntsler, J H 1993, *The Geography of Nowhere: The Rise and Decline of America's Man-Made Landscape*, Simon and Schuster, New York.

Laitos, J and Carr, T 1999, 'The Transformation on Public Lands', *Ecology Law Quarterly*, vol. 26, 140–242.

Lang, A 1973, *Crown Land in New South Wales: The Principles and Practice Relating to the Disposal of and Dealings with Crown Land*, Butterworths, Sydney.

Lehmann, S 1995, *Privatizing Public Lands,* Oxford University Press, New York.

Lucero, L 2010, 'Stop the Beach Renourishment – Six Perspectives', *Planning and Environmental Law,* vol. 62, no. 9, 5–6.

Loux, A 1993, 'The Persistence of the Ancient Regime: Custom, Utility and the Common Law in the Nineteenth Century', *Cornell Law Rev.*, vol. 79, 183–218.

Lovett, J 2010, 'Progressive Property in Action: The Land Reform (Scotland) Act 2003' *Nebraska Law Rev.*, vol. 89, 739–820.

McKee, S 2000, 'Conservation Easements to Protect Historic Viewsheds: A Case Study of the Olana Viewshed in New York's Hudson River Valley', in J Gustanski and R Squires (eds), *Protecting the Land: Conservation Easements Past, Present and Future,* Island Press, Washington, DC.

Macpherson, C B 1999, 'The Meaning of Property', in *Property: Mainstream and Critical Positions,* University of Toronto Press, Toronto, Ontario.

Mayo, T 2000, 'A Holistic Examination of the Law of Conservation Easements', in J Gustanski and R Squires (eds), *Protecting the Land: Conservation Easements Past, Present and Future,* Island Press, Washington, DC.

Meine, C 2004, *Correction Lines Essays on Land, Leopold, and Conservation,* Island Press, Washington, DC.

Merrill, T W 1998, 'Property and the Right to Exclude', *Nebraska Law Rev.*, vol. 77, 730–755.

Mitchell, J 2008, 'What Public Presence? Access, Commons and Property Rights', *Social and Legal Studies,* vol. 17, 351–67.

Montgomery, C 2014, *Happy City: Transforming Our Lives Through Urban Design,* Farrar, Strauss and Giroux, New York.

Nazer, D 2004, 'The Tragicomedy of the Surfers' Commons', *Deakin Law Rev.*, vol. 9, 655–713.

Nelson, R 1995, *Public Lands and Private Rights: The Failure of Scientific Management,* Rowman and Littlefield Publishers, Lanham, MD.

O'Keefe, J 1967, *The Law and Practice Relating to Crown Land in New Zealand,* Butterworths, Wellington.

Olson, M 1968, *The Logic of Collective Action: Public Goods and the Theory of Groups,* Harvard University Press, Cambridge, MA.

Ostrom, E 1990, *Governing the Commons: The Evolution of Institutions for Collective Action,* Cambridge University Press, New York.

Page, J 2011, 'Towards a Sustainable Paradigm for Property', *Property Law Journal,* vol. 1, 86–96.

Page, J and Brower, A 2007, 'Property Law in the South Island High Country – Statutory Not Common Law Leases', *Waikato Law Rev.*, vol. 15, 48–63.

Parker, D 2004, 'Land Trusts and the Choice to Conserve Land with Full Ownership or Conservation Easements', *Nat. Res. J.*, vol. 44, 483–518.

Peloso, M and Caldwell, M 2011, 'Dynamic Property Rights: The Public Trust Doctrine and Takings in a Changing Climate', *Stan. Envtl. L.J.*, vol. 30, 51–120.

Penalver, E 2005, 'Property as Entrance', *Virginia Law Rev.*, vol. 91, 1889–1972.

Penalver, E 2009, 'Land Virtues', *Cornell Law Rev.*, vol. 94, 821–88.

Philp, M 2008, 'The No-Go Zones', *North and South,* August.

Public Land Law Review Commission 1970, *One Third of the Nation's Land: A Report to the President and to the Congress,* Public Land Law Review Commission, Washington, DC.

Raymond, L 1997, 'Viewpoint: Are Grazing Rights on Public Lands a Form of Private Property?', *Journal of Range Management*, vol. 50, no.4, 431–38.

Raymond, L 2003a, *Private Rights in Public Resources*, Resources for the Future, Washington, DC.

Raymond, L 2003b, 'Sovereignty Without Property? Recent Books in Public Lands', *Nat Res. J.*, vol. 43, 313–29.

Rieser, A 1991 'Ecological Preservation as a Public Property Right: An Emerging Doctrine in Search of a Theory', *Harv. Envtl. L. Rev.*, vol. 15, 393

Rose, C M 1986, 'The Comedy of the Commons: Custom, Commerce, and Inherently Public Property', *Univ. Chicago Law Rev.*, vol. 53, no. 3, 711–81.

Rose, C M 1990, 'Property as Storytelling: Perspectives from Game Theory, Narrative Theory, Feminist Theory', *Yale Journal of Law & the Humanities*, vol. 2, 37–57.

Rose, C M 1992, 'Rhetoric and Romance: A Comment on Spouses and Strangers', *Georgetown Law Journal*, vol. 82, 2409–21.

Rose, C M 1994, 'Seeing Property' in *Property and Persuasion Essays on the History, Theory, And Rhetoric of Ownership*, Westview Press, Boulder, CO.

Rose, C M 1996, 'A Dozen Propositions on Private Property, Public Rights and the New takings Legislation', *Wash. and Lee L. Rev.*, vol. 53, 265–98.

Rose, C M 1998a, 'Joseph Sax and the Idea of the Public Trust', *Ecology L. Q.*, vol. 25, 351–62.

Rose, C M 1998b, 'The Several Futures of Property: Of Cyberspace and Folk Tales, Emission Trades and Ecosystems', *Minn. L. Rev.*, vol. 83, 129–82.

Rose, C M 2003, 'Romans, Roads and Romantic Creators: Traditions of Public Property in the Information Age', *Law and Contemporary Problems*, vol. 66, 89–110.

Rose, C M 2006, 'Property and Language, or the Ghost of the Fifth Panel', *Yale Journal of Law and the Humanities*, vol. 18, 1–28.

Round, D 2011, *Foreshore and Seabed Public Access*, available at: www.nzcpr.com/guest217.htm.

Sax, J 1969, 'The Public Trust Doctrine in Natural Resource Law: Effective Judicial Intervention', *Michigan Law Rev.*, vol. 68, 471–566.

Sax, J 1980a, *Mountains Without Handrails: Reflections on the National Parks*, University of Michigan Press, Ann Arbor, MI.

Sax, J 1980b, 'Liberating the Public Trust Doctrine from its Historical Shackles', *U.C. Davis L. Rev.*, vol. 14, 185–94.

Sax, J 1982, 'Some Thoughts on the Decline of Private Property', *Wash. L. Rev.*, vol. 58, 481–96.

Sax, J 1984a, 'The Claim for Retention of the Public Lands', in S Brubaker (ed.), *Rethinking the Federal Lands*, Resources for the Future, Washington, DC.

Sax, J 1984b, 'Do Communities Have Rights? The National Parks as Laboratories of New Ideas', *University of Pittsburgh Law Rev.*, vol. 45, 499–511.

Sax, J 1992, 'Property Rights and the Economy of Nature: Understanding *Lucas v. South Carolina Coastal Council*', *Stan. L. Rev.*, vol. 45, 1433–55.

Sax, J 2011, *Ownership, Property and Sustainability*, University of Utah Press, Salt Lake City.

Scheiber, H 1984, 'Public Rights and the Rule of Law in American Legal History', *Cal. L. Rev.*, vol. 72, 217–51.

Silverstone, S 1974, 'Open Space Preservation through Conservation Easements', *Osgoode Hall L.J.*, vol. 12, 105–24.

Singer, J 2000, *Entitlement: The Paradoxes of Property*, Yale University Press, New Haven, CT.

Singer, J 2006, 'The Ownership Society and Takings of Property: Castles, Investments, and Just Obligations', *Harv. Envtl. L. Rev.*, vol. 30, 309–38.

Singer, J 2009, 'Democratic Estates: Property Law in a Free and Democratic Society', *Cornell Law Rev.*, vol. 94, 1009–62.

Singer, J 2010, 'Property Norms Construct the Externalities of Ownership', in G Alexander and E Penalver (eds), *Property and Community*, Oxford University Press, New York.

Souder, J and Fairfax, S 2000, 'In Lands We Trusted: State Trust Lands as an Alternative Theory of Public Ownership', in C Geisler and G Daneker (eds), *Property and Values: Alternatives to Public and Private Ownership*, Island Press, Washington, DC.

Sprankling, J, Coletta, R and Mirow, M C (eds) 2006, *Global Issues in Property Law*, West Academic Publishing, St. Paul, MN.

Squillace, M 1988 'Common Law Protection for our National Parks' in D Simon (ed.) *Our Common Lands Defending the National Parks*, Island Press, Washington, DC.

Stevens, J 1980, 'The Public Trust: A Sovereign's Ancient Prerogative Becomes the People's Environmental Right', *U.C. Davis L. Rev.*, vol. 14, 195–232.

Sydenham, A 2002, 'The Countryside and Rights of Way Act 2000: Balancing Public Access and Environmental Protection?' *Envtl. L. Rev.*, vol. 4, 87–100.

Ubhi, N and Denyer-Green, B 2004, *Law of Commons and Town and Village Greens*, Jordan Publishing, Bristol.

Underkuffler, L 2003, *The Idea of Property: Its Meaning and Power*, Oxford University Press, Oxford.

Waldron, J 1985, 'What is Private Property?', *Ox. J. Legal Stud.*, vol. 5, 313–49.

Waldron, J 1991, *The Right to Private Property*, Oxford University Press, New York.

Waldron, J 1992, 'Homelessness and The Issue of Freedom', *UCLA Law Rev.*, vol. 39, 295–324.

Wilkinson, C 1980, 'The Public Trust Doctrine in Public Land Law', *U.C. Davis Law. Rev.*, vol. 14, 269.

Chapter 3

The obviousness and obliviousness of common property

3.1 Introduction

Common property is arguably the greatest victim of private property's dominance. It is 'seen' (if at all) as marginal, tragic, or anachronistic,[1] yet Carol Rose, American property jurist, describes it as 'oddly ubiquitous', a paradox where common property is *obvious* in its frequency, but *oblivious* to precise identification (Rose 1998, p.132).

This chapter will examine traditional and contemporary manifestations of common property, and the theories and myths that surround its application to natural resource management. These diverse perspectives reveal that common property has much to add to a vibrant property mosaic, a putative contribution disproportionate to its apparent size or profile. The chapter will then assess common property's understated strengths, the centrality of use rights, an inherent sociability, its environmental norms and values and its locally-generated resilience, before concluding with its overstated weaknesses, its tarnished image and near-invisibility.

That we see common property through the overblown prism of its so-called failures has pushed it to the periphery. Yet to dismiss it as marginal is to overlook its potential. It also ignores the notion that common property is more 'obviously there' than our obliviousness to it suggests. The identification of common property in any given landscape requires a conscious concerted effort that rewards the viewer with an enriched mosaic of property types.

3.2 Traditional common property

Common property in its traditional form was, and remains, intrinsically linked to an agrarian, village-based, pre-industrial conception of society. In England, 'common land had a significant role in ... agricultural life', (Ubhi and Denyer-Greene 2004, p.4) and remains most prevalent outside metropolitan areas.[2] In Europe, ongoing common property models have been studied as irrigation cartels in rural Spain (Ostrom 1990, pp.69–82) and centuries-old land tenure patterns in isolated mountainous cantons in the Swiss Alps (Netting 1981).

This agrarian (and historicized) paradigm is reflected in Jeanette Neeson's description of traditional common rights.

> The interest which a commoner has in a common is ... to eat the grass with the mouths of his cattle, or to take such other produce of the soil as he may be entitled to ... The soil itself, the land, was not the commoner's but the use of it was. That use was common right. Its history had important consequences for small landholders, rural artisans and landless labourers in 18th century England ... their very sense of who they were and how well they lived were all in part dependent on [it].
>
> (Neeson 1993, p.1)

Common lands reflected the (once) central importance of agriculture to the English economy, in particular the open-field system of agricultural practice. Common lands since Norman times comprised the waste lands of the manor, uncultivated, unenclosed lands outside the lord's individual *demesne*, or lands held by tenants under copyhold or customary freehold tenure (Ubhi and Denyer-Greene 2004, pp.34–5). Rights of common are legal interests in land, incorporeal hereditaments in the nature of profits *a prendre* ('profits'), a non-possessory right to enter someone else's land and remove some thing or produce off that land. As *Gale on Easements* (Gaunt and Morgan 2002), the authoritative text, points out, while all rights of common are profits, not every profit is a right of common, since some profits may be enjoyed individually, or severally with others, not necessarily in common with a defined class.

Traditional Anglo common law common rights are capable of classification into one of four categories: rights of common appendant;[3] rights of common appurtenant;[4] rights of common in gross;[5] and rights of common by reason of vicinage.[6] Since 1970, rights in common in England must be registered to remain valid and enforceable under the *Commons Registration Act 1965* (UK), thus rendering these categories, for all practical purposes, obsolete.

Importantly, common rights are not public property rights, they are vested in members of a locality, or to a defined class of persons within that locality, and operate as 'legal rights over the surface of lands, exercise(d) together or in common' (Hoskins and Stamp 1963, p.4). Thus, strangers from outside a locality are not entitled to access common lands, or exercise privileged use rights.[7] A third party (historically the manorial lord, but now often local borough councils) holds title, and their use of the land is assured in common with that of the commoners. While use rights such as pasturage are the most prevalent,[8] other common rights include the gathering of wood, turf, or gorse for heating (turbary), the gathering of timber for repair of fences and houses (estovers), fishing in common streams (piscary), access across the countryside,[9] the gleaning of crops,[10] the gathering of wild foods such as nuts, mushrooms and berries, and recreational uses, including rights of air and exercise.[11] The diversity of common rights varies according to local custom and usage. 'In reality on the ground, the range of common produce was magnificently broad, the uses to which it was put was minutely varied, and the defence of local practice was determined and often successful' (Neeson 1993, p.313).

The commons were also more than a platform for natural resources; they were an integral component of community. As Neeson surmises, common rights had deeper social meaning and implication. '[T]he broad relationships engendered by independence of the wage enhanced leisure and community time, while access to the openness of the commons brought solitude … each usage of common waste created a sense of self; it told commoners who they were, a part of a tribe' (ibid., p.180). The common lands themselves were 'literally and metaphorically common ground', a space where 'contact, familiarity and exchange' established connections between commoners and others of mutuality and respect (ibid., p.182).

The enclosure movement that culminated in the late eighteenth and early nineteenth centuries represented the loss of much customary common right, and more broadly the wholesale transfer of property rights from the community to the individual, and from the landless to the landed.[12] It also triggered social upheaval, emigration and massive demographic change, and as argued more broadly in this book, a fundamental realignment of our conception of property. Yet, elsewhere in Europe, common property rights proved more durable, in the forests and meadows of alpine communities, common property remains a functioning component of social and economic activity.

Anthropologist Robert Netting studied a 'closed corporate community', the village of Torbel in alpine Switzerland in the early 1970s, and 'the ecological balance achieved between its inhabitants and the environment' (Netting 1981, p.vii). Netting described a patchwork of private and communal tenure that had existed from the mid fifteenth century, a deliberately planned and inter-connected pattern of land ownership that achieved an ecological and economic equilibrium 'created and maintained by intensive human effort for the physical benefits it could confer … private good and gain are weighed against village well-being and security' (ibid., p.225).

Village-owned common property in Torbel generally comprises less productive higher altitude holdings;[13] pastures used for summer grazing and alpine woodlands managed sustainably for annual fuel and timber needs. Common property also includes usufructs over alpine passes, used historically for inter-village access, hunting, the collection of stones for foundations and roofing slate, and the cutting of alpine grasses as a fodder supplement. Rights to common property, dating from 1453, are restricted to citizens of Torbel. Non-citizens who acquired private land in the village did not necessarily obtain common rights, while citizens who sold their private property in the village relinquished their common rights. 'Although outsiders could be admitted at the pleasure of the community, competition for obviously scarce resources was decisively restricted. The definition of citizenship was equivalent to erecting a barrier around the community' (ibid., p.60). The village rigorously self-managed and policed individual access to communal resources, such that in the 1970s, at the time of Netting's extended stay at Torbel, there was no evidence of any 'tragedy of the commons'. Rather, 'common holdings and corporate administration by the village promote three things; an efficiency of utilization that would be threatened by fragmented private ownership, the potential for maintaining yields by enforced conservation; [and] the equitable sharing of necessary resources by all group members' (ibid., p.63).

> [t]he Torbel case ... reflects a situation in which clearly differentiated individual property and communal property exist side by side ... It appears that the historic persistence of both types of property in a single community must be explained in ecological terms rather than solely as a projection of certain cultural or ethnic origins or the artefact of some system of legal ideas.
>
> (ibid., p.63)

In the New World, traditional common property found little traction in emerging colonial societies. In New South Wales, despite commons being set aside from 1804 to satisfy the need for grazing lands in populous districts (Campbell 2007, p.246), early settlers demonstrated scant interest in common title. A seemingly limitless frontier available for freeholding, an alien social context and recent memories of displacement from common lands in England or Scotland, rendered common title a brief footnote in the history of settler land tenure. As John McLaren observes:

> For people denied customary rights and displaced from the enjoyment of rights in common, the prospect of securing the clearest and most durable of rights over land in the colony, 'their land', must have proven seductive and seemed necessary to their survival and prosperity.
>
> (McLaren 2001, p.135)

Nonetheless in New South Wales, the legislature has considered the remnant tenure worthy of retention; the *Commons Management Act 1989* (NSW) is the current statute that regulates about 200 commons in that state. When the bill was debated in 1989, commons were originally needed for 'milking cows, maintaining food supplies ... keeping horses for transport, and for providing a source of fuel for local agricultural labourers' (Campbell 2007, pp.260–61). While such agrarian uses persist, more contemporary rationales embrace recreation. Use of commons is restricted to persons who meet defined eligibility criteria to be entered on a commoners' roll,[14] usually town residents or nearby farmers. Non-commoners are effectively strangers to the use of the land, and their unauthorized use of the commons is enforceable through trespass. Commoners elect a 'commons trust', which manages the common, and establishes by-laws and management plans.[15]

In the USA, particularly in northern New England,[16] local common rights developed informally. As Eric Freyfogle describes, early America was a 'polyglot world, in terms of the legal ideas, and land-use and land tenure practices that people brought with them across the Atlantic' (Freyfogle 2007, p.53). As a form of customary practice, local residents in the New England thus used unenclosed rural lands for open grazing, hunting, fishing, and collecting firewood and berries, in ways understood as common practice in their 'home country'.[17] However, common rights were insecure and short-lived. By the mid nineteenth century, courts

> [l]ooked askance at customary practices that were not in line with the common law and its clear definition of trespass. They were particularly suspicious of customary arrangements in which multiple people had rights to use the land at the same time... Local customary practices became suspect. The common law, including a nearly full right of landowners to exclude, was gaining the upper hand.
>
> (ibid., p.54)

Traditional common property is captive to both its rich and ancient social history, and its agrarian, pre-industrial settings. It may be legally 'frozen' in the uplands and village greens of rural England, across small country towns in New South Wales, or balancing on a Swiss Alp. Yet the 'idea' of traditional common property has potential to escape these confines, and take root in more modern forms and contexts. This is seen next in the concept of 'limited common property', a model that builds on its historical antecedence, yet adapts to modern exigency.

3.3 Modern limited common property

Carol Rose argues that we need to consider and refine our thinking about 'limited common property', a property type that was 'neither entirely individualistic nor entirely public'. Rose defines 'limited common property' as property 'held as a commons among the members of the group, but exclusively vis-à-vis the outside world' (Rose 1998, p.132). This 'inside commons/outside private property' structure is the key to a wider seeing of modern limited common property. We are oblivious to the ubiquity of limited common property because we are conditioned to see only the private external shell (Hamilton and Bankes 2010, p.36). As a consequence, we tend to ignore the significance of the 'inside commons'.[18]

Yet this preoccupation disguises the fact that individual private title has a capacity to accommodate communal rights. Alvin Esau's observation is made in the context of the communal title of religious communities in North America, but it has wider implications:

> Our law actually displays a 'deep reverence for the group, as long as it assumes corporate or quasi-corporate form.' By incorporating, the group right can be articulated as an individual property right and this group right can be vindicated in the law.
>
> (Esau 2005, pp.217–18)

Esau's articulation of the 'inside commons/outside private property' dichotomy allows 'inside-law communal norms' to take the form of 'outside-law arrangements' (ibid., p.209), hence allowing the norms of group ownership to be compatible with the individualized law of fee simple title. Taking this dichotomy as a guide, limited common property materializes more readily. Inner-city company title units, ski lodges,[19] surf life-saving clubs (Brower and Page 2011), community gardens or a floor of barrister's chambers[20] all exemplify the potential for modern limited common property. Rose argues that non-public collective property is all around us, 'many of us live in co-ops and condominiums, [and] most of us belong to institutions that collectively own property – clubs, churches, and the like' (Rose 2000, p.484). All share a structure where internalized common use rights of 'community' members lie beneath the surface of private fee simple title.

In essence, the defining feature of modern limited common property is its *structure*. Specifically, title is vested in an external entity (typically incorporated) with member *use* rights a consequence of entity membership. Thus, in inner-city company or co-operative title units, a company holds the real property title; individual shareholders enjoy rights of use, exclusive rights of occupancy over the unit to which the share relates, and shared use rights to lifts, foyers and other common areas. By contrast, strata title apartments remain substantively private property, as the ownership structure is dominated by individual fee simple titles. However, body corporate-owned facilities in the apartment complex – lifts, gardens, pools, driveways, stairwells, visitor parking bays etc. – may constitute modern limited common property, such that the typical property 'split' is one of dominant private/peripheral common.

Conversely, the *use or purpose* of the property holding does not characterize modern limited common property. If, as asserted, company title units, ski lodges, surf life-saving clubs, community gardens or barrister's chambers are variants of modern limited common property, then their wide divergence of use defies any 'common purpose' definition. Nor is modern limited common property necessarily contingent on the *number* in the communal group. It is the universal nature of the common use right that is critical (albeit subject to internal variance[21]), a unity of 'ownership' with some analogy to a private joint tenant's four unities of possession, interest, time and title.

Robert Ellickson extends the concept of modern common property beyond structure, or the need for any formal external entity, corporate or otherwise. Ellickson's study of the property-like norms of the 'household' (2008), yield original observations about common property by focusing on the content and substance of relevant domestic arrangements. Ellickson sees common property in shared dormitory rooms, and describes multi-person households as limited-access 'commons', with complex mixes of private and common space (Ellickson 2008, pp.117–19). Ellickson's expansive model illustrates that modern limited common property is remarkable for its ubiquity and unseen incidence.

3.4 Common property: the natural resource perspective

Garrett Hardin's seminal *The Tragedy of the Commons* (1968) gave enormous impetus to an assumption that common property regimes were inevitably and remorselessly on a trajectory towards tragedy. This tragedy describes the 'degradation of the environment to be expected whenever many individuals use a scarce resource in common' (Ostrom 1990, p.2). Hardin exemplifies the tragedy by describing the 'rational' herder of cattle, who overstocks an open access pasture by adding more and more cattle. Hardin argues that the individual rational herder's self-interest is served by increasing the number of cattle feeding on the pasture. Conversely any loss occasioned by the deterioration of the paddock is delayed and dispersed amongst all herders using the resource. In short, the herder's individual benefit from overstocking outweighs the shared cost of loss of productivity.

> Each man is locked into a system that compels him to increase his herd without limit – in a world that is limited. Ruin is the destination toward which all men rush, each pursuing his own best interest in a society that believes in the freedom of the commons.
>
> (Hardin 1968, p.1244)

Hardin's solution to averting the tragic outcome of common property involves either privatization of the resource, such that market forces ordain its best and highest use, or state intervention to directly and centrally regulate the resource. The clear inference is that common property is an inferior and tragic tool for resource management. Hardin's terminology of the 'tragedy of the commons' has passed into everyday use,[22] and further entrenches an institutional bias against the commons that can be traced to the enclosure period, when the privatization of so-called 'waste-lands' was lauded as a victory for efficiency and modernity in improvement discourse (Graham 2010, pp.51–84).

Elinor Ostrom rose to prominence by calling out the 'remorseless' inevitability of Hardin's thesis. Ostrom placed Hardin's tragedy in context, as a work influenced by powerfully similar theories in vogue in the 1960s and 1970s. In particular, Ostrom cites the Prisoner's Dilemma game, a theory that provoked intense academic interest,[23] and Mancur Olson's 1965 book *The Logic of Collective Action.* Prisoner's Dilemma involves resource users embarking on rational strategies that lead to third-best outcomes, more formally known as 'Pareto-inferior equilibrium outcomes' (Ostrom 1990, pp.3–5). The appeal of the theory lies in the paradox of rational decisions leading to irrational outcomes, an end result not dissimilar from an inevitable, fatalistic tragedy. Similarly, Mancur Olson's work affirms the rational supremacy of individual self-interest over collective good.

> Unless the number of individuals is quite small, or unless there is coercion, or some other special device to make individuals act in their common interest, rational self-interested individuals will not act to achieve their common or group interests.
>
> (Olson 1965, p.2)

Olson's basic premise is that a participant in the use of a natural resource, who cannot be excluded from the benefits of a collective good, has no incentive to contribute voluntarily to that collective good. Olson's rational actor bears strong analogy to Hardin's rational herder.[24]

Ostrom offers an alternative to Hardin's 'either/or' private or state answer to averting the tragedy. Ostrom's 'third way' to resolve the commons problem is common property itself, successful *common pool resource* (CPR) institutions that defy the erstwhile logic of unremitting environmental degradation, and act as an effective tool for natural resource management. Ostrom identifies a number of successful CPR institutions (Ostrom 1990, pp.58–102) (including the Swiss village of Torbel studied by Robert Netting) that escape the rigidity of Hardin's public–private divide, and mirror the argument for property plurality. 'Institutions are rarely either private or public – "the market" or "the state". Many successful CPR institutions are rich mixtures of "private-like" and "public-like" institutions defying classification in a sterile dichotomy' (ibid., p.14).

In trying to discern what made some CPRs 'long enduring' and 'robust', and others not, Ostrom identifies and analyses seven factors that help successful CPRs break the 'shackles of a commons dilemma' (ibid., p.21).

They are: *clearly defined boundaries* that 'close' the common area and the rights of users to extract common resources; a *convergence* between use rights and prevailing local conditions; non-static *collective-choice arrangements* that allow the modification of resource rules as exigency demands; effective *self-monitoring*; *graduated sanctions* for users who violate resource rules, enforced by other users or the collective community; low-cost *conflict-resolution mechanisms*; and *minimal external interference* in the community's self-governance and self-enforcement (ibid., pp.90–101). The simplicity of Ostrom's research lies in its isolation of the key indicators of functionally healthy common property arrangements.

Ostrom's defence of common property builds on an earlier rejection of the universality of Hardin's tragedy thesis in an article by Ciriacy-Wantrup and Bishop in 1975. Ciriacy-Wantrup and Bishop develop a conceptual framework for common property, defining it as 'a distribution of property rights in resources in which a number of owners are co-equal in their rights to use the resource' (Ciriacy-Wantrup and Bishop 1975, p.714), and then use this definitional framework to attack a fundamental flaw in Hardin's argument, his equating of the open access commons with the internally regulated commons: 'Common property is not "everybody's property"... [to confuse the terms is to] slur fundamental institutional relationships.' (Ciriacy-Wantrup and Bishop 1975, p.715). They further argue that the evidence of economic history of common property is not the inevitable tragedy that Hardin's herder analogy alleges, but a mixed bag of success and failure. Indeed, common property can be helpful for modern problems of natural resource policy. 'Common property, with the institutional regulation it implies, is capable of satisfactory performance in the management of natural resources, such as grazing and forest land, in a market economy' (ibid., p.721). Common property overcomes many problems of private property; it delivers a larger spatial perspective in land management,[25] it may be more suited to certain physical locations, or overcome human or technological limitations 'that make individual propertization difficult' (Rose 1998, p.139).

Many scholars have subsequently criticized Hardin's tragedy thesis on the basis of either or both of these two flaws: the confusion between open access and limited commons, and the simplistic glossing over of successful commons management precedents.[26] Eric Freyfogle comments:

> Other scholars had spent lifetimes studying common property regimes, including common grazing lands, and they knew full well that common property arrangements sometimes worked just fine, with nothing like the tragedy Hardin predicted. What Hardin had described was essentially an open-access commons, one in which outsiders could show up at any time and start using it or in which existing users could increase their use at will.
>
> (Freyfogle 2007a, p.160)

Similarly Doris Fuchs refers to

> Literature on common property resources [that] provides empirical evidence against a necessary link between common pool resources and collective failure. This literature emphasizes that Hardin's tragedy of the commons generally applies to open-access resources, but often is not the outcome for common property resources. Numerous case studies ... illustrate that groups of appropriators can jointly and sustainably manage natural resources.
>
> (Fuchs 2003, pp.59–60)

One upside of the natural resource perspective on common property is the insight it provides into successful common property regimes. Ostrom's seven-factor analysis has been previously traversed. Fuchs similarly identifies related factors that 'foster the ability of joint appropriators from a resource to overcome collective action problems', including group homogeneity, the presence of leadership, the ability to exclude outsiders, and an ability to communicate and learn (Fuchs 2003, p.60). Freyfogle talks of responsive institutions, succession planning and fair management by resource users (Freyfogle 2003, p.172). Ellickson's study of American pioneer settlements emphasizes group efficiency; he concludes that common property is more efficient for 'large events', due to increased returns to scale and the spreading of risk (Ellickson 1993, pp.1322–23). Such insights in turn instil confidence in others to advocate the common property model as a solution to resource scarcity. Thus, Edward Barbanell (2001) recommends common property as a sustainable resource management tool for water security in the Colorado River basin in America's West. Similarly, Evan van Hook (1993) advocates the 'ecocommon', a common property management model for sensitive ecosystems and buffer zones adjoining resource-dependent communities.

Another upside is the clarity it brings to conceptual definitions of common property. When emphasis is placed on the exploitable resource, and the rights of eligible appropriators to access that resource, coherent definitions of common property, and common property rights, ensue. This clarity minimizes the risk of misunderstanding, and elevates common property from esoteric curiosity to feasible alternative. Fuchs defines common property as 'resources for which the exclusive title is in the hands of a group of individuals. This group has control over access to the resource, is frequently backed in this capacity by the state, and has general decision-making capacity over the resource' (Fuchs 2003, p.49). Barbanell's definition is 'a state of affairs where (only) the members of the resource community have limited rights to use the resource, and where such limits are determined by a process of collective choice ... [made] by members of the resource community' (Barbanell 2001, p.67). Contrast these resource-premised definitions to traditional articulations such as 'rights of commoners ... to eat the grass with the mouths of his cattle' (Neeson 1993, p.1). Common property is transformed from museum exhibit to viable property option through the prism of natural resources.

The obvious downside is the oft-cited, instantly recognizable tragedy of the commons. Like William Blackstone's 'sole and despotic' trope, Hardin's noetic tragedy taints common property with its broad-brush application, and overwhelms the detail of any counterargument. Thus, William Lucy and Catherine Mitchell's argument for the replacement of private property by a notion of stewardship rejects common property as a viable alternative because it is 'almost as problematic when applied to land … as private property.' (Lucy and Mitchell 1996, p.579) Lucy and Mitchell canvass both a 'strong' and a 'weak' common property, the 'strong' version features unrestricted use with attendant risks of 'over-consumption, over-use or pollution.' (ibid., p.581) The 'weak' interpretation entails some regulation of access, but the authors conclude that 'we do [not] know of any account of common property that fills this gap' (ibid.). For Lucy and Mitchell, the myth of tragedy is all-consuming. Dealing with this powerful yet misleading narrative is a burden that modern common property must accommodate. The dominant discourse of common property overstates its weaknesses and understates its strengths. To restore balance, common property's weaknesses must be understood in context, and its strengths highlighted.

3.5 The strengths of common property

3.5.1 Sociability

The sociability of common property is the measure by which it contributes to community and social cohesion. Sociability is an underrated attribute of property, which is, after all, a social institution (Rose 2014). An inherent strength of common property is its ability to 'counteract the individualised and exclusive notion of property ... by regarding property as that which potentially brings a community together rather than that which separates it into exclusive units' (Davies 2007, p.127).

Jeanette Neeson saw eighteenth-century English common property as more than a platform for natural resources, it was literally 'common ground', a place where commoners could interact, and develop concepts of identity and relation to place. In the early 1970s, idealistic rural communalists again looked to property to provide some social meaning for both self and the collective.[27] Today the phenomenon of the community food garden speaks to similar desires. Sociability is a strength shared with public property, although arguably common property may be a more effective agent for sociability because the 'group' to which it relates is smaller and more identifiable.

The impact of the enclosure period in diminishing the link between property and sociability cannot be underestimated. Nicole Graham calls it a time of 'immense geosocial significance … [that] sheds light on the ongoing necessity and cost of the separation of people and place in dominant forms of contemporary property law' (Graham 2010, p.83). Andrew Buck describes it as a period of

> [a] hardening and concretion of the notion of property in land, and the rectification of usages into properties which could be rented, sold, or willed … The process of dispossession did not involve legal decisions alone, but also changes in assumptions, which were themselves reflected in language and rhetoric. What was involved … was the creation of a mindset conducive to the acceptance and operation of market-oriented concepts of property.
>
> (Buck 2006, pp.24–25)

This 'hardening' squeezed aside alternative conceptions of property that did not have realizable value in money or commodity terms. Pushed to the periphery, or indeed off the edge, were more settled values of property, sociable values that connected people to place.[28] Yet the post-enclosure paradigm shift was not completely extinctive of such settled values. Academic Leigh Davidson describes his 'home' interest in communal land in northern New South Wales in the early twenty-first century as 'liberating'.

> We can only sell it to someone who has been accepted by the community as a member. In other words, we probably can't liquefy our assets and move on with any appreciable amount of capital. This arrangement has many advantages. For example we don't waste time wondering if we would be better off living somewhere else, so we have a commitment to place and community.
>
> (Metcalf 1995, p.52)[29]

Re-connecting property with 'place and community' is a latent attribute of common property. It is a value worthy of wider infusion into mainstream property discourse.

3.5.2 Use rights

Common property rights are exclusively rights to use. They are proprietary interests in the nature of non-private profits or easements. By contrast, private property rights are mainly possessory, with a smattering of second-tier usufructs. Public property rights lack developed definition, but may be generically characterized as diffuse rights of enjoyment. By a process of elimination, common property becomes the default standard-bearer for rights of use.

Use rights occupy an uncomfortable place in modern property, yet another consequence of the hegemony of private property. The right to exclude garners far greater attention and enforcement. This is despite Honore's listing of 'the right to use' as second in his list of eleven property incidents (Honore 1961, p.113). Use rights, beyond a core few, lack proprietary gravitas, are dismissed pejoratively as personal rights or relegated down the property hierarchy.[30] As Laura Underkuffler explains:

> [t]he almost absolute protection for rights to exclude and devise must be contrasted with the 'sliding scale' of protection afforded to other property rights. Other rights ... are simply not held with the same sense of inviolable protection; their protection is far more a matter of collective whim. For example the right to use – in particular, the right to protect or to enhance value through continuation of pre-existing, permitted use – has been consistently characterized as 'less protected' or 'less compelling' than other property interests.
>
> (Underkuffler 2003, p.25)

Their 'less compelling' status mirrors the equally ambiguous standing of common property. Yet, use rights have much utility and potential significance. The 'tailoring of use rights' to land resources is the *modus operandi* of US natural resources law (Freyfogle 2007b), a mindset with much to offer traditional property doctrine. Conceptually, the usufruct enlivens the feasibility of simultaneous right holders and multiple ownerships. Conversely, dominion entrenches a sterile monopoly. As Freyfogle predicts, 'once we begin to focus on specific use-rights, we may begin to question many existing property arrangements' (Freyfogle 1988, p.1551).

The well-recognized right of way easement exemplifies how use rights enable a complex simultaneity. Their grant does not exhaust other co-existing uses of the easement site; leaving the burdened landowner free to use their land provided access is not impaired. Nor is the easement itself absolute; it is subject to restrictions and constraints. Consider however if access was protected by common law lease, where exclusive possession is integral. The lease leaves little scope, theoretical or practical, for other complementary rights to subsist, but for the freeholder's reversion. On common land, the simple easement example is exponentially diversified. There, multiple uses occur contemporaneously, exercised by different owners under different rights. If the image of the easement is an intermittent link joining burdened and benefited landowners, common property is an inter-connected, complex, at times disruptive 'web of interests', the allegory of Tony Arnold's reconstituted image of property (Arnold 2002).

Raw exclusory power suffocates property diversity by devouring the theoretical oxygen that enables other rights, including use rights, to co-exist. That is why common property, and its emphasis on use, not dominion, is important. Use rights place property rights in context, as mere sticks in a greater whole. Use rights are 'context dependent rather than abstract' (Freyfogle 1988, p.1545). They also invite the logical corollary that because a simultaneous plurality of uses is possible, ideally use rights should be compatible and sustainable, rather than 'resource-intensive [with] short-term orientation' (Bosselman 2008, p.15). Importantly, use rights de-couple possession from ownership.

The right to use and enjoy is also a pathway for concepts such as stewardship. Freyfogle predicts a heightened place for use rights in his 'Bill of Rights for the Responsible Landowner'.[31]

> Perhaps we need to apply more broadly the idea that all of nature remains in a sense in public hands, with private owners receiving only prescribed rights to use.
>
> (Freyfogle 2007c, p.141)

Freyfogle's right to use has as its jural correlative a duty not to degrade, to act as steward.[32] Pioneering conservationist Aldo Leopold famously articulated 'stewardship' in terms of his much quoted 'land ethic', a responsibility that was the concomitant of the right to use.

> We abuse land because we regard it as a commodity belonging to us. When we see land as a community to which we belong, we may begin to use it with love and respect ... [t]hat land is a community is the basic concept of ecology, but that land is to be loved and respected is an extension of ethics.
>
> (Leopold 1966, p.x)

Use rights may enable property duties by removing the all-consuming spatial inherency of possessory rights to fill the available void. This tendency is evidenced with private rights, freehold or leasehold (Page and Brower 2007), and their conflation of exclusive possession. If the extremes of 'despotic dominion' are less polarizing, and use rights achieve credible parity with possession, duties, including environmental obligations of stewardship, may begin to populate the space vacated by private property's conflated right to exclude.

Christopher Rodgers argues that environmental stewardship is enhanced when a use-premised conceptualization of property replaces one dominated by an ownership discourse. Rodgers describes a 'resource allocation model of property rights' comprising 'elements or strands of *utility* that combine to make up the constituent elements of a land interest'

(Rogers 2009, p.557, emphasis added). Use rights transform the landowner from an entity with absolute control, to the holder of a 'residuum of socially permitted power over land resources ... a state-approved usufruct.' (ibid., p.557) Property rights allocate access to a resource, and the terms upon which that resource is used (ibid., p.551). Rodgers places primacy on use, not possession, and the consequent dividend is an environmentally responsible stewardship of land.

The centrality of use rights presents an opportunity for common property, as both a role model for new conceptualizations of property, and possible enabler of property obligations. And if Freyfogle's prediction for use rights comes to pass, common property may be an unintended beneficiary of their resurgence.

3.5.3 Proportionality and moderation of use

The norms and values of common property are important in the implications they pose for property's future direction, and its 'quest for an environmental ethic' (Rose 1994, pp.14–31). They have a distinctly environmental resonance. 'There are great bodies of law about common property, and they revolve around an ethic of moderation, proportionality, prudence and responsibility to the others who are entitled to share in the common resource' (ibid., p.25).

Rose argues that such values should influence property rhetoric, such that our rights and relationships with land are seen through the prism of a 'gift' rather than a 'given'. Sustainability is a natural consequence of these values of restraint, not the inexorable 'tragedy' pre-destined to befall common property.

Such qualities of common property are not a recent invention. In eighteenth-century England, common property did not fail for 'tragic' reasons of unsustainable or irresponsible use. As Nicole Graham observes:

> The death of the laws and customs of the commoners and the peasant economy was not brought about by any intrinsic failure or inevitable collapse. Contrary to the claims of the improvers (those who stood to benefit from enclosure), the laws and customs of the commoners were neither unproductive nor non-viable.
>
> (Graham 2010, p.54)

Klaus Bosselmann likewise cites a rich tradition of sustainable land use in Europe dating from the end of the fourteenth century to the beginnings of the noneteenth century, when common property systems (known in German as 'Allemende') institutionalized principles of sustainable land use. Informing Allemende practices were ethics of land use where 'land was respected as an essential ingredient of life with humans being mere users', and where land could only be 'owned within the limit of ecological sustainability' (Bosselmann 2008, p.14)

Bosselmann describes this human–nature relationship as one of stewardship, arising from restrictions on land use imposed by an overarching structure of common property rights. Common property imposed restrictions of both a practical and ethical nature, the latter comprising 'an important ecological limitation ... the relational context of land use rights ... regarded as heritage from the past and obligation for the future' (ibid., p.14).

3.5.4 *Local, vernacular and resilient*

That common property is historically a localized phenomenon is likewise an under-regarded strength. Common property rules have been described as 'vernacular' micro-laws that 'define and stabilize a community and unite its members ... to protect the resources of a commons'. Such localism builds on the traditional nature of common property rights to be 'self-policing and stable without exogenous institutional backup' (Weston and Bollier 2013, p.229). Where motivated communities want to bolster self-sufficiency, common property models present long-forgotten structural advantages that emphasize group self-reliance and institutional resilience.

Weston and Bollier cite the rise of local food collectives or the development of community forests as emerging examples of an organic, self-organized localism that employs commons mechanisms to enact resilient ends, that 'promote permaculture, rebuild local infrastructures ... cultivate local provisioning of food, build renewable fuel sources, and insulate their communities from the vagaries of [globalism]' (Weston and Bollier 2013, p.234). If the future of property law is 'local', as Nicole Graham foresees, then that future will likely engage with common property.

Yet, the strengths of common property remain intangible, ill defined or in the case of rising localism, it is too early to tell if they will endure. Belonging to place, or 'group-hood' values are 'warm and fuzzy' concepts. It is far easier to see common property's weaknesses.

3.6 The weaknesses of common property: profile and reputation

The flaws of common property are its obscurity and tarnished reputation. In the latter case, this is understandable given the normative force of Hardin's tragedy thesis. But the former is perplexing. We have lost the skill to 'see' common property. Legal historian John McLaren attributes this in the first instance to a 'selective historical amnesia', a 'forgetfulness' of the common rights enjoyed within the settlers' living memory at home in England or Scotland (McLaren 2001, p.135). This forgetfulness, conscious or otherwise, transformed into a societal or corporate loss of knowledge as the generations passed. McLaren's explanation is relatively simple; we cannot 'see' common property if we no longer know what common property is, or what it represents.

Carol Rose identifies more modern factors for the obliviousness of limited common property, and its problematic place in western legal traditions. Such obliviousness is *odd* because 'common property itself is actually ubiquitous, if unremarked' (Rose 1998, p.132). Rose cites a combination of economic and cultural reasons for this myopia. Economically, common property is perceived to be inefficient, its rules are internally complex and unwieldy when compared to individual private property. This unwieldiness is particularly exacerbated in the case of alienability or its enforcement (ibid., p.140). Membership of the entitled group is often amorphous: who belongs and who does not is not always readily defined, and common property's responsive, dynamic nature to resource availability means that resource rules fluctuate over time and according to exigency. The economic stability or assuredness demanded of property takes a slightly different, less comfortable form for common property.

Culturally, Rose submits that communal property claims are often made by groups 'somehow deemed inappropriate to make claims of entitlement' (ibid., p.141). These claims by groups with questionable social status offend social notions of the *propriety* of property ownership. Joseph Singer claims that our sense of propriety plays a significant role in resolving ownership disputes and 'public concepts of entitlement' (Singer 2000, p.190). For Kevin and Susan Gray, 'a deep subtext of propriety has always pervaded the social and legal definition of "property"' (Gray and Gray 1999, p.13). Margaret Davies explores the resonance of property's propriety, the idea that 'property is there to reflect and cement propriety – the proper order of the social and political spheres' (Davies 2007, p.12). The social status of the property claimant is often problematic for common property, whether they are landless commoners, indigenous peoples,[33] or 'long-haired hippies' in 1970s rural intentional communities (Page 2010). The combination of unconventional communal claim and dubious social status 'overlap and conspire' against common property and its seeing (Rose 1998, p.141).

Rose (later and separately) added a third reason for common property's problematic profile, at least in the American common law. Politically, informal customary governance fell out of favour with American courts in the mid nineteenth century. Community practices that gave rise to customary forms of collective property were 'mired in the swamps of medieval feudalism, hierarchy, and rigidity' (Rose 2000, p.486). Rather, laws (including property laws) should be made by forward thinking, democratically elected representatives; not communities looking backwards to history. Common property was no longer in vogue with progressive, democratic ideals of law making.

Lastly, as previously traversed, the reputation of common property has been tainted by the stigma of Garrett Hardin's 'tragedy of the commons'. This essay has become a 'bellwether in the debate on community versus individual rights' (Grinlinton and Taylor 2011, p.vii). But it is worth repeating that Hardin was not talking of internally regulated common property when he advanced his tragedy thesis, but rather 'open access' property, the unregulated commons.[34] Tragedy's counterargument is that properly regulated common property may be its antithesis (Ciriacy-Wantrup and Bishop 1975; Bosselmann 2008, pp.13–15), a potential 'comedy of the commons' (Rose 1986). Yet this counter-argument faces an uphill task in overcoming the pervasive, crowding-out 'white noise' of the commons tragedy.

3.7 Conclusion

Common property is a multi-faceted paradox. It is simultaneously 'there' and 'not there' in terms of presence and visibility. It is both anachronistic and a mooted model for future natural resource management. It is stuck in its historical milieu, yet the idea of common property can take root in unlikely modern contexts. It is tragic or comedic. On the 'inside' it is communal and inclusive, but on the 'outside' it is private and exclusive. It was removed from property consciousness by enclosure, but its rights are incapable of being physically enclosed. It is vulnerable yet persistently resilient.

This chapter has canvassed the traditional and less traditional forms of common property. From rights of pasturage, to twenty-first century urban forms and natural resource theory, the diversity and insight of common property is rich but underestimated. Despite (or because of) its manifest internal contradictions, common property adds vital layers of diversity and complexity to the expansive notion of property diversity. It is a small but important piece in the property mosaic because of the qualities it brings to property, its emphasis on use, community, and non-commodity values, and a propensity to infuse wider property discourse with its paradoxical originality. In sum, its influence outweighs its size. To lose sight of common property is to pauperize the property mosaic, and in turn diminish the potential of property to sustain human landscapes.

Notes

1 The eighteenth-century enclosure movement exemplified this phenomenon in terms of common property. As a consequence, common property is criticized as economically inefficient, socially improper, or a "tragedy of the commons" waiting to happen.

2 Common land in 2004 comprised 'some 550,000 hectares – about 4% of the total land area in England and Wales ... Surprisingly just over 51% of all registered commons in England are less than 1 hectare in area, and only 1.3% are

1,000 hectares or more in area. Just over half of England's common land is in Cumbria and North Yorkshire' (Ubhi and Denyer-Greene 2004).

3 Rights of common annexed to lands by operation of law that existed as at *Quia Emptores 1290.*

4 Rights of common attached to a particular parcel of land.

5 Rights of common not attached to any particular parcel of land.

6 Permissive rights of common that arise when two common lands adjoin or are contiguous.

7 Unless statute otherwise permits access, Countryside Rights of Way Act 2000 (UK).

8 Pasturage generally referred to 'cattle', being animals needed to plough the land (horses), or animals needed to manure the arable land, such as *cattle proper*, and sheep. Variants to *pasture* include vesture and herbage. Rights of pasture could be limited to specific numbers of cattle through 'stinting' (Neeson 1993, p.114). Alternatively, on some lands, rights of pasture could only be exercisable at specified times of the year ('commonable lands'), pigs (pannage), geese, and goats were separate common rights (Ubhi and Denyer-Green 2004, pp.27–30).

9 'To local people almost entirely employed in agriculture ... there simply was no notion of rights of access onto the common separate from the rights and incidents of rights of common. With the massive urbanisation of the 19th century, and the disengagement of many people from agricultural activities, many commons came to be seen to have separate or additional recreational purposes' (Ubhi and Denyer-Green 2004, p.133).

10 The collecting of the remains of a harvest left in the fields.

11 Customary activities include cricket, Morris dances and village fairs (Hoskins and Stamp 1963, p.4).

12 In 1963 a Royal Commission on Common Lands reported there were 1.5 million acres of commons in England and Wales (Hopkins and Stamp 1963).

13 '[T]he high mountain catchment basin of Torbel's principal irrigation stream also was treated as common land ... guarding the vital water rights of the village' (Netting 1981, p.68).

14 Sections 10 & 12 Commons Management Act 1989 (NSW).

15 Part 2 Commons Management Act 1989 (NSW).

16 In the USA, common property is said to survive in 'property niches'. Historically it existed 'in the form of woodlots and pastures in New England and the antebellum South, and among the Hispanic and Indian communities of the Southwest' (Geisler 2000, pp.72–73).

17 Freyfogle argues that a large proportion of early immigrants were Celts, who had a disrespect for the English common law of property.

18 By contrast, American law has been accommodating of 'liberal common property', collective property characterized by internal private governance and liberal exit. Examples include corporations, cooperatives and condominiums (Rose 2000, pp.486–87).

19 For example, the Peninsula Ski Club Inc. owns the Peninsula Ski Club in Mt. Hotham, Victoria. Formed in 1975, ownership of debenture stocks in the association entitles members to use rights over the ski lodge, built on subdivided Crown leasehold. The lodge comprises unallocated member's accommodation, a communal kitchen, dining area, lounge, and other common facilities, such as a dry room and laundry.

20 Legal historian Wilfred Prest's observation to the author. Personal conversation, December 2009.

21 For example, 'stinting' in traditional common property.

22 Ostrom argues that Hardin was not the first to coin the term (Ostrom 1990, pp.2–3).
23 Ostrom cites more than 2,000 articles devoted to Prisoner's Dilemma theory by 1975 (Ostrom 1990, p.5).
24 The supremacy of the rational actor has since been challenged, with altruism or 'uncommon decency' (Singer 2000, pp.1–17).
25 Freyfogle uses as an example the 'Tilbuster Commons' on the Northern Tablelands of NSW, where 'private landowners lease their private lands to a collectively managed grazing co-operative. Their combined lands are worked in concert – like open field farms of centuries ago- with their animal herds mingled' (Freyfogle 2007, pp.99–100; also Williamson et al. 2003).
26 Davies 2007, p.73; Barbanell 2001, p.112; Godden 2011, pp.249–72; Rose 1993, p.1025.
27 The plethora of rural communes that appeared in the early 1970s provided the venue for a generational journey in personal spiritual discovery. Peter Cock personalized this when he wrote in 1979, 'My basic concerns were ... similar to those of people within the alternatives movement. I was asking: Who am I? What am I going to become? How will I live? What do I need and want ... I was dissatisfied, feeling the fruitlessness of protest and seeking something more meaningful than being a graduate in money-making' (Cock 1979, p.2; also Munro-Clark 1986, p.33).
28 Freyfogle sees the two competing values of property as 'settled' versus 'intensive'.
29 *The Northern Star* newspaper describes ownership at Dharmananda in the following terms; 'If a person leaves they are not paid for their buildings or their share in the trust ... The community feels that because members cannot sell their shares, there is an incentive to make the community work' (Corcoran 1988).
30 Native title rights are perceived as 'weak' because of their communal nature (Godden 2011, pp.249–72).
31 Sax likewise incorporates use rights in his concept of 'qualified private ownership' (Sax 1971, p.154).
32 However, Hohfeld would consider the right to use a *privilege* if it was to invoke a commensurate *duty* (Hohfeld 1913).
33 Rose claims that American law was hostile to common property as a 'historically self-serving myopia' that ignored the collective property claims of Native Americans (Rose 2000).
34 One example of an unregulated commons was the American rangeland prior to the enactment of the Taylor Grazing Act of 1934.

References

Arnold, C A 2002, 'The Reconstitution of Property: Property as a Web of Interests', *Harvard Environmental Law Rev.*, vol. 26, 281–364.

Barbanell, E 2001, *Common Property Arrangements and Scarce Resources: Water in the American West*, Praeger Publishers, Westport, CT.

Bosselmann, K 2008, *The Principle of Sustainability*, Ashgate, Aldershot.

Brower, A and Page, J 2011, 'Property Rights Across Sustainable Landscapes: Competing Claims, Collapsing Dichotomies, and the Future of Property', in D Grinlinton and P Taylor (eds), *Property Rights and Sustainability: The Evolution of Property Rights to Meet Ecological Challenges*, Brill-Nijhoff, Leiden.

Buck, A 2006, *The Making of Australian Property Law*, Federation Press, Sydney.
Campbell, E 2007, 'Rights of Common in New South Wales: A History', *Legal History*, vol. 11, pp.243–63.
Ciriacy-Wantrup, S and Bishop, R 1975, 'Common Property as a Concept in Natural Resources Policy', *Nat. Resources J.*, vol. 15, pp.713–27.
Cock, P 1979, *Alternative Australia Communities of the Future*, Quartet Books, London.
Corcoran, K 1988, 'The Search for a Better Way', *The Northern Star* (Lismore), 24 August.
Davies, M 2007, *Property Meanings, Histories, Theories*, Routledge, Abingdon.
Ellickson, R 1993, 'Property in Land', *Yale L.J.*, vol. 102, pp.1315–1400.
Ellickson, R 2008, *The Household: Informal Order Around the Hearth*, Princeton University Press, Princeton, NJ.
Esau, A 2005, 'The Establishment and Preservation of Hutterite Communalism in North America, 1870–1925', in J McLaren, A Buck and N Wright (eds), *Despotic Dominion, Property Rights in British Settler Societies*, UBC Press, Vancouver, BC.
Freyfogle, E 2003, *The Land We Share: Private Property and the Common Good*, Island Press, Washington, DC.
Freyfogle, E 2003, *The Land We Share: Private Property and the Common Good*, Island Press, Washington, DC.
Freyfogle, E 2007a, *Agrarianism and the Good Society: Land, Culture, Conflict and Hope*, University of Kentucky Press, Lexington.
Freyfogle, E 2007b, *Natural Resources Law Private Good and Collective Governance*, Thomson West, St. Paul, MN.
Freyfogle, E 2007c, *On Private Property: Finding Common Ground on the Ownership of Land*, Beacon Press, Boston.
Fuchs, D 2003, *An Institutional Basis for Environmental Stewardship: The Structure and Quality of Property Rights*, Kluwer Academic, Dordrecht.
Gaunt, J and Morgan, P (eds) 2002, *Gale on Easements* (17th edn), Sweet & Maxwell, London.
Geisler, C 2000, 'Property Pluralism', in C Geisler and G Daneker (eds), *Property and Values Alternatives to Public and Private Ownership*, Island Press, Washington, DC.
Godden, L 2011, 'Communal Governance of Land and Resources as a Sustainable Property Institution', in D Grinlinton and P Taylor (eds), *Property Rights and Sustainability: The Evolution of Property Rights to Meet Ecological Challenges*, Brill-Nijhoff, Leiden.
Graham, N 2010, *Lawscape: Property, Environment, Law*, Routledge, Abingdon.
Gray, K and Gray, S 1999, 'Private Property and Public Propriety', in J McLean (ed.), *Property and the Constitution*, Hart Publishing, Oxford.
Grinlinton, D and Taylor, P 2011, 'Introduction', in D Grinlinton & P Taylor (eds), *Property Rights and Sustainability; The Evolution of Property Rights to Meet Ecological Challenges*, Brill-Nijhoff, Leiden.
Hamilton, J W and Bankes, N 2010, 'Different Views of the Cathedral: The Literature on Property Law Theory', in A. McHarg et al. (eds), *Property and the Law in Energy and Natural Resources*, Oxford University Press, Oxford.
Hardin, G 1968, 'The Tragedy of the Commons', *Science*, vol. 162, no. 3859, 1243–48.
Hohfeld, W 1913, 'Some Fundamental Legal Conceptions as Applied in Legal Reasoning', *Yale Law Journal*, vol. 23, 16–59.

Honore, A M 1961, 'Ownership', in A G Guest (ed.), *Oxford Essays in Jurisprudence*, Oxford University Press, Oxford.

Hoskins, W G and Stamp, D 1963, *The Common Lands of England & Wales*, Collins, London.

Leopold, A 1966, *A Sand County Almanac with other Essays on Conservation from Round River*, Oxford University Press, New York.

Lucy, W and Mitchell, C 1996, 'Replacing Private Property: The Case for Stewardship', *Cambridge Law J.*, vol. 55, no. 3, 566–600.

McLaren, J 2001, 'The Canadian Doukhobors and the Land Question: Religious Communalists in a Fee Simple World', in A Buck, J McLaren and N Wright (eds), *Land and Freedom: Law Property Rights and the British Diaspora*, Ashgate, Aldershot.

Metcalf, B 1995, *Co-operative Lifestyles in Australia: From Utopian Dreaming to Communal Reality*, UNAW Press, Sydney.

Munro-Clark, M 1986, *Communes in Rural Australia: The Movement Since 1970*, Hale & Ironmonger, Sydney.

Neeson, J M 1993, *Commoners: Common Right, Enclosure and Social Change in England, 1700–1820*, Cambridge University Press, Cambridge.

Netting, R 1981, *Balancing on an Alp: Ecological Change and Continuity in a Swiss Mountain Community*, Cambridge University Press, Cambridge.

Olson, M 1968, *The Logic of Collective Action: Public Goods and the Theory of Groups*, Harvard University Press, Cambridge, MA.

Ostrom, E 1990, *Governing the Commons: The Evolution of Institutions for Collective Action*, Cambridge University Press, New York.

Page, J 2010, 'Common Property and the Age of Aquarius', *Griffith Law Review*, vol. 19, no. 2, 172–96.

Page, J and Brower, A 2007, 'Property Law in the South Island High Country: Statutory Not Common Law Leases', *Waikato Law Rev.*, vol. 15, 48–63.

Raff, M 1998, 'Environmental Obligations and the Western Liberal Property Concept', *Melb. Univ. Law Rev.*, vol. 22, 657–92.

Rodgers, C 2009, 'Nature's Place? Property Rights, Property Rules and Environmental Stewardship', *Cambridge Law Journal*, vol. 68, no. 3, 550–74.

Rose, C M 1993, 'Environmental Lessons', *Loyola of Los Angeles Law Review*, vol. 27, 1023–47.

Rose, C M 1994, 'Given-ness and Gift: Property and the Quest for Environmental Ethics', *Envtl. L.*, vol. 24, 1–31.

Rose, C M 1998, 'The Several Futures of Property: Of Cyberspace and Folk Tales, Emission Trades and Ecosystems', *Minn. L. Rev.*, vol. 83, 129–82.

Rose, C M 2000, 'Left Brain Right Brain and History in the New Law and Economics of Property' (2000) *Oregon Law Rev.*, vol. 79, 479–92.

Rose, C M 2014, 'The Law is Nine-Tenths of Possession: An Adage Turned on its Head', *Arizona Legal Studies*, Discussion Paper No. 14–13, p.14. available at http://ssrn.com/abstract=2435329

Sax, J 1971, 'Takings, Private Property and Public Rights', *Yale L.J.*, vol. 81, 149–86.

Singer, J 2000, *The Edges of the Field Lessons on the Obligations of Ownership*, Beacon Press, Boston.

Ubhi, N and Denyer-Green, B 2004, *Law of Commons and Town and Village Greens*, Jordan Publishing, Bristol.

Underkuffler, L 2003, *The Idea of Property: Its Meaning and Power,* Oxford University Press, Oxford.

van Hook, E 1993, 'Note, The Ecocommons: A Plan for Common Property Management of Ecosystems', *Yale L. & Pol. Rev.*, vol. 11, 561–96.

Weston, B and Bollier, D 2013, *Green Governance: Ecological Survival, Human Rights, and the Law of the Common,* Cambridge University Press, New York.

Williamson, S, Brunckhorst, D and Kelly, G 2003, *Reinventing the Common: Cross-Boundary Farming for a Sustainable Future,* Federation Press, Sydney.

Part II

The implications of property diversity for place, community and obligation

Chapter 4

Seeing property diversity, its core elements

4.1 Introduction: the imaginings of property

From time to time, the transformative potential of property has been glimpsed, serendipitous-like imaginings of the many and different 'futures of property' (Rose 1998). In 1964, Charles Reich saw property as the vanguard of an emerging civic compact, a New Property right to 'government largess' that would address social inequity. In the early 1970s, Christopher Stone was inspired by the constantly evolving nature of property to imagine that trees had legal standing, while Joseph Sax (1971) envisaged an environmental future where public property rights were equal to their private equivalents. In the twenty-first century, Jedediah Purdy (2010) argues for a new approach to property to address the existential threat of climate change. When confronted with insurmountable challenge, scholars aspire to property and invoke in it an imagination of seemingly limitless potential.

Re-imagining property in land is the thrust of this chapter. Premised on Carol Rose's ideas of 'seeing' property (Rose 1994), the inter-disciplinary influences of legal geography and sustainable urban design, and paradigm-shifting unorthodoxies such as property marginality (van der Walt 2010), this chapter describes and details a theory of *property diversity* as an imaginative, new way of seeing property. To see the mosaic that is property diversity is to imagine a 'different attitude towards land and the nature of land ownership' (Sax 1992, p.1445), a reconceptualization that escapes the myopic private paradigm, and faithfully reflects the heterogeneity of our many relationships with land.

Section 2 commences this chapter by articulating the guiding principles of a doctrine of property diversity in land. Section 3 then deconstructs the constitutive elements of the diverse property mosaic, incorporating aspects of preceding chapters devoted to private, public and common property. The diversity of property type (in physical and valorized form), and expansive understandings of landed interests and ownerships, is each explored in turn, re-conceptualizing, piece by piece, this imaginative envisioning of property.

4.2 Defining principles of a theory of property diversity

It is trite to observe that without diversity, there can be no mosaic. This section outlines the core tenets that give structure and content to a nascent theory of property diversity in land.

Property diversity sees the fullest range of property patterns in human landscapes, dense mosaics of the private, public and common estates, and hybrid variants in between that collectively explain the propertied truth of 'who gets to do what and where' (Freyfogle 2007, p.107). It also sees property patterns holistically, their connections and interactions. Diverse property is likewise contextual, grounded in place, not de-physicalized abstraction. It favours use rights over possession, and situates exclusion alongside inclusion. It celebrates that property is multivalent, and it embraces eclecticism, the idea that property is particularized, variable and occasionally untidy. Last, it acknowledges that diverse property is best seen through performance, reiterative acts that reinforce that property is constantly enacted in divergent ways.

4.2.1 Diverse property in land is visible

Rose argues that 'seeing property is ... an act of imagination [that] opens the door to ... persuasion.' By contrast, an inability to see property is a 'kind of imaginative disability' (Rose 1994, p.285). Rose's seeing arises through four media: as pictures, metaphors, narratives and illusion. The first three have especial resonance for property diversity. By accentuating difference, diverse property shifts the seeing of property in landscapes from near-invisible abstraction to contextual relief.

To see diverse property as pictures is to recognize its many visual markers or physical indicia. For private property it may be the fences, locked gates, or keep out signs that 'yell' of exclusion (Rose 1985). For public property, it may be well-trodden grassed paths, crowded beach foreshores or 'please close the gate' signs that speak of inclusion. Pictures may also show ambiguity, blurred overlaps where public and private converge equivocally. Pictures include maps, scaled representations (Santos 1987) that enable complex visualities to be reduced to simple, easily understood images. Maps 'bring [property] data together in a single perceptible space' (Rose 1994, p.277) and reveal unexpected connections. 'The map, far from stifling the imagination, invites the viewer to reflect on the story behind the case' (ibid., p.277).

To reflect on sub-textual stories is to segue into the seeing of property as narrative. Rose writes of 'the battered remnants of last century's fences, meandering ... though the blissfully resurgent woods ... a vision [that] reveals the impermanence and pathos of property's aspirations to eternity' (Rose 1994, pp.286–87). Property's narratives 'enlist the visual imagination to tell a story about property' (ibid., p.289). Classic property stories are those of tragedy, improvement, or scarcity, sweeping morality tales that entrench private dominance and drown out alternative narratives. More mundane, but equally significant stories are those of everyday commerce or sociability, acted out on private or public lands. Narratives also anchor people to place, telling us where we belong and where we do not; the folklore that orients owners and non-owners alike through a sense of continuity from past to present.

To see property as metaphor is more nuanced. Yet Rose argues that apartment owners typically see property in terms of metaphor, a larger bundle for their private condominium, and an altogether different and reduced one for common or shared areas. To see property as metaphor is to accentuate property's duality, at one level the divisibility of its sticks, and at the other, to 'reclaim a sense of the whole and the relatedness of the various elements of entitlement' (ibid., p.282).

To see property in land is more likely where there is contrast, where there is a visible 'warp and woof' (Leopold 1999, p.168) in the property patterns of human landscapes. Seeing patchworks of private, public and common property, or the variegated stories they tell, accentuates difference. Conversely, seeing is less likely when camouflaged in a property monotone. Rose saw property in the 'forceful and imperious landscape' of Hawaii, islands of striking physicality where 'people who live there seem to take an unusual interest in property law, and ... know a great deal about it' (Rose 1994, p.267). In such places, seeing property is intuitive, it 'hits you in the eye'.

> The landscape has directed Hawaii's property law to an intense concern for issues of land and water; but the intervention of property law, in its various guises, has in turn affected the landscape. Those effects are visible too: the waterworks, the patterns of cultivated and natural vegetation, the tall buildings in Oahu and the low ones in Kauai, these matters are creatures of law ... most particularly the law of property.
>
> (ibid., pp.267–68)

It is no accident therefore that the case studies in Chapter 5 are mostly found in landscapes of striking physicality. It is easier to see and explain property diversity where it does hit you in the eye. But once recognized, its patterns can manifest anywhere.

4.2.2 Diverse property sees land as an inter-connected whole

Once seen, property diversity then shifts the imaginative focus from the artificially imposed lines that divide land parcels to the holistic landscape in between and across the lines. It refutes the paradigm that looks 'to the lines first, not the land upon which the lines were laid' (Meine 2004, p.201), and affirms an intuition that 'the straight edges of our constructed environment [are] narrow pencils of shadow ... dark mortar joining the parts of the world together' (Carter 2009, p.1).

Joseph Sax's prescient 'economy of nature' observes, 'viewing land through the lens of nature's economy reduces the significance of property lines' (Sax 1992, p.1445). Its consequence is an understanding that land is inextricably interconnected as 'part of an ecosystem' (ibid., p.1438). The 'backwards looking' alternative is one where land is inert, and owners share no obligation to participate in the natural or ecological services that their lands collectively provide. Emphasizing the systemic (what Sax calls 'ecosystemic') reflects that 'connections dominate' (ibid., p.1445).

Connections between, and within, private, public and common land holdings have greater capacity to avoid Eric Freyfogle's 'tragedy of fragmentation', the private stasis that paralyzes human landscapes. The inter-connective mosaic is an overarching mechanism that measures the impact of land use externalities. Metaphorically, the mosaic is analogous to Tony Arnold's 'webs of interests' (Arnold 2002), or Henry Smith's 'architectural' or 'modular' property model (Smith 2012), except that it inserts the full panoply of property tiles into the seeing. Its antithesis is the disaggregated bundle of rights, where universal stick rights readily detach, and any one stick may relate to another. As Smith wryly notes, the bundle 'picture' treats property in an 'atom-counting fashion, which is fine as far as it goes. But what we still need is a theory of how the pieces fit together' (Smith 2012, p.1709). Property diversity starts to provide such a picture.

4.2.3 Diverse property rights are use rights

Sax's economy of nature also re-conceives ownership rights in land as use rights, not rights to possess, or rights of dominion. His usufructuary model draws analogies with water, where the private right to extract is subservient to the community's dependence on the resource. Use rights 'serve two masters, the community and the individual' (Sax 1992, p.1453).

Rose and Freyfogle likewise see parallels between water and emergent use rights in land. Rose invites readers to imagine a paradigm where water is property in land's 'chief symbol'.

> We might think of property rights ... in quite a different way. We might think of rights ... as more fluid and less fenced-in ... as entailing less of the Blackstonian power of exclusion and more of the qualities of flexibility, reasonableness ... moderation, and attentiveness to others.
>
> (Rose 1996, p.351)

Freyfogle (1988) predicts that were property law to develop like water law, property rights would begin to resemble use rights that accommodate their context, and the similar rights of others.

Use rights escape from theory to practice in natural resources and public lands law. This vast jurisprudence of property in natural resources offers an instructive counter-point to traditional Anglo-common law approaches to real property (Scott 2008). Natural resources (whether extractive or non-extractive) are capable of capture, monetization and transfer. Yet property in natural resources is overwhelmingly couched in the terminology of permits, licences, concessions or privileges; rights predicated on use, not possession. Importantly, use rights permit the sharing of resources, since uses are not automatically mutually exclusive. Thus, in the American rangelands, private rights to graze share the public domain with public rights of recreational access (Page 2009). Natural resources law, like water law, has avoided the yoke of possession, and fostered instead long-standing policies of 'multiple use, sustained yield.'

Use rights are desirable for many reasons. They enable and reflect the reality of multiple rights co-existing in the one parcel of land. They are consistent with the common law's view of property rights as relative not absolute. And the grant of a private use right does not exhaust or consume residual public rights in land. Even where exclusive, use rights focus on the proper question of exclusivity of access to the resource, not the falsely conflated right to exclude (Katz 2008, p.277). As Sax identifies, use rights are more attuned to an ecological perspective, concentrating on the tangible resource, how it relates to other inter-connected resources, and ultimately, each resource's finitude.

While the common law does not eschew the usufruct completely, its incorporeal hereditaments are hierarchically inferior, typically burdens on possessory estates rather than templates for the future imaginings of property in land. By contrast, diverse property rights reverse this logic, since public and common rights to land are use rights. Rather than exceptions to the possessory rule, private use rights are seen in pluralist context.

4.2.4 Diverse property in land is contextual

John Orth's identification of the unifying themes of the American common law of property reveals in its opening paragraphs a profound truism. Orth writes, '[a]ll property law is local ... the place where the land lies' (Orth 2010, p.vii). His efforts to reach generic conclusions only make sense when applied to 'some specific time and place'. Legal geographers agree, describing the law as inherently 'world-ed' (Braverman et al. 2014, p.1).

Orth's plain observation runs counter to the prevailing orthodoxy that property rights are universalized relations between persons about things. In the propertied world, place is irrelevant. Having reached its abstract apogee with Wesley Hohfeld's analysis of relations between jural persons (1913), abstraction's end game is famously that of illusion (Gray 1991). For Nicole Graham, the paradigm of placeless-ness means, 'that property is not about things, that property is not really "real", [and] that property is de-physicalised' (Graham 2010, p.7). Nicholas Blomley (2004) observes that modern property has been emptied of all its heterogeneity and distinctiveness. Yet such critiques, descriptions of the universalizing tendencies of post-enclosure property, jar with Orth's simple logic.

Theodore Steinberg takes property's detachment from place to absurd lengths when writing of the 'folly of owning nature' (Steinberg 1995). Steinberg cites private appropriations of the surface of the Moon, or property disputes over the weather, as comedic attempts to own that which is beyond capture. 'It is a tribute to the colonizing impulse at the heart of property law that it has been able to encroach' into these surreal realms. Steinberg warns that a world where everything can be converted into property may be a creative one, but it is also 'an impoverished ... dangerous world as well' (Steinberg 1995, p.165).

The destructive perversity that Steinberg identifies is however a consequence of the over-reach of private appropriation. As Graham and Blomley agree, property was not always so place-less. Graham observes that pre-enclosure common property was diverse, localized and heterogeneous, while Blomley sees resistance to enclosure as an ongoing subtext of modern property. Such resistance can be seen in the idiosyncratic claims to property that Blomley documents in his home city of Vancouver, evidence that at least some property is still local.

Examples of contextual property include the Scottish right to roam discussed in this book's Introduction. A more recent illustration is found at Te Urewera in New Zealand's North Island. Te Urewera is a vast area of natural wilderness, an 'ancient and enduring [land], a fortress of nature, alive with history; its scenery abundant with mystery, adventure, and remote beauty.'[1] In 1954, the New Zealand government, in acknowledgment of these values, gazetted Te Urewera as national park. Yet, 60 years later, its park status was revoked. In its stead, the *Te Urewera Act 2014* vested ownership of Te Urewera in the land, such that the land became the owner, and the owner became the land.[2] Seemingly, Te Urewera fulfils (and extends) Christopher Stone's prophecy that trees would have standing, as a natural land-owning entity in its own legal right (Stone 1972). But such a conclusion is only half right, since the propertied story of Te Urewera is deeply contextual. For two centuries, Te Urewera was contested territory, home to the Maori Tūhoe people, yet claimed by the colonial (and post-colonial) New Zealand Crown. This contest left a legacy of 'large scale land confiscations, brutal military campaigns and unjust land purchases'.[3] This history yielded two parallel worlds, the 'Western construct' of protected national park (Ruru, 2014) and the Maori reality, where sovereignty, let alone title, had never been surrendered.[4] By 2014, this tension resolved in the *Te Urewera Act*, a unique legislative response to history, conflict and ultimately reconciling cultures. The Act disestablished the national park, vested title to the land *in* the land, and established a management board comprising Crown and Tūhoe representatives.[5] The Act also serves mundane functions, deeming Te Urewera as inalienable registered land under the Torrens title system, and giving it an individual tax status. Te Urewera's uniqueness stems not so much from Stone's inexorable trajectory towards rights for natural objects, as the compelling narratives of its special-ness, of its misty, mountainous and spiritual place.

Diverse property reaches back to the rights of pre-enclosure commoners, as much as it incorporates the dissentient voices of Blomley's poor and unpropertied. It finds contemporary form in the accommodation of Tūhoe and Pakeha at Te Urewera.[6] And it agrees with Orth's intuitive assertion that property is local, the place where the land lies.

4.2.5 Diverse property privileges neither exclusion nor inclusion

Property diversity also recognizes that exclusion cannot be understood in isolation. In the case of private property, the right to exclude has always been qualified by exigency.[7] In the case of public property, the under-theorized right of inclusion (Page 2013) is a critical foil to private property's exclusion. Even common property is paradoxically exclusive on the outside, but inclusive within. Exclusion provides an incomplete, unsatisfactory account of property. As Hanoch Dagan observes 'large slabs of property doctrine' devoted to 'co-operative relationships' would need to be discarded if exclusion was its sole premise.

> Numerous property rules, prescribing the rights and obligations of members of local communities, neighbors, co-owners, partners, and spouses cannot be fairly analyzed under the exclusion paradigm.
>
> (Dagan 2006, pp.85–86)

In stark contrast, the central logic of property uniformity is that property 'center[s] around the idea of exclusion' (Balganesh 2012, p.1892). To classify an interest as a property right 'entails endowing it with an exclusionary significance' (ibid., p.1899). Yet, Balganesh is forced to create a 'plausible' category of quasi-property to explain those interests that fall outside the exclusion thesis (ibid., pp.1924–25).

Property diversity does not compel its proponents to take absolutist or implausible positions. Instead it recognizes that exclusion and inclusion are two-halves of the one dialectic, where property is shaped by the constant interaction, and at times overlap, of each irresistible force. Dagan's delicate 'balance of property values' (2011) is one where the diversity of context, and the particularity of resource, determines the contours of property's form, and its commensurate proportionality of inclusion and exclusion.

4.2.6 Diverse property in land is multivalent

Another central logic of property diversity is that it is more varied and multivalent than the private liberal paradigm supposes. This extends not only to the seeing of the public and common estates, and their respective property norms, but also to the seeing of private property's long ignored social and communitarian values.

As noted, Dagan argues that monistic, totalizing theories of property are incomplete in their account of the lived experiences of property (Dagan 2011, pp.57–75). Instead, he endorses a pluralistic account. Pluralism reflects a truth of property law that recognizes 'different meanings of ownership in different social contexts and with respect to different resources' (ibid., p.72). Once relieved of the burden of monism, heterogeneity can be acknowledged for what it is; 'a testimony of property law's appreciation of the significance of facilitating multiple forms of human interaction.' Because 'free people have diverse ends, diverse forms of property are necessary to realize those ends' (ibid., pp.72–73).

Diverse property enacts Dagan's theories. Different meanings of ownerships do arise according to context and the nature of the resource, even if the common law is sometime loathe to put different names to it.[8] And it is both reasonable and desirable, as Dagan argues, for property to have more than one set of principles, since the institution is not a monolith.

4.2.7 Diverse property in land is eclectic

The flipside of diverse property is that it is untidy. If real not abstract, then by necessity it is customized to context. Such untidiness could be simply explained – ownerships vary according to context and resource. However, another interpretation is more problematic – that customized property is unpredictable and unstable, in short, unworthy of property status.

The latter interpretation aligns with the closed list view of property mandated by the 'meta-principle' of *numerus clausus* (Merrill and Smith 2000). Brendan Edgeworth says that it

> expresses the stringency of the common law's approach to property rights, particularly over land. In essence, the principle holds that landowners are not at liberty to customize land rights, in the sense of re-working them in an entirely novel way to suit their particular individual needs and circumstances.
>
> (Edgeworth 2006b, pp.387–88)

Numerus clausus prescribes that there are only so many estates, servitudes and security interests that the law will recognize as things of property. If the interest under scrutiny is outside that list, then 'it will be impotent against successors in title' (ibid., p.389). Unlike the liberties of contract law, parties are not free to create new categories of enforceable property. Thomas Merrill and Henry Smith justify such restrictiveness on the drily economic argument that 'excessive information costs' are imposed on third parties where property interests are non-standard, such that any resultant interest is 'sub-optimal' (Merrill and Smith 2000, pp.26–27).[9]

Yet, the edifice that is *numerus clausus* is not as imposing as first appears. It is a creature of the civil law, not the common law. Elsewhere, Smith explains that *numerus clausus* must be seen in its historical milieu, a doctrine designed 'for the wholesale stripping of feudal custom out of [French civilian] property law' (Smith 2009, p.35). Prior to 2000, it was prominent by its absence in the common law (Merryman 1963). As Merrill and Smith admit, the deeply implicit principle 'has no [common law] name' (Merrill and Smith 2000, p.4). Indeed, it is more a 'pigeon holing exercise' (ibid., p.11), a norm of judicial self-governance that assumes that the creation of new property rights is solely a legislative concern (ibid., p.58).

Away from *numerus clausus*, the values of untidiness in property have been more generally observed. Rose (1988) sees property law optimally as a self-adjusting balance between the certainty of crystalline statute and the pragmatism of the common law's mud. Muddying the waters may be messy, but it provides necessary relief to the jagged, unintended consequence of statute. Joseph Singer goes further, arguing that contrary to the intuitive view, flexible *standards* are more important to predictability in property law than fixed and certain *rules* (Singer 2013). Singer calls these variables the *rules of reason* that 'rule property law.' The reasons that courts 'eschew clarity in favor of ambiguity' is that '[p]roperty law is simply too complicated and too contextually nuanced to be rigidly defined by categorical rules' (Singer 2013, p.1404). Ambiguity is on balance more useful to property law than not, promoting 'moral reflection', the 'shaping' of property rights to reflect human values, and regulating the 'systemic effects' of the exercise of individual property rights vis-à-vis the rights of others (ibid., p.1434).

To recognize that diverse property is customized is to accept its nuance. But that does not concede that it is unprincipled. There is a middle course between the extremes of property's polarities, the rigidity of the closed list, or the infinite possibilities of laissez-faire customization. Judges refer to the guidance of property's 'principled parameters' (Wonnacott 2006). Henry Smith sees the mediation of 'things' as giving property its stable *in rem* character (Smith 2012, p.1691). Hanoch Dagan likewise demonstrates that plurality can be reconciled with principle (Dagan 2011, p.53). Eclecticism is a challenge to property's central logic, the uncritical assumption that property is what we expect it to be. But it is also 'a mindset that is conformist, unreflective, and narrow' (van der Walt 2010), in short, unimaginative.

4.2.8 Diverse property in land is performed

Last, diverse property is best understood through its doing. Performance theory is a legal geographic proposition that property is a 'relational effect, not a prior ground ... brought into being by the very act of performance' (Blomley 2013, p.32). In other words, doing does not merely describe or represent property, but it enacts, such that property becomes a reality through its performance. Blomley says when applied to property, performance theory challenges private modalities that recognize only two temporal moments: property's initial creation, and any later transfer of title. Instead, time is always important, as performance belongs in the constant acts of doing. Importantly, the constancy of performance over time has a citational effect, as one 'more or less successful act ... cites other performances, and in so doing, compels future similar performances' (ibid., p.36).

If private property is, as Blomley analogizes, the 'more or less successful' performance of everyday acts like mowing lawns or building fences (ibid., p.36; Blomley 2014), then public property is enacted by kicking footballs around the park, sunbathing on the beach or hiking in national parks; while common property is enacted by community gardening or swimming in your club's member-only pool. Collectively, these performances of diverse property are faithful depictions of its lived experience.

Performance theory is liberating. It unfreezes the arcane rules that limit our imagination of what is property in land. To use a Dagan metaphor, performing property diversity is akin to playing 'a complex piece of music with full orchestration' compared to the private monotone's singular 'melody line [that] risks missing most of the performance' (Dagan 2011, p.72).

Reimagining landed property as a diverse mosaic is to shift focus, to lift our eyes from the self-limiting hegemony that is the private ownership paradigm. It is to see something familiar, but from a different, much higher vantage point. In gaining altitude, we see the constraints that bound our current imaginings of property and the narrowness of our vision. Section 3 proceeds to identify the constituent elements of the diverse mosaic that this heightened perspective throws into sharper relief.

4.3 What comprises the diverse property mosaic? Types and values and interests and ownerships

The diverse property mosaic is a converged model, where property types and their commensurate values intersect with a plethora of interests and divergent concepts of ownership. It is a jumbled mix of orthodox and *sui generis*, drawing hybrid strength from its heterogeneity. It is a full and sometimes cacophonous symphony, not a solo melody line.

This section deconstructs this symphony into its constituent parts. First, it examines property *type* – private, public and common property in land – and their respective values. Second, it describes the mosaic's elements, the melange of property *interests* in land, corporeal, incorporeal and otherwise, that spills across the boundaries of type. Third, it canvasses the many meanings of *ownership* both within and beyond the private model.

4.3.1 A confluence of property type: physical and normative

The mosaic is a seeing of private, public and common *in situ*, a rendering of a faithful image of propertied human landscapes, an unedited seeing of all property types. While somewhat artificial,[10] what distinguishes one property type from another is, to borrow bundle terminology, 'how the quality and content of the bundle of rights varies in practice, and who holds the sticks' (Barnes 2009, p.11).

With private property, the 'who' question is fairly straightforward. Jeremy Waldron describes this as the 'single organizing idea' of private property that a 'certain specified person is able to determine how a specified resource is to be used' (Waldron 1991, pp.59–60). The quality of the private right is typically secure and exclusive.

By contrast, there is frequent misapprehension as to meanings of the common and public estates. Many jurists lump non-private property into a single 'collective' category. Others talk of 'state' property. Others confuse the two. Michael Brill observes that common property provides for community life, a sociability 'with people you somewhat know', while public property provides for public life and a shared sociability 'with a diversity of strangers' (Brill 2002, p.50). As we have seen, common property is not public property; it refers to use rights vested in community members who derive their propertied relationship with land through communal membership. Outsiders are trespassers on common lands. Rose says that common property is more 'obvious' than we suppose, seen in clubs, associations and condominiums. Indeed, its obviousness is so commonplace, we are 'oblivious' to its seeing. In contradistinction, the 'who' in public property is opaque. Again, Rose posits that ultimately the public stick-holder is not the state, or its agencies, but the diffused, 'unorganized public at large' (Rose 1986).

The universalizing perception that property and private property are synonymous yields maps of landscapes that are one-sided; accounts of place that fail to record the 'striking evidence of other divergent and often oppositional understandings ... of property [with their] very different spatial representations and practices' (Blomley 2004, p.55). To map property diversity however offers the possibility of restoring substance to 'all the complexities and particularities that give[s] meaning on the ground' (ibid., p.68).

Property diversity also yields a normative mosaic commensurate to the grounded patterns of private, public and common property. Private values promote efficiency, exclusivity and security. Collectively, they have unleashed land's economic potential, and the acquisition of private wealth through commoditization. Public values provide a welcome foil; inclusion, and a macro-sociability premised on the widest 'comedy of the commons'. Public property in land is also democratic, a forum open to all, while away from the maddening crowd, public spaces allow for self-contemplation and solitude. Critically, public property fulfils a function of propriety, where the public estate endows well-ordered communities with a capacity for human flourishing. The normative mosaic is completed by the under-regarded values of common property; the micro-sociability of community and belonging, its environmental norms of prudence, responsibility and moderation, and its example of localized use rights untainted by tragedy. Each imbues 'important graces, tolerances and social learnings … becoming lost to us' (Brill 2002, p.49), as community and public life is displaced by an 'exaggerated private domain' (ibid., p.51).

The exaggeration that Brill identifies is not always simply one of private versus public normative dominance. It is also a skewing of the relative values of private property itself. Private property is more complex and multivalent than its exclusionary rhetoric suggests. It has values important to personhood: the protection of privacy, the promotion of self-expression, or the securing of personal autonomy and choice (Alexander 2013). It also has overlooked or forgotten social and communitarian values.

> Less has been written about private property's collective or communitarian values.... Such understandings are equally important in explaining and justifying private property, and in simply understanding the institution's fullest, socially situated dimensions.
>
> (Lametti 2010, p.4)

Gregory Alexander sees private property's collective values in terms of 'inclusiveness', the opportunity to join and belong, and 'community', the facilitating of social relations (Alexander 2013). These values reflect the reality that much of contemporary sociability occurs on private land, 'the strip, shopping malls, atriums of skyscrapers, casinos, sports arenas, amusement parks, racetracks' (Brill 2002, p.53). Brill observes that the modern migration of public or community life to private space has the curious effect of masking the inherent sociability of private property. He attributes this to the less esteemed sociable activities that occur in these private commons, the consumptive hedonism of 'spectacle, entertainment, and … commerce and trade' (ibid., p.53).

4.3.2 An array of real property interests

Not only is the property mosaic one of diverse types and values, it is also a compendium of diverse real property interests: a functioning system of corporeal estates, incorporeal interests, and *sui generis* partnerships of public, private and community owners. Its individual parts may appear to operate in isolation (Smith 2012), yet the mosaic is optimally an integrated network, best understood as a functioning whole. As the sum of many parts, this section will attempt to categorize, and in turn identify, those real property interests that make up each loose category of the mosaic. As a precursor to Chapter 5, each interest will also be viewed through the prism of good land use ends.

4.3.2.1 Corporeal estates

Modern real property interests may be simultaneously abstract and corporeal; a paradox not often seen for the curious anomaly it presents. However, as a traditional classification, it is convenient for the purposes of property diversity with its implicit admission that (at least some) property in land is tangible, and hence contextual.

Corporeal estates in modern land law usually comprise the fee simple and freehold life estate. In some jurisdictions, the fee tail may limp on. If one discards the feudal fiction of chattels real, the leasehold is another corporeal estate in land. Each is an interest in the diverse mosaic, a right to use for a duration that varies from an infinite uncertainty to a certain term of years.

The fee simple is the most important of the modern corporeal estates, indeed it is universalizing and totalizing of the category as a whole. Yet, despite its near omnipotence, the absence of scholarly scrutiny of the fee simple is another paradox. Simon Douglas notes, 'surprisingly little is written about its content', perhaps because of our 'strong intuitive grasp of what it means to own land' (Douglas 2013, p.359). Douglas posits that fee simple owners enjoy 'open ended' liberties to use land,[11] a right better explained by the under-scrutinized right to use than the dominant exclusion thesis (ibid., p.360). As a property tool for sustainability, the fee simple is a blunt instrument with limitations. Seen within the property monotone, it manifests in private environmental organisations purchasing conservation lands, either in perpetuity or through revolving fund transactions. As a stand-alone strategy, the fee simple is limited by high acquisition costs, succession issues where ownership is ostensibly perpetual, or the belief that conservation is not served by retreat into enclaves (Fairfax et al. 2005, p.254). Richard Brewer lists 'transactions costs, initial capital expenses, and costs of continuing stewardship' (Brewer 2003, p.133). State-owned national parks and conservation reserves represent the public fee simple. They are impacted by similar restraints, the scarcity of taxpayer dollars and identical concerns about enclave retreat.

The life estate is more an outlier. It is rarely cited in sustainability literature, despite it possessing a common law doctrine concerned with intergenerational consequence, the law of waste. While a possessory estate, its doctrines strongly focus on use rights of the life tenant, be it rights to income, timber or emblements.

> In a sense all landowners are life tenants, albeit the fee simple owner has an estate of potentially infinite duration … All landholders hold their interests for the benefit of posterity as well as their own use … [as] trustees for the future.
>
> (Cribbet 1986, p.40)

Corporeal estates should be seen in context, as one category in a diversity of real property interests. Similarly, within the category, the fee simple needs to be seen as one freehold estate, and not the defining paradigm. A consequence of seeing corporeal estates through this taxonomic context is to recognize what is common to all corporeal estates, an entitlement to use land distinguished by different durations.

4.3.2.2 Incorporeal/less than fee interests

The diversity of real property interests is more apparent with incorporeal interests. Easements and covenants are regular features of propertied landscapes, and along with the lesser known profit *a prendre,* positively or negatively regulate the use of land. However, as discussed, incorporeal interests are typically seen as burdens on corporeal estates, hierarchically less significant, and thus diminished.

Easements have been adapted to good land use ends, protecting scenic corridors, or securing unimpeded sunshine to solar collector panels. Limitations include the need for transactional consent and a common law reticence to protect aesthetic values. However, statutory intervention can supervene.[12] Covenants, positive and restrictive, likewise are widely employed to achieve environmental outcomes, such as protecting wind access to turbines. In particular, positive covenants can impose stewardship obligations on future landowners, again with the assistance of statute.[13] For example, conservation covenants protect biodiversity corridors, open space and so on (Farr 2008, pp.93–94, pp.120–23). More novel applications include the preservation of dark sky preserves (Nagle 2010; Page, Brower and Welsch 2013). The ancient profit *a prendre* can also be re-tooled, such as a device to sequester carbon, but its essentially extractive nature is problematic.[14] The common law's adaptability also leaves open the potential for obsolete incorporeal hereditaments to be future tiles in the diverse mosaic. These include the rent charge, franchise, (Gray 2010b, p.248), or profit *a rendre* (Edgeworth 2006a).

Nor is the property mosaic restricted to traditional incorporeal interests. Imaginative *sui generis* rights such as grass banks (Register 2006, p.261), solar access rights (Corbett and Corbett 2000, p.35, p.163) or conservation banks (Nagle 2010, pp.86–87) expand the seemingly exponential plurality of what can constitute an incorporeal interest in land.

4.3.2.3 Public/private/community partnerships

Other interests in land fall outside, or cross over, the arbitrary distinction of corporeal versus incorporeal. Sally Fairfax and her colleagues describe the rise of collaborations between public, private and community actors as the defining feature of modern conservation.

> Multiple agents now own partial interests in a single parcel of land for a wide variety of purposes that are often in conflict. The result … is an interlocking network of policies and actors that defies easy categorization. Neither regulatory or market based, neither public nor private, the result is best described as an emerging mosaic of claims on land.
>
> (Fairfax et al. 2005, p.8)

Several factors make these partnerships the new norm. These include a changing philosophy of governance, fluctuating conservation goals, variable economic conditions, or changing ideas about property (Fairfax et al. 2005, pp.9–11). The latter is apposite. Post-bundle, 'a continuous reinterpretation of property has resulted in complex ownership ideas and … increasingly fragmented and intricate arrangements among public and private actors' (ibid., p.10). Fairfax concludes on balance that this is a good thing, representing 'at best … a new, collaborative and sophisticated approach that can approximate the elusive win-win model so frequently touted in conservation circles' (ibid., p.272).

Multi-ownership collaborations can be formally structured and documented,[15] or they may be informal groupings that just happen in response to threat or exigency. Amnon Lehavi describes such haphazard groupings as 'limited management commons' or 'Spontaneous Communities' (Lehavi 2013, pp.166–67). While governance of formal joint ventures may depend on black letter law and enforceable rules, governance of informal groupings often depends on a blend of law, social norms and co-operative strategies (Garnett 2012).

The rise of the amorphous multi-owner partnership demonstrates a diversity of interests in land that transcends traditional classifications. Instead of being confined to the all-pervasive, all-encompassing fee simple, property diversity offers the imaginative possibility of so much more.

4.3.3 A diversity of ownerships

This section concludes by canvassing the conceptual breadth of what constitutes 'ownership', both from within and outside, the private paradigm. Within the property monotone, ownership of land demands that property-ness is restricted to state-enforced private rights that run with the land. Concepts of private ownership only vary as to the measurable impact of their external effects. At one end of this short spectrum, an owner may be sovereign of their 'castle'. At the other, their ownership is (variously described) as a 'citizenship, good neighbor or environmental' construct (Singer 2006). The castle view is a rhetorically powerful caricature, where the despotic owner is supposedly free to raise the drawbridge, and ignore trans-boundary effects of adverse land uses. Singer is highly critical of this interpretation, preferring the latter understandings because they import obligation alongside property right, and take account of harmful land uses.

> The citizenship model rests on the notion that owners have obligations as well as rights ... Obligation is inherent in liberalism, but the castle and market models marginalize it. They seek to suppress consciousness of the obligations inherent in ownership, to draw our attention away from them.
>
> (Singer 2006, p.330)

Ownership can also embrace common property rights of ownership, described as 'ownership without possession' (Neeson 1993). Ownership of public property is far more contestable and esoteric, a diffuse 'sum of interests in which the individual concerned has no greater claim than any other member of the public.'[16]

Alternative claims to 'what is ours' derive legitimacy from theories such as Andre van der Walt's 'marginal' perspective on property law, where the analytical focus is on 'dissent and contention rather than consensus' (van der Walt 2010, p.103). In a similar vein, Blomley argues that the ownership claims of society's marginalized, concretized in claims to community-owned property, are acts of resistance against the ongoing enclosure of non-private rights. Apart from contest, other bases for collective ownerships include adherence to customary practice, or the observance of social norms (Ellickson 2008).

To claim a vested interest in such an amorphous subject matter is to articulate non-paradigmatic ideas like 'property as belonging'. Davina Cooper argues that this 'quite different understanding' of property yields an ownership that captures the everyday life and minutiae of community. Cooper does not dismiss the private ownership model, but says that its deficiency lies in its failure to capture the full picture of what ownership entails. By ignoring property's norm of inclusion, private ownership 'not only misses but also misrecognizes what is going on' (Cooper 2007, p.659). Ultimately, the gap between ownership as 'belonging' and illusory ownership, such as Kevin Gray's proprietary place in a queue (Gray 2010a) is wafer thin. Yet, despite its jarring with property's central logic, the literature continues to give voice to these alternative claims. Importantly, property diversity, by its inclusiveness, is open to this vast array of ownerships. Thomas Merrill's 'property strategy' perhaps unintentionally sums up this open-ended approach, noting that wherever there is a resource and access to it, the property strategy is at work. Critically, the strategy operates beyond 'rights that enjoy the imprimatur of law' (Merrill 2012, p.2075).

4.4 Conclusion

To see property diversity requires imagination, an openness to acknowledge the 'property-ness' of things outside comfortable yet complacent assumptions. In re-imagining property from this higher vantage point, the diverse mosaic presents as an inter-connected, at times untidy network, performed by an array of private, public and common actors, and their hybrid collaborators. It infuses diverse property values into human landscapes, and functions through a working system of real property interests that are traditional and novel. Its senses of ownership are broad, and reflect the vast diversity of relationships that people have with their propertied landscape.

Having examined its core attributes and constitutive elements, it is timely to test property diversity beyond simple description. The following chapter sets out to do this through three different means, its goal to reveal that in actual place 'there is a diversity of property on the ground' (Blomley 2004, p.9).

Notes

1 S. 3(1) Te Urewera Act 2014 (NZ).
2 S. 11(1) Te Urewera Act 2014 (NZ).
3 See: www.doc.govt.nz/news/media-releases/2014/tuhoe-claims-settlement-and-te-urewera-bills-passed/
4 The Tūhoe were never signatories to the 1840 Treaty of Waitangi, the constitutional document between the British Crown and many Maori iwi.
5 Initially the board membership is equally split between Tūhoe and Crown, but at the end of the first 3-year term, the Tuhoe will be dominant with 6 board members out of 9.
6 Pakeha are European New Zealanders.
7 *State v. Stack* 277 A.2d 369 (N.J. 1971).
8 For example, the freehold life *tenant* and leasehold *tenant* are different ownerships.
9 The 'Monday watch' exemplifies a property right that imposes excessive information processing costs on later owners.
10 The boundaries of type are porous, seen in hybrids like the modern shopping mall (Kunstler 1993, pp.119–20).

11 These liberties may be constrained by external regulations such as planning or environmental law, but their 'open-ended' nature remains unimpaired (Douglas 2013, p.359).
12 For example, the US scenic easement is statutory.
13 The rule in *Austerberry Corporation* precludes the burden of positive covenants running with land, but in many jurisdictions statute validates positive covenants, see e.g. s 97A Land Title Act 1994 (Qld).
14 See e.g. s 88AB(2) Conveyancing Act 1919 (NSW).
15 See e.g. the Malpai Borderlands Trust (Rose 1998, p.178).
16 *Stow v. Mineral Holdings (Australia) Pty Ltd* (1977) 51 ALJR 672, 679.

References

Alexander, G 2013, 'Property's Ends: The Publicness of Private Law Values', *Cornell Law Faculty Working Papers*, Paper 107.

Arnold, C A 2002, 'The Reconstitution of Property: Property as a Web of Interests', *Harvard Environmental Law Rev.*, vol. 26, 281–364.

Balganesh, S 2012, 'Quasi-Property, Like, But Not Quite Property', *U. Pa. L. Rev.*, vol. 160, 1889–1925.

Barnes, R 2009, *Property Rights and Natural Resources*, Hart Publishing, Oxford.

Blomley, N 2004, *Unsettling the City: Urban Land and the Politics of Property*, Routledge, New York.

Blomley, N 2013, 'Performing Property: Making the World', *Canadian Journal of Law and Jurisprudence*, vol. 26, no. 1, 23–48.

Blomley, N 2014, 'Learning from Larry: Pragmatism and the Habits of Legal Space', in I Braverman, N Blomley, D Delaney and A Kedar (eds), *The Expanding Spaces of Law: A Timely Legal Geography*, Stanford University Press, Stanford, CA.

Braverman, I, Blomley, N, Delaney, D and Kedar, A 2014, 'Expanding the Spaces of Law' in I Braverman, N Blomley, D Delaney and A Kedar (eds), *The Expanding Spaces of Law: A Timely Legal Geography*, Stanford University Press, Stanford, CA.

Brewer, R 2003, *Conservancy: The Land Trust Movement in America*, University Press of New England, Hanover, NH.

Brill, M 2002, 'Problems With Mistaking Community Life for Public Life', *Places*, vol. 14, no. 2, 48–55.

Carter, P 2009, *Dark Writing Geography, Performance, Design*, University of Hawai'i Press, Honolulu.

Cooper, D 2007, 'Opening up Ownership: Community Belonging, Belongings, and the Productive Life of Property', *L. & Soc. Inq.*, vol. 32, 625–64.

Corbett, J and Corbett, M 2000, *Designing Sustainable Communities: Learning from Village Homes*, Island Press, Washington, DC.

Cribbet, J 1986, 'Concepts in Transition: The Search for a New Definition of Property', *U. Ill. L. Rev.*, 1–42.

Dagan, H 2006, 'Property and the Public Domain' *Yale Journal of Law and the Humanities*, vol. 18, 84–93.

Dagan, H 2011, *Property, Values and Institutions*, Oxford University Press, New York.

Douglas, S 2013, 'The Content of a Freehold: A 'Right to Use' Land', in N Hopkins (ed.), *Modern Studies in Property Law*, Hart Publishing, Oxford.

Edgeworth, B 2006a, 'Profits a rendre: A reincarnation?', *Australian Property L. J.*, vol. 15, 1–11.

Edgeworth, B 2006b, 'The *Numerus Clausus* Principle in Contemporary Australian Property Law', *Monash Univ. L. Rev.*, vol. 32, 387–419.
Ellickson, R 2008, *The Household: Informal Order Around the Hearth*, Princeton University Press, Princeton, NJ.
Fairfax, S, Gwin, L, King, M A, Raymond, L and Watt, L 2005, *Buying Nature: The Limits of Land Acquisition as a Conservation Strategy, 1780–2004*, MIT Press, Cambridge, MA.
Farr, D 2008, *Sustainable Urbanism Urban Designs with Nature*, Wiley, Hoboken, NJ.
Freyfogle, E 1988, 'Context and Accommodation in Modern Property Law', *Stanford L. Rev.*, vol. 41, 1529–1556.
Freyfogle, E 2007, *Agrarianism and the Good Society: Land, Culture, Conflict and Hope*, University of Kentucky Press, Lexington.
Garnett, N S 2012, 'Managing the Urban Commons', *Uni. Pa. L. Rev.*, vol. 160, 1995–2027.
Graham, N 2010, *Lawscape: Property, Environment, Law*, Routledge, Abingdon.
Graham, N 2011, 'Owning the Earth', in P Burdon (ed.), *Exploring Wild Law: The Philosophy of Earth Jurisprudence*, Wakefield Press, Kent Town, Australia.
Gray, K 1991, 'Property in Thin Air', *Cambridge. L.J.*, vol. 50, 252–307.
Gray, K 2010a, 'Property in a Queue', in *Property and Community*, Oxford University Press, New York, NY.
Gray, K 2010b, 'Regulatory Property and the Jurisprudence of Quasi-Public Trust', *Sydney Law Rev.*, vol. 32, 221–41.
Hohfeld, W 1913, 'Some Fundamental Legal Conceptions as Applied in Legal Reasoning', *Yale Law Journal*, vol. 23, 16–59.
Katz, L 2008, 'Exclusion and Exclusivity in Property Law' *Univ. Toronto Law J.*, vol. 58, 275–315.
Kuntsler, J H 1993, *The Geography of Nowhere: The Rise and Decline of America's Man-Made Landscape*, Simon and Schuster, New York.
Lametti, D 2010, 'The Objects of Virtue', in G Alexander and E Penalver (eds), *Property and Community*, Oxford University Press, New York.
Lehavi, A 2013, *The Construction of Property: Norms, Institutions, Challenges*, Cambridge University Press, Cambridge.
Leopold, A 1999, *For the Health of the Land: Previously Unpublished Essays and Other Writings*, Island Press, Washington, DC.
Meine, C 2004, *Correction Lines Essays on Land, Leopold, and Conservation*, Island Press, Washington, DC.
Merrill, T W 2012, 'The Property Strategy', *Uni. Pa. Law Rev.*, vol. 160, 2061–95.
Merrill, T W and Smith, H E 2000, 'Optimal Standardization in the Law of Property: The Numerus Clausus Principle', *Yale L. J.*, vol. 110, 1–110.
Merryman, J 1963, 'Policy, Autonomy, and the Numerus Clausus in Italian and American Property Law', *Am. J. Comp. L.*, vol. 12, 224–31.
Nagle, J C 2010, *Laws Environment: How the Law Shapes the Places We Live*, Yale University Press, New Haven, CT.
Neeson, J M 1993, *Commoners: Common Right, Enclosure and Social Change in England, 1700–1820*, Cambridge University Press, Cambridge.
Orth, J 2010, *Reappraisals in the Law of Property*, Ashgate, Burlington, VT.
Page, J 2009, 'Grazing Rights and Public Lands in New Zealand and the Western United States: A Comparative Perspective', *Natural Resources Journal*, vol. 49, 403–432.

Page, J 2013, 'Towards an Understanding of Public Property', in N Hopkins (ed.), *Modern Studies in Property Law*, Hart Publishing, Oxford.

Page, J, Brower, A and Welsch, J 2015, 'The Curious Untidiness of Property and Ecosystem Services: A Hybrid Method of Measuring Place', *Pace Environmental Law Review*, vol. 32, 756–90.

Purdy, J 2010, *The Meaning of Property: Freedom, Community, and the Legal Imagination*, Yale University Press, New Haven, CT.

Register, R 2006, *Ecocities: Rebuilding Cities in Balance with Nature*, New Society Publishers, Gabriola Island, BC.

Reich, C 1964, 'The New Property', *Yale Law.J.*, vol. 73, 733–87.

Rose, C M 1985, 'Possession as the Origin of Property', *Univ. Chicago Law Rev.*, vol. 52, no. 1, 73–88.

Rose, C M 1986, 'The Comedy of the Commons: Custom, Commerce, and Inherently Public Property', *Univ. Chicago Law Rev.*, vol. 53, no. 3, 711–81.

Rose, C M 1988, 'Crystal and Mud in Property Law', *Stanford L. Rev.*, vol. 40, 577–610.

Rose, C M 1994, 'Seeing Property' in *Property and Persuasion Essays on the History, Theory, And Rhetoric of Ownership*, Westview Press, Boulder, CO.

Rose, C M 1996, 'Property as the Keystone Right?', *Notre Dame L. Rev.*, vol. 71, 329–69.

Rose, C M 1998, 'The Several Futures of Property: Of Cyberspace and Folk Tales, Emission Trades and Ecosystems', *Minn. L. Rev.*, vol. 83, 129–182.

Ruru, J 2014, 'Tūhoe-Crown Settlement: The Te Urewera Act 2014', *Maori L. Rev.*, available at: http://maorilawreview.co.nz/2014/10/Tūhoe-crown-settlement-te-urewera-act-2014/

Scott, A 2008, *The Evolution of Resource Property Rights*, Oxford University Press, Oxford.

Santos, B de S 1987, 'Law: A Map of Misreading: Toward a Postmodern Conception of Law', *J. Law & Soc'y*, vol. 14, 279–302.

Sax, J 1971, *Defending the Environment: A Strategy for Citizen Action*, Knopf, New York.

Sax, J 1992, 'Property Rights and the Economy of Nature: Understanding *Lucas v. South Carolina Coastal Council*', *Stan. L. Rev.*, vol. 45, 1433–55.

Singer, J 2006, 'The Ownership Society and Takings of Property: Castles, Investments, and Just Obligations', *Harv. Envtl. L. Rev.*, vol. 30, 309–38.

Singer, J 2013, 'The Rule of Reason in Property Law', *UC Davis L. Rev.*, vol. 46, 1369–434.

Smith, H 2009, 'Community and Custom in Property Law', *Theoretical Inq. L.*, vol. 10, 5–41.

Smith, H 2012, 'Property as the Law of Things', *Harvard Law Rev.*, vol. 125, 1691–726.

Steinberg, T 1995, *Slide Mountain, or The Folly of Owning Nature*, University of California Press, Berkeley, CA.

Stone, C 1972, 'Should Trees Have Standing? Toward Legal Rights for Natural Objects', *S. Cal. L. Rev.*, vol. 45, 450–501.

Waldron, J 1991, *The Right to Private Property*, Oxford University Press, New York.

van der Walt, A J 2010, 'The Marginality of Property', in G Alexander and E Penalver (eds), *Property and Community*, Oxford University Press, New York.

Wonnacott, M 2006, *Possession of Land*, Cambridge University Press, Cambridge.

Chapter 5

Seeing property diversity, in theory, place and picture

5.1 Introduction

This chapter advances the 'seeing' of property diversity in three divergent and unconventional ways. First, it locates its telltale signs in the literature of *sustainable communities.*[1] Second, it observes the 'worlded-ness' of diverse property through three case studies, one in New Zealand, and two in the USA. Third, it seeks to enliven, and importantly, envision property diversity through the medium of the photograph. Each approach is premised on the simple, yet imaginative idea that property diversity is more obvious than we suppose.

One important implication of this chapter is the identification and description of the little remarked convergence between sustainable, so-called liveable communities, and their property diversity. What this chapter does not set out to do, however, is to make the correlative claim that property diversity *per se* is determinative of their liveability. But it does note the overlap, and observes its happy felicity.

5.2 Property diversity in sustainable communities literature

Nicholas Blomley says 'the centrality of the ownership model renders other modalities of ownership invisible' (Blomley 2004, p.9). Yet, recent literature of sustainable communities suggests otherwise. It observes that communities showcased as successful models of 'liveability' feature property diversity in their design or functioning. In so doing, this literature reveals diverse property to be visible in erstwhile unapparent ways.

This section begins with Jane Jacobs' seminal study of American urban space in the early 1960s, *The Death and Life of Great American Cities.* Jacobs deduced that vibrant cities possess *city diversity*, a complex quality of 'intricate urban mixtures' (Jacobs 1961, p.150). To generate a requisite 'exuberant diversity', Jacobs isolates four conditions as indispensable; that communities must serve more than one primary function;[2] that city blocks should be short and 'opportunities to turn corners ... frequent'; that a 'closely grained' mingling of buildings of variable age and condition is essential, and that there is a 'sufficiently dense concentration of people' (ibid., pp.150–51). Significantly, city diversity relies on a congenial interplay of public and private property.

> In our American cities, we need all kinds of diversity, intricately mingled in mutual support ... Public and quasi-public bodies are responsible for some of the enterprises that help make up city diversity – parks, museums, schools, auditoriums, hospitals, some offices, some dwellings. However most city diversity is the creation of incredible numbers of different people and different private organizations ... planning and contriving outside the formal framework of public action. The main function of city planning and design should be to develop ... cities that are congenial places for this great range of unofficial plans, ideas, and opportunities to flourish, along with the flourishing of the public enterprises.
>
> (ibid., p.241)

Jacobs relies on the private estate, and its values of commerce, sociability, and personhood, to do diversity's heavy lifting. Yet it cannot do it alone, public property is an anchor around which a multiplicity of private uses swirl. It is incumbent on the public estate to entrench itself at key locations that 'add effectively to diversity', and then to 'stand staunch ... while (private) money rolls around ... and begs them to roll over' (ibid., pp.254–55). The public–private interaction is symbiotic, city diversity requires well-positioned, defiantly staunch public amenities, compact city blocks criss-crossed by a network of walkable public streets, lanes and sidewalks, and a vibrant blend of private land uses in close and dense proximity.

Jacobs' work is pioneering in its prescience, its intuitive yet simple understanding of what makes successful cities flourish.[3] *The Death and Life of Great American Cities* was first and foremost a call for city diversity, but it also highlighted the interaction between public and private land as a critical way to achieve and maintain that diversity. This was the concept echoed 30 years later, in James Howard Kunstler's *The Geography of Nowhere* (1993). In 2013, Stephen Wheeler similarly advocates 'compact, balanced, mixed-use communities rather than single-use monocultures' as the basis for sustainable land use (Wheeler 2013, p.137). Other writers continue to borrow and reflect on Jacobs' core ideas.[4]

Using Rose's ways of seeing property described in Chapter 4, this section argues that property diversity may be seen in an analogous fashion in sustainable communities literature. First, it may be seen as Rose's literal picture, visible in a community's physical layout of private, public and common spaces. Optimally, these property patterns result in the convivial neighbourhoods envisaged by 'new urbanists', where parks, community food gardens, cycle ways and walkable streets and sidewalks successfully integrate with surrounding private property.[5] Second, (and as a corollary of the first), diversity can be seen as a narrative, the stories by which a community's propertied physical environment add to, or detract from, its social capital. Third, property diversity can be seen as a metaphor of competing property values, principally the contest of communitarian versus individual, analogized in Gregory Alexander's 'property as commodity' versus 'property as propriety' dialectic (1997).

5.2.1 *Property diversity as picture*

Seeing property diversity as a picture is to recognize its separate constitutive parts, the discrete elements that comprise the variegated patchwork of private, public and common lands, the physical infrastructure of community. Two components of this patchwork are sidewalks and open spaces, the subject of much study in sustainable communities literature. Each is visible (either because of its presence or absence), each illustrates the importance of public or community property contributing to the liveability of sustainable communities and each highlights the interaction of private and non-private property in urban settings.

The sidewalk was *the* principal focus of Jacobs' three opening chapters.[6] Sidewalks (along with streets and lanes) are foundational to the small city block, one of Jacobs' four generators of city diversity. As public conduits, sidewalks provide countless opportunities for planned and unplanned civic interactions, where street corners 'are often turned'. Pre-dating Carol Rose's writings on the sociability of public property (1986), Jacobs describes Boston's North End in 1959 as a place 'alive with children playing, people shopping, people strolling, people talking … [a] street atmosphere of buoyancy, friendliness and good health' (Jacobs 1961, p.9). Fast forward 50 plus years, and the sociability of the public sidewalk continues to resonate. In 2013, Jeff Speck isolates walkability as the most meaningful indicator of urban vitality. '[W]hat works best in the best cities is walkability' (Speck, 2013, p.4). Conversely, the 'twin gods of Smooth Traffic and Ample Parking' have rendered downtowns 'places that are easy to get to but not worth arriving at' (ibid.).

An alternative perspective on sidewalks is that of legal geographer Nicholas Blomley, and his identification of an all-pervasive 'pedestrianism' as the dominant logic of sidewalk governance (Blomley 2011). He argues that sidewalks are purely functional spaces for pedestrian circulation, 'a conduit for purposeful, directed flow' (Blomley 2011, p.12). Interestingly, pedestrianism proves a rare counter-example to the erstwhile unidirectional propensity of private property to erode public space. Sidewalks are 'staunch' defenders of the public realm that resist private encroachments into the public right of free flow and passage.[7] Despite being a 'fragile commons' or 'finite public resource' (ibid., p.32), Blomley observes a policing of sidewalks that rarely acquiesces to the private appropriation of public space (ibid., p.93). Indeed, the opposite is often truer: 'in Vancouver the sidewalk has been expanded and enhanced by set-back requirements that in essence reclaim a slice of private space for the public streetscape' (Register 2006, p.131). That sidewalks are so defiantly *public* sharpens the visibility of property diversity in urban landscapes.

Like the sidewalk, public open space is a regular subject of discourse in sustainable community literature. Ian McHarg's *Design With Nature* (1969) is widely acknowledged as a leading work on the links between open space and sustainable urban design. McHarg argues that 'nature should be integrated into the metropolis', emphasizing the ecological services that open space provides to cities (McHarg 1969, p.67). He also maps open space to urban contexts, putting into green relief its (then) declining incidence (ibid., p.57). Such maps 'hit you in the eye', visualizing a rudimentary picture of private and public property. Later literature developed this further, arguing that parks, urban forests, green belts, community gardens, treed street verges and 'naturalized private backyards' (Roseland 2009, p.45), collectively contribute to indicators of city sustainability (Bell and Morse 2008). These include the presence of ecological corridors and wildlife habitat, the provision of recreational opportunities, the reduction of the urban heat island effect, better drainage and water quality, increased absorption of pollutants and increased community space and aesthetics (Roseland 2009, pp.45–47). Open space (public, common and private) inculcates the natural environment into urban living, such that cities are seen as 'granite gardens', environments within, not outside nature (Spirn 2009, p.140).

Interestingly, Jacobs did not list parks as one of her four diversity drivers. Indeed, she observed of Boston's North End that 'it has little parkland ... everything conceivable is presumably wrong in orthodox planning terms' (Jacobs 1961, p.35). More important than open space was sociability, driven by 'very small blocks ... badly cut up with "wasteful" streets.' Open space can also have a dark side: for example, poorly frequented parks may be sites of antisocial activity, or green belts on city fringes have the potential to become perverse 'greed belts' (McHarg 1969). Such conflicting arguments suggest that seeing property diversity, as a literal picture, is but one component in the overall structural diversity of sustainable cities (Brill 2002). Arguably, more significant is the relationship between a propertied urban environment and its accrued 'social capital', the collective narratives that these property pictures tell and entrench in civic culture.

5.2.2 Property diversity as narrative: building social capital

Rose saw 'property as narrative' as one of the key, if underrated, aspects of her scholarship (Rose 2006). For Rose, property is a form of storytelling. It explains leaps in doctrinal logic, or smooths over the implausibility of the common law's fictions. Its corollary is that property is 'persuasion', a complex, multi-layered tale that must engage and convince its listener for the particular form of property to prosper.[8] In sustainable communities literature, property narratives are discerned in the way that property patterns enrich or pauperize social capital. Diverse property recounts stories of inter-connectivity, sociability and inclusion. Conversely, private uniformity tends to speak of isolation, exclusion and dislocation (Calthorpe 2009).

Mark Roseland describes social capital as the glue that holds communities together, 'the shared knowledge, understandings and patterns of interactions that a group of people brings to any productive activity, the relationships, networks, and norms that facilitate collective action' (Roseland 2009, p.9). Social capital is a unique public good in that it does not wear out by use, but if unused, its fragility translates to rapid deterioration. Moreover, it is hard to create, resists confected construction, and is non-transferable. In sustainable communities literature, a principal objective is to locate and multiply a community's social capital (Calthorpe 2009, p.10).

Reliant on formal and informal interactions, a community's built, propertied environment creates the opportunities that either enable or impede social capital. Formal interactions (such as planned meetings or sporting events) are integral to 'building social capital between otherwise disparate and isolated people'. Critically, they can only happen 'where there is a place for them to occur' (Eicher and Kawachi 2011, p.121). Equally important are informal interactions: impromptu encounters whose efficacy depends on physical factors such as 'street layout, (private) building features ... the width of sidewalks' (ibid., p.122). Whether transactions in private shops or businesses, or encounters on streets, parks, sporting fields, or community clubs or associations, the frequency (and hence social capital value) of planned or unplanned interactions is multiplied where the built environment is mixed and diverse.[9] It is a recurrent theme of sustainable communities literature that '[t]here is a positive association between social capital and communities with mixed uses, access to civic amenities, and walkable neighborhoods' (Ewing et al. 2011, p.160).

Social capital is commonly located in so-called 'third spaces', community-shared 'living rooms' (Beatley 2009, p.335), in which social interactions occur away from home or work. Third spaces and social capital are intimate in both their cause and effect, the more time spent in them the greater the return, but 'conversely the more time people spend away from the public eye at home, the more disinvestment there is in community social capital' (Eicher and Kawachi 2011, p.122). Community food gardens meet the definition of viable third spaces. Providing for urban food production not only meets sustainability criteria such as cooling cities, reconnecting people to the food chain, or reducing the carbon footprint of food transport, but it also enhances urban conviviality through social interaction (Capon and Thomson 2011, pp.370–71). Howard Frumkin and Jared Fox are two of many scholars who observe that community gardens build a sense of community, encourage mental and physical well-being, and restore blighted neighbourhoods (Frumkin and Fox 2011, p.237). At a broader level, third spaces are focal points around which we derive happiness, the bounty of an excess of social capital.

> Happiness is a house of many rooms, but at its core is a hearth around which we gather with family, friends, the community, and sometimes even strangers to find the best part of ourselves.
>
> (Montgomery 2014, pp.38–39)

For the most part, communities with high levels of social capital tend to be pedestrian or bicycle oriented, successful 'walkable cities' (Speck 2013). Pedestrian travel promotes a 'cycle of informal social interaction' that builds a much stronger sense of community (Howden-Chapman, Stuart and Chapman 2010). By contrast, automobile-centric urban sprawl tends to be associated with built environment characteristics that make chance encounters less frequent. Its consequence is that civic life suffers (Eicher and Kawachi 2011, p.123). Urban sprawl is characterized in this literature as typically 'a suburban world of cul-de-sacs, detached single-family houses, single-use zoning and dependence on automobiles' (Calthorpe 2009, p.89), a predominantly private landscape. Peter Calthorpe sums up the significance of the pedestrian, and its propertied context.

> Without the pedestrian, a community's common ground – its parks, sidewalks, squares and plazas – become useless obstructions to the car. Pedestrians are the lost measure of a community.
>
> (ibid., p.90)

Hollie Lund's empirical study of the relationship between the urban physical environment and its creation of a sense of community strongly suggests that pedestrian-friendly settings contribute to the development of a richer social environment (Lund 2002). She compared a TN (traditional-era neighbourhood) with a MSN (modern suburban neighbourhood) in Portland, Oregon. In the former, with its compact rectangular blocks, structured public and semiprivate space, and local stores and neighbourhood facilities, there was a reported higher sense of community. Much of this sentiment was based on residents' ability to engage in 'pleasure-driven strolling trips' that arise where 'strollers feel like being part of the neighborhood or feel like running into or socializing with their neighbors' (Lund 2002, p.310). By contrast, MSN residents tended to drive, or engage in 'purposeful destination walks' to neighbourhood shops located on MSN fringes, the net effect being a decreased sense of community.

Conversely, a lack of community common space pauperizes its stock of social capital. Roseland observes, that 'a community must have commons', meeting places or clusters where social interactions occur (Roseland 2009, p.11). '[A] lack of common space impairs community self-image', and the resultant emphasis on the private domain discourages participation. In its quest to multiply social capital, sustainable communities literature stresses the desirability of many different thoughtful sites of social interaction, a potential enlivened and enlarged by property diversity.[10]

Diverse property tells more than the singular or dominant story. In particular, its narratives embrace the idea of diffuse ownerships (Singer 2000) beyond the orthodox private model, sociable tales of community gardeners and strolling pedestrians, of belonging to physicalized third spaces outside the private realm. Such narratives speak of enhanced and frequent interaction, invoking (as sustainable communities literature theorizes) multiplied social capital. The propertied landscape of new urbanists, and their fostering of social capital through physical urban design (Roseland 2009, pp.141–42), is one that incorporates key tenets of property diversity, a serendipitous yet noteworthy convergence.

5.2.3 Property diversity as a metaphor of values

Rose's third way of seeing property, as metaphor, is also discernible in sustainable communities literature. It occurs as the symbolic representation of property's competing individualistic and communitarian values. While private 'lawscapes' (Graham 2010) chiefly enact the values of the former, the composite mosaic makes room for the latter. And in recognizing that property is multivalent, the mosaic also highlights the inherent tension between the two.

This tension forms the basis of Alexander's important dialectic of modern property law: property as commodity versus property as propriety (Alexander 1997). Alexander argues that the ascendant market-oriented view of property is only half-right. He traces the history of American legal thought from the eighteenth century to argue that property is not monistic, that it has 'multiple meanings and multiple traditions' (Alexander 1997, p.7), and that one half of this continuity is a view of property as propriety. This Alexander defines as 'property [as] the material foundation for creating and maintaining the social order, the private basis for the public good' (ibid., p.1). Importantly, this dialectic has 'normative commitments', with property as commodity based on the value that the 'market is the primary mechanism for mediating individual preferences within society' (ibid., p.3).

In sustainable communities literature, Kent Portney uses a similar historical narrative to argue that sustainability indicators should not only measure environmental factors, but should also actively foster communitarian values in modern cities (Portney 2003, pp.130–49). In this way American cities will then faithfully reflect their shared but presently skewed traditions of individualism and communitarianism.

> To many advocates of sustainable communities, making cities livable requires changing the fabric of civil society. To state it succinctly, the concept of sustainable communities is fundamentally communitarian in nature ... it is a question of public values.
>
> (ibid., pp.127–28)

For Portney, sustainability cannot be realized until communitarian values effectively counter the adverse effects of 'rampant individualism'.[11] This occurs when 'great import is placed on the function of civil society, the institutions and social processes that influence how residents interact' (ibid., p.125). Public space is Portney's metaphor for such values. In San Francisco, public space is green space, measured by proximity to natural settings, parks or treed street corridors. In Seattle, it is access to public cultural amenities such as libraries and galleries (ibid., p.11).

Many sustainability indicators are likewise indicia of property diversity. The strategic siting of civic property amidst the private estate; dense, compact networks of sidewalks and public rights of way; the virtues of mixed land use; thoughtful interactions of public and private property in land that generate social capital; or the values of public and community space, all exemplify a common ground, one that speaks to new paradigms, and acknowledges the shared flaws of the old.

This literature also illustrates that property 'penetrates everywhere in the realm of daily life' (Steinberg 1995, p.9). Theodore Steinberg uses case studies, 'Indians along a river, farmers in a desert, oil companies on a lake' to illustrate this point (ibid., p.9). In a similar case-based study of the effects of environmental laws, John Nagle observes 'there is a special need ... to recover the importance of place in environmental law' (Nagle 2010, p.252). The same holds true for property. Re-physicalizing property to place is to engage in what Blomley calls 'resistant re-mapping'. Section 3 adopts this theme, situating property diversity to case study place, an act of resistance to a paradigm that poorly describes the landscapes in which it is sited.

5.3 Mapping property diversity to place

The locations selected in this part are convenient in that they are, to varying degrees, the subject of existing study. In at least two cases, they are also Rose's 'imperious' landscapes, places of great natural beauty where 'property hits you in the eye.' These two factors make the task of describing or 'mapping' the property mosaic somehow easier and more credible. However, these locations are not exceptional, all human landscapes are 'intensely propertied' (Blomley 2004), such that any locale, mundane or otherwise, could form the content of this exercise.

The settings vary from rural through coastal peri-urban to suburban. In the first case, the mosaic is binary, the replacement of one failed public tile with a viable other. In the second, a new mosaic replaces an earlier, more singular property mix. In the third, the mosaic is elaborately designed, a greenfield suburb well known for its sustainability and sense of community. These micro-studies infer that each place is better for its property diversity, in terms of either community ethos, the instituting of Aldo Leopold's 'good land use', or both. The primary objective of this section is to simply identify and situate the diverse property mosaic to actual place. As stated earlier, its objective is not to claim that property diversity is the sole or dominant driver for each community's liveability, but merely that it is observable, and thus noteworthy.

5.3.1 Otago Central Rail Trail, New Zealand

This 150km rail trial is a publicly owned corridor that stretches from Middlemarch to Clyde in the Central Otago region of New Zealand's South Island. The trail connects to a functioning rail line from Middlemarch to Dunedin.

Construction of the now disused railway line commenced in 1879 and was completed in 1921. Prior to World War II, the line carried passengers from the rural region to the region's main city of Dunedin, and freighted fruit, livestock and wool (Otago Central Rail Trail Trust 2004, p.11). Its slow demise began in the immediate post-war years when passenger services gave way to cars, and rail freight lost the regulatory protection that state-owned railways once enjoyed.[12] In 1990, the line was closed and dismantled, leaving a derelict public corridor vulnerable to private encroachment.[13] The slow loss of government services and enterprises (including the railway) formed a pattern of 'long decades of decline that dispirited the community. So much so, that when the idea for the Rail Trail was first put to the people living along the track, they wondered why anyone would pedal or walk through this barren land with no history' (ibid., p.12).

The Department of Conservation (DoC) purchased the corridor from New Zealand Railways in 1993 with the intention of developing the nation's first rail trail. In an era of declining public ownership, this investment was a significant counter-example. Acquired as a recreation reserve,[14] DoC realized that community ownership was vital to its long-term viability (ibid.). In 1994, the Otago Central Rail Charitable Trust was formed, its stated purpose to

> Establish, develop and maintain the trail and any part of it for public recreation and enjoyment, and to assist and coordinate with the Department of Conservation, any local or regional authority or other group or person … Walking, cycling and horse riding uses of the trail shall be paramount.[15]

The Trust became the 'face of the project … gathering support for the trail as a recreational facility, ensuring its sustainability, coordinating its promotion and fundraising' (ibid., p.12). With financial and community support from the Trust, DoC re-built the line from 1994 to 2000, re-surfacing the former tracks, re-decking bridges, and restoring historic infrastructure such as ganger's huts, viaducts and culverts.

The re-development of the rail corridor faced widespread opposition from adjoining private landowners. Farmers feared interferences with agricultural practices and unchecked trespass. Many thought the corridor should be used for grazing, with sections sold to neighbouring landowners. Today, most farmers are happy to be proved wrong. Many embrace the commercial opportunities that recreationalists provide, establishing lodgings, coffee carts, or food outlets along the track. The public agency's investment has breathed economic life back into moribund rural communities, and restored the region's pride in its history. Once sceptical private landowners agree with the sentiment that 'DoC had shown a lot of foresight and should be congratulated'.[16]

The trail passes through a majestic, empty landscape of mountains, high country valleys and tussock grasslands, interspersed by small service towns, a land of schists and tors and climatic extremes. Its stark, rugged natural beauty engenders a sense of belonging that Otago poet Brian Turner describes as 'the surpassing glory of our right habitation of place' (Turner 2012, p.14). He writes of the landscape invoking in him a strong land ethic, a duty of stewardship 'underpinned by an acceptance that life is not all about us but about what's *all* about us' (ibid.). The advent of the trail has enhanced good land use:

> since its completion many communities have become actively involved in developing the trail further, helping and initiating replacement and restoration of station buildings and creating shade-giving plantings of native trees.
>
> (Otago Central Rail Trail Trust 2004, p.14)

Significantly the statutory basis for the trail mandates that 'those qualities of the reserve which contribute to the pleasantness, harmony, and cohesion of the natural environment and to the better use and enjoyment of the reserve shall be conserved', including water, soil, and forest values.[17]

The property mosaic in the Central Otago is a largely private landscape of grazing farms and small urban holdings connected by a 150km public conduit, a thin ribbon of public land that now defines the propertied landscape. Although legally structured as a recreation reserve, the partnership between DoC and the Otago Central Rail Trust diffuses DoC's ostensible title to the trail, adding a further nuanced layer of community ownership. Meanwhile the trail's status as statutory reserve impresses upon the agency's bare title a beneficial ownership on behalf of all New Zealanders,[18] akin to Rose's 'unorganized public', where the sociability of visiting cyclists becomes the public estate's core rationale. The presence of a vibrant public estate also enhances the value of nearby private lands, engenders a renewed sense of community in the towns along the trail (McGregor and Thompson-Fawcett 2011), and inserts into the landscape a statutory obligation to protect natural and scenic resources. The surrounding private estate also shapes the contours of the public right. A code of conduct requires trail users to 'leave gates as you find them, not disturb stock, and not to venture onto private property' (Otago Central Rail Trail Trust 2004, p.25), accommodating private values such as productivity and privacy in the exercise of the public right. The trail also fulfils Alexander's property as propriety; property's capacity to enable well-lived human lives, through the shared sociability of fellow trail users, physical exercise, and the solitude of wide, open spaces.

5.3.2 The Sea Ranch, California

Approximately three hours driving time north of San Francisco, astride the San Andreas Fault and beside a winding California State Highway 1, The Sea Ranch is a planned community that features a diverse mosaic of private, common and public interests in land. Sited along ten miles and 4,000 acres of rugged Sonoma County coastline, The Sea Ranch is rich in its sense of place. Its propertied patterns shape the contours of a distinct community informed from its inception by a 1960s Aquarian ethos of 'living lightly off the land' (Halprin 2002, p.287).

Devised as an 'open' and 'exploratory' architectural experiment (Lyndon 2009, p.82), The Sea Ranch has long struggled to reconcile its environmental ideals with its later reputation as an enclave of private wealth. Landscape architect, Lawrence Halprin was instrumental to its early design. His overarching aim was to create

> [a] feeling of overall place, a feeling of community in which the whole was more important than the parts ... if the whole could link buildings

> and nature ... then we could feel that we had created something worthwhile which did not destroy, but rather enhanced the natural beauty we had been given.
>
> (Lyndon and Alinder 2004, p.19)

Before 1963, when the developer Oceanic Properties bought the 'Rancho del Mar', the landscape's property patterns were simple and unadorned; a large, privately owned ranch, with a history of cattle farming and redwood logging (Clark 2009). The public estate was minimal, a dormant public trust in the empty wet sands, and an equally dormant public interest in unprotected coastal vistas. Indeed, the purchase by Oceanic Properties did not change property patterns in the immediate term, as one private owner merely replaced another.

However, in 1965, a residents' association was formed in which newly constituted common property was vested.[19] The insertion of common land diversified the propertied landscape, all part of a design vision heavily influenced by the 'establishment of large stretches of commons that would preserve the dominance of the natural setting'; an effort to share the landscape rather than having it 'sequestered in separate private ownerships' (Lyndon and Alinder 2004, p.19). Thereafter, fifty per cent of all open space would be 'held in common for all Sea Ranchers to own and enjoy' (Halprin 2002, p.35). The commons served environmental and aesthetic functions, where 'large areas of commonly held land ... ensure the perpetuation of the coastal ecology' (Lyndon and Alinder 2004, p.19). Commons also had social implication in ways that echo Jeanette Neeson's bonds of belonging.

> The land held in common, particularly the commons in the coastal meadows became a focal point of shared interest. Management of this treasured asset was expressed as a community responsibility, not a task for individual property owners looking out for their own parcels ... That no one citizen exclusively owned a piece of the natural resource - the resource that is the very foundation of the community ... defied conventional development wisdom and cemented a bond of common interest.
>
> (Sexton 1995, p.35)

By the late 1960s, public access to wet sands was a burgeoning issue in a rapidly growing California. At The Sea Ranch, it manifested in heated, often bitter contest between private right holders and public claimants. The community's reputation as an enclave of private privilege gained traction, and groups such as 'Californians Organized to Acquire Access to State Tidelands' (COAST) complained that the development effectively privatized public beach access along the ten-mile coastline. An early agreement with Sonoma County traded 100 acres of public parklands for limited public access rights over the ten miles of coast, however its terms attracted trenchant criticism (Dyer 1972, pp.573, 585–86). In 1972, as a result of the passage of the Californian Coastal Zone Conservation Act, planning powers were transferred to the newly formed North Central Coastal Commission, which favoured wider and more universal public access. Throughout the 1970s, the Commission acted to halt new development at The Sea Ranch, hoping its planning veto would eventually resolve the access standoff. Ultimately, the public interest prevailed as an effective component of the landscape.[20] In 1980, the State of California by legislative intervention guaranteed five dedicated access easements, a near halving of house sites, and preserved scenic corridors from California Highway 1.

The Sea Ranch illustrates a shift from property monotony in the early 1960s, to its present-day architecture of property diversity. This conscious reconstruction has not been seamless or smooth, as its stop-start narrative of controversy attests. Nor has it been perfect, with private dominance overly accentuating the 'outside private shell' of its common coastal meadows that remain visibly off limits. But the change did improve and clarify public property rights of access and vista, particularly compared to its earlier monistic iteration. And within The Sea Ranch, the diverse common/private property structures integrated community and social cohesion, creating a sense of the whole rather than an aggregate of sequestered housing lots;[21] stewardship ideals were enacted by covenants that gave effect to 'lightly living with the land'; and the shared nature of the landscape emphasized co-existing use, not exclusive dominion. To see The Sea Ranch today is to see deliberate patterns of diverse property; private housing adjoining communal meadows and community infrastructure, posted beach access, and public coastal vistas mandated by statute. Such contemporary diversity reflects a pioneering design philosophy that from its origins, sought to diminish overt indicia of private dominion.

> Fences enforcing property lines are discouraged … Where houses are very close together, fences are considered necessary for privacy and for screening cars, but not for demarcating property lines. An intentionally fuzzy line is desired for the boundary between individually owned and community property.
>
> (Sexton 2002, p.36)

Just as the San Andreas Fault produced its 'visually imperious' geography and gave the landscape its subterranean 'geologic confetti' (Collier 1999, p.3), the confetti-like patterns of diverse property are rarely far from the surface. In the chiefly architectural literature devoted to The Sea Ranch, telltale signs of property diversity speak to its unique sense of place. Even fences tell nuanced tales beyond the simplistic yelling of exclusion.

> [As a] model for quiet, thoughtful delineation of common boundaries ... the long row of simple board fence at the property line is made as a common face for the public realm, and not as an individuated expression of the private properties beyond it. It speaks of continuity and public purpose ... a place that shows respect for the private worlds of each house, as well as for the common realms of street and meadow.
>
> (Lyndon and Alinder 2004, p.55)

5.3.3 Village Homes, Davis, California

The third study is another planned community, the suburb of Village Homes in Davis, California. A greenfield project, its first homes were built in 1975 with the final build in 1982. It has been called 'one of the most important and inspiring built examples of sustainable community design in the United States' (Francis 2003, p.xi).

The designers of Village Homes sought to realize two radical objectives, 'helping people live more lightly on the land, and creating a sense of community' (Corbett and Corbett 2000, p.8).[22] Determined to avoid outcomes of 'only private houses and private yards' (ibid., p.3), design innovations included narrower, no-through streets, small housing clusters of eight dwellings, the extensive use of paths and cycle ways,[23] and the dedication of 25 per cent of the site to public and community open space. The latter includes 12 acres of greenbelts and open space, 12 acres of common agricultural land, two village greens and a community swimming pool and meeting centre (Francis 2003, p.47). The common lands are themselves subdivided into three typologies; household commons, greenbelt commons and agricultural lands, in which all Village Homes residents hold common property interests. The neighbourhood constitution specifies three sanctioned uses of the commons, 'enjoyment, flowers and food, and profit' (Francis 2003, p.36), the latter two referring to widespread planting of edible vegetation (Corbett and Corbett 2000, p.39), and a 300-tree almond orchard that raises income to offset neighbourhood fees. Apart from utilitarian and aesthetic purposes,[24] the common spaces also enhance sociability by providing 'a place and a reason for people to come together, thereby allowing a sense of community to develop' (ibid., p.32).[25] Importantly, these commons are 'lived-in' landscapes, where good land use is performed; they are not manicured, detached spaces.

> There are people actually using these open spaces – walking, digging, or playing for example. When empty, there are physical traces of use such as garden furniture, tools, and children's toys. Together this activity communicates a sense of stewardship – people caring for and feeling attached to where they live.
>
> (Francis 2003, p.11)

Mark Francis compares Village Homes to the rest of Davis, internationally renowned in its own right for urban sustainability. Taylor observes that visitors to Davis typically fail to perceive the city's reputation, with its conventional, largely private suburban layout. Yet in Village Homes, with its patent common spaces, sustainability is more persuasive, it 'hits you in the eye'.

Village Homes displays several interesting features of diverse property. First is the blurring of boundaries, particularly between private and non-private space. The household commons deliberately blend private into common, residences front and overlook the common gardens, not the street, and the differentiation between 'heavily vegetated private and shared land' is indiscernible (Corbett and Corbett 2000, p.37). Covenants preclude internal dividing fences, only carefully planted hedges, trees, or shrubs provide a substitute for privacy. Private outdoor courtyards segue effortlessly into common orchards and drainage watercourses; here the emphasis is on use, not demarcated dominion. If there is any sense of boundary, it is the line that divides Village Homes from the rest of Davis, not internal boundaries within the suburb (Corbett and Corbett p.140).

Second, and a consequence of the first, is a tangible sense of diffused ownership of common land. This vesting translates into lower crime rates.

> Residents have planned and maintained their commons, they have a vested interest in the spaces, and they have every right to protect these areas from intruders. Even the more public greenbelts are less vulnerable to vandalism than an adjacent park.
>
> (ibid., p.144)

Third, is a strong recognition by residents of the distinction between public and common property. This manifests in disputes where outsiders pick fruit from community orchards. Residents enforce their common rights to the produce, posting signs indicating that the fruit trees are on community not public land, and warning against unauthorized picking (Francis 2003, p.67).

In the official typology of 'open space', there is an explicit characterization of 'streets, bicycle and pedestrian paths, and central greens' as public lands, while 'community vineyards and orchards, and household commons' are common lands. This recognition of the diversity of non-private property, especially the legal distinction between public and common, is rare. While not an 'imperious' natural setting, the constructed landscape of Village Homes has become one where, as Rose predicts, people see property and debate its implications.

5.4 Seeing property diversity in photographs

The Sea Ranch, Village Homes and Central Otago are three disparate landscapes that share one common denominator: the visibility of their diverse property. In each community, indicators of property diversity are to varying degrees evident – their heightened sense of shared use, the significance of context, or the unique fusion of property values that dilute the private hegemony. These brief case studies illustrate that diverse property can be redacted to place. This chapter closes by repeating this same point, but through another medium, by depicting property diversity in its literal, pictorial form.

Figure 5.1 The right to exclude, Gold Coast, Australia

The right to exclude is both dominant and domineering in private property discourse. The US Supreme Court says it is 'one of the most treasured strands in an owner's bundle of property rights'. Jerry Anderson says modern property has 'canonized' the right, placing it at the top of the judicial 'woodpile' without regard to context, community values or social norms. Its spectral monopolization has rendered other property types invisible, and produced Nicole Graham's monotonous 'lawscape' where the specialness of place is irrelevant.

Figure 5.2 The private fence, Sonoma County, California

Carol Rose 'sees' abandoned fences as symbolic of private property's 'impermanence and pathos' and a refutation of its pretence of unchanging fixity. It is also symbolic of Theodore Steinberg's 'folly of owning nature'.

Figure 5.3 Southampton Common, UK

Southampton Common in the UK was an example of 'traditional' common property. Today it signifies the misunderstandings about the nature of property other than private property. Its open access as a park has effectively transformed it into public land.

Figure 5.4 Clunes Common, New South Wales, Australia

The Clunes Common in NSW illustrates the transportability of traditional ideas of common property, where use rights of the land are restricted to members of the association in whom the common rights are vested. Public access to the grounds is however permitted, again indicating a blurring of non-private property type at the edges.

Figure 5.5 The high country public estate, Lake Tekapo, New Zealand

In this image, Crown pastoral tenure in the NZ high country abuts public conservation land. The fence line to the right of the tramper's hut represents the boundary line. It also represents the powerful rhetorical force of the private right to exclude to devour other co-exisiting rights, effectively landlocking and precluding public access to the hut on the conservation estate.

Figure 5.6 Wet sands/ dry sands

The wet and dry sands of beaches signifies the boundary line between private littoral lands and inherently public property under the US doctrine of the public trust. Public rights of access to such public lands across dry sands is problematic, and varies between US jurisdictions.

Figure 5.7 Fence lines in the New Zealand high country, Lake Tekapo

This boundary fence separates two forms of public lands, one the conservation estate, and another encumbered by a private right to graze. The fence is practical (in keeping sheep enclosed) but also symbolic of the propensity of the private right to conflate and extinguish co-existing public property rights in the context of vast, empty landscapes, such as the NZ high country.

Figure 5.8 The New Zealand public–private bach, Rangiototo Island, New Zealand

The bach is a New Zealand icon; a vernacular early twentieth-century private right to use built on public foreshore, often without planning permission. If 'what we see is what we get', this image suggests at first blush the typical intersection of public and private property. If we 'see' deeper however, we get public foreshore, eclectic private rights to use, and unseen indigenous foreshore rights.

Figure 5.9 Abstraction collides with context – Coal Seam Gas (CSG) public art, Southern Cross University, Lismore, New South Wales

Opponents of coal seam gas (CSG) exploration seek to 'zip' up their lands, as this public art at Southern Cross University, NSW demonstrates. This art speaks to a certain desire to re-physicalize property rights in land, a defence against separable and abstract property sticks, such as the right to exploit divisible resources.

Figure 5.10 Protecting community property against CSG exploration, Northern Rivers, New South Wales

This road sign talks of collective property being 'protected by community' against CSG incursion. It has strong parallels to Nicholas Blomley's study of collective property claims in Vancouver's Downtown Eastside (Blomley 2004).

Figure 5.11 The Otago Central Rail Trail, New Zealand I

Figure 5.12 The Otago Central Rail Trail, New Zealand II

The Otago Central Rail Trail in NZ is a thin ribbon of public property that transects this rural region. It epitomizes the values and rationales of public property in land, the likes of a democratic sociability with strangers, recreation, and the human need for solitude. These foster Gregory Alexander's 'property as propriety', the forgotten half of the property dialectic, a capacity for public infrastructure to enhance well-lived civic lives.

Figure 5.13 Sumner, New Zealand

A well-used public footpath zigzags through private lands, creating a 'walkable' neighbourhood where chance encounters accrue social capital.

Figure 5.14 Public path and private farmland, Taylors Mistake, New Zealand

This coastal walking track in New Zealand also crosses over private farmland. Exclusion and inclusion overlap as private and public uses share the same landscape.

Figure 5.15 Sociable public street scenes, Lismore, New South Wales

The sociability of public property in land is Carol Rose's 'comedy of the commons', sociable street scenes where 'the more is the merrier'.

Figure 5.16 Public handball courts, Los Angeles, California

Again, public property in land provides the physical and metaphorical space and infrastructure for egalitarianism, as these public handball courts at Venice Beach, Los Angeles enact.

Figure 5.17 The Sea Ranch, California

At The Sea Ranch, an ethos of 'living lightly off the land' sees property lines blur, as private houses adjoin communal meadows. However, common property remains off-limits to outsiders.

Figure 5.18 The Otago Central Rail Trail, New Zealand III

Seeing property through Joseph Sax's 'economy of nature' blurs the significance of property lines. We see the land in between and across boundaries, not the markers that dissect it into atomized, disconnected parcels. Here, empty landscapes such as the Central Otago in NZ are largely uncluttered with the indicia of (at least private) property.

Figure 5.19 Coastal landscape, Port Stephens, New South Wales

Coastal landscapes are visually imperious ones, where property, as Carol Rose explains, 'hits you in the eye'. Here the property mosaic is more apparent, with a well-trodden grassed path asserting public rights over what otherwise appears to be private land.

Figure 5.20 The Otago Central Rail Trail, New Zealand IV

Private rights encroach readily on vulnerable public ones. Here a truck depot encroached onto abandoned rail tracks on the Otago Central Rail Trail in NZ. It took years for the Department of Conservation to rectify the unauthorized private trespass.

Figure 5.21 Open space covenants, Southland, New Zealand

'Seeing' incorporeal public property, protected open space covenants in the New Zealand countryside.

Figure 5.22 Manicured front lawns and sidewalks, Beverly Hills, California

Nicholas Blomley says the public sidewalk is a staunch and vigorous defender of the public estate. Here, the sidewalk comes up against Georgette Poindexter's neatly manicured lawn, which she describes as a suburban 'idolization of the private realm', one that eviscerates community and other collective values.

Figure 5.23 Peninsula Ski Lodge, Mt Hotham, Victoria, Australia

Modern common property can be seen in the unlikeliest and most everyday of places. Here, a ski lodge at Mt Hotham, Victoria operates on common property principles, as an outside private shell with inside communitarian use rights for a small community of lodge members, and their (paying) guests.

Figure 5.24 Santa Monica Community Garden, California I

Sue Farran's account of an 'extraordinary return to the land' describes new and evolving relationships between people and land. This phenomenon is 'seen' through a resurgence of interest in community gardens, orchards and allotments. Farran argues this 'return to the land' poses challenges to orthodox land law, with its innovative tenures (such as crop-shares and tree-leases) and its re-emphasis on the social and cultural values of property (Farran 2013).

Figure 5.25 Santa Monica Community Garden, California II

This sign at the Santa Monica Community Garden in California is interesting in its Lockean articulation of private property in a distinctly hybrid context. Private rights are asserted in a publicly accessible forum, but where use rights to garden and cultivate are restricted to eligible communal members.

5.5 Conclusion

Chapters 4 and 5 canvass the expansive and imaginative idea of property diversity. Importantly, this chapter has sought out its telltale signs in the literature of sustainable communities, situated it to three specific studies in two common law jurisdictions and reduced it to a visual seeing. In so doing, this chapter transports the concept of property diversity to a disciplinary, grounded, and visualized place. The chapter ends where this book's mid-point journey began, with Carol Rose's homespun words about the transformative power of imagination.

> There is an old adage, told of plain people and plain things: what you see is what you get. Property seems plain in this way too: what you see is what you get. With property, the nature of 'things' imposes their own constraints. Yet even with those, what you see in property is what you and others have talked yourselves into about those 'things'; and given some imagination, you may talk yourselves into seeing something else, with all the effects on understanding and action that a new 'envisioning' may bring.
>
> (Rose 1994, p.297)

For some centuries, we have talked ourselves into seeing a narrow picture of property in land. Perhaps a fresh burst of imagination; a new envisioning may 'talk us into seeing something else'. As Charles Reich exhorted over 50 years ago in his unrealized call to action, it may be timely to see a 'new property', a re-conceptualization that captures all of its rich, diverse and imaginative forms (Reich 1964).

Notes

1 This term covers diverse disciplines: urban planning, architecture, landscape architecture, public policy, urban design, and so on.

2 This compels the sharing of common spaces at different times by different people.

3 Jacobs also writes of cities lacking four *indispensable* conditions: 'virtually all of Detroit is weak on ... diversity ... it is a ring superimposed upon ring of failed gray belts' (Jacobs 1961, p.150).

The 2012 film *Detropia* cites low population density and diffuse city blocks as instrumental in Detroit's decline, and affirms Jacobs' 'great blight of dullness' (ibid., p.357).

4 For example, 'Great neighbourhoods' possess walkable size, a mix of land uses and housing types, an integrated network of walkable streets, and sites reserved for civic purposes: 'civic buildings should occupy landmark sites that are the permanent anchors for community pride' (Farr 2008, p.130). Michael Brill writes of 'public buildings that are proudly located' (Brill 2002, p.51).

5 New urbanism 'asserts that communities must be designed to re-establish and reinforce the public domain, that our districts must be human-scaled, and that our neighborhoods must be diverse in use and population' (Calthorpe 2009, p.90).

6 See Jacobs (1961): 'Chapter 2 – The use of sidewalks: safety'; 'Chapter 3 – The use of sidewalks: contact', and 'Chapter 4 – The use of sidewalks: assimilating children'.

7 'An encroachment is inherently private, entailing an unlawful intrusion onto public property by a private actor' (Blomley 2011, p.48).

8 For example, the tenancy by entireties survives in North Carolina by constantly re-inventing its story (Orth 2010, pp.35–45).
9 'Regular customers of a shop, users of a park ... members of such groups may not necessarily know each other ... yet are an immense reservoir of energy and imagination' (Roseland 2009, p.11).
10 A 'thoughtful interaction' of public, private, semi-private and common land enhances 'civicness' (Roseland 2009, p.11).
11 These include the NIMBY syndrome (Portney 2003, pp.130–53).
12 In 1961, road freight could only be carried for a maximum of 48km.
13 In Oturehua, a privately owned freight depot began parking trucks across the disused corridor, effectively privatizing the public land. In the early 1990s when DoC started to plan the Rail Trail, it took several years to discontinue the illegal private use, notwithstanding the land never passed out of public ownership. Private conversation, Graeme Duncan, Wedderburn, 29 December 2012.
14 Sect. 17(1) Reserves Act 1977 (NZ). The public has 'freedom of entry and access to the reserve' under s 17(2)(a).
15 It has 4 trustees and a patron 'who provide a geographic spread along the trail and who come from a diverse range of business and community backgrounds' (Otago Central Rail Trail Trust 2004, pp.64–65).
16 Graeme Duncan, *Community Head of Steam – From a Rail to a Trail*, video, undated.
17 Sect. 17(2)(c)(d) *Reserves Act 1977* (NZ).
18 *Gibbs v. The New Plymouth District Council* [2006] NZHC 231.
19 A declaration of covenants, conditions and restrictions regulated building materials and design, and imposed a strict landscape plan where houses were clustered to mimic the coastal landscape of ridgelines, pastures and hedgerows.
20 Calif. Coastal Zone Conservation Act of 1972, Cal. Pub. Res. Code SS 27000 *et seq.*
21 The governing principle was a vision of a 'social community for people of like minds, with a love of nature ... for whom living lightly on this land" was central' (Halprin 2002, p.287).
22 These aims remain central to the community, see Village Home's website at: www.villagehomes.com
23 Paths connect housing clusters and provide meeting and interactive places for residents, an echo of Jacobs' drivers of city diversity.
24 The greenbelt commons also act as natural drainage swales (Corbett 2000, pp.43–47).
25 Up to 80 per cent of residents regularly participate in communal activities, a factor attributed to 25 per cent of the land being devoted to common open space (Corbett 2000, pp.140–42).

References

Alexander, G 1997, *Commodity and Propriety: Competing Visions of Property in American Thought 1776–1970*, University of Chicago Press, Chicago.

Beatley, T 2009, 'Planning for Sustainability in European Cities', in S Wheeler and T Beatley (eds), *The Sustainable Urban Development Reader*, Routledge, Abingdon.

Bell, S and Morse, S 2008, *Sustainability Indicators: Measuring the Immeasurable*, Earthscan, London.

Blomley, N 2004, *Unsettling the City: Urban Land and the Politics of Property*, Routledge, New York.

Blomley, N 2011, *Rights of Passage: Sidewalks and the Regulation of Public Flow*, Routledge, Abingdon.

Brill, M 2002, 'Problems With Mistaking Community Life for Public Life', *Places*, vol. 14, no. 2, 48–55.

Calthorpe, P 2009, 'The Next American Metropolis: Ecology Community and the American Dream', in S Wheeler and T Beatley (eds), *The Sustainable Urban Development Reader*, Routledge, Abingdon.

Capon, A and Thompson, S 2011, 'Built Environments of the Future', in A Dannenberg, H Frumkin and R J Jackson (eds), *Making Healthy Places: Designing and Building for Health, Well-being, and Sustainability*, Island Press, Washington, DC.

Clark, S 2009, *Images of America The Sea Ranch*, Arcadia Publishing, San Francisco.

Collier, M 1999, *A Land in Motion: California's San Andreas Fault*, University of California Press, Oakland.

Corbett, J and Corbett, M 2000, *Designing Sustainable Communities: Learning from Village Homes*, Island Press, Washington, DC.

Dyer, D 1972, 'California Beach Access: The Mexican Law and the Public Trust', *Ecology L.Q.*, vol. 2, 571–611.

Eicher, C and Kawachi, I 2011, 'Social Capital and Community Design', in A Dannenberg, H Frumkin and R J Jackson (eds), *Making Healthy Places: Designing and Building for Health, Well-being, and Sustainability*, Island Press, Washington, DC.

Ewing, R, Meakins, G, Bjarnson, G and Hilton, H 2011, 'Transportation and Land Use', in A Dannenberg, H Frumkin and R J Jackson (eds), *Making Healthy Places: Designing and Building for Health, Well-being, and Sustainability*, Island Press, Washington, DC.

Farr, D 2008, *Sustainable Urbanism: Urban Designs with Nature*, Wiley, Hoboken, NJ.

Farran, S 2013, 'Earth Under the Nails: The Extraordinary Return to the Land', in N Hopkins (ed.), *Modern Studies in Property Law*, 7th edn, Hart Publishing, Oxford.

Francis, M 2003, *Village Homes: A Community by Design*, Island Press, Washington, DC.

Frumkin, H and Fox, J 2011, 'Contact with Nature' in A Dannenberg, H Frumkin and R J Jackson (eds), *Making Healthy Places: Designing and Building for Health, Well-being, and Sustainability*, Island Press, Washington, DC.

Graham, N 2010, *Lawscape: Property, Environment, Law*, Routledge, Abingdon.

Halprin, L 2002, *The Sea Ranch: Diary of an Idea*, Spacemaker Press, Berkeley, CA.

Howden-Chapman, P, Stuart, K and Chapman, R (eds) 2010, *Sizing Up the City: Urban Form and Transport in New Zealand*, Steele Roberts, Wellington.

Jacobs, J 1961, *The Death and Life of Great American Cities*, Random House, New York.

Kuntsler, J H 1993, *The Geography of Nowhere: The Rise and Decline of America's Man-Made Landscape*, Simon and Schuster, New York.

Lund, H 2002, 'Pedestrian Environments and Sense of Community', *J. Planning Educ. & Res.*, vol. 21, 301–12.

Lyndon, D 2009, 'The Sea Ranch Qualified Vernacular', *J. Arch. Ed.*, 81–89.

Lyndon D and Alinder, J 2004, *The Sea Ranch*, Princeton Architectural Press, New York.

McGregor, S and Thompson-Fawcett, M 2011, 'Tourism in a Small Town: Impacts on Community Solidarity', *Int. J. Sustainable Society*, vol. 3, 174–89.

McHarg, I 1969, *Design With Nature*, Natural History Press, Garden City, NY.
Nagle, J C 2010, *Laws Environment: How the Law Shapes the Places We Live*, Yale University Press, New Haven, CT.
Orth, J 2010, *Reappraisals in the Law of Property*, Ashgate, Burlington, VT.
Otago Central Rail Trail Trust 2004, *From Steam Trains to Pedal Power: The Story of the Otago Central Rail Trail*, Otago Central Rail Trail Trust, Dunedin.
Portney, K 2003, *Taking Sustainable Cities Seriously, Economic Development, the Environment, and Quality of Life in American Cities*, MIT Press, Cambridge, MA.
Register, R 2006, *Ecocities: Rebuilding Cities in Balance with Nature*, New Society Publishers, Gabriola Island, BC.
Reich, C 1964, 'The New Property', *Yale Law.J.*, vol. 73, 733–87.
Rose, C M 1986, 'The Comedy of the Commons: Custom, Commerce, and Inherently Public Property', *Univ. Chicago Law Rev.*, vol. 53, no. 3, 711–81.
Rose, C M 1994, 'Seeing Property' in *Property and Persuasion Essays on the History, Theory, And Rhetoric of Ownership*, Westview Press, Boulder, CO.
Rose, C M 2006, 'Property and Language, or the Ghost of the Fifth Panel', *Yale Journal of Law and the Humanities*, vol. 18, 1–28.
Roseland, M 2009, *Toward Sustainable Communities*, New Society Publishers, Gabriola Island, BC.
Sexton, R 1995, *Parallel Utopias: The Quest for Community*, Chronicle Books, San Francisco.
Singer, J 2000, *Entitlement: The Paradoxes of Property*, Yale University Press, New Haven, CT.
Speck, J 2013, *Walkable City, How Downtown Can Save America One Step at a Time*, Farrar, Straus and Giroux, New York.
Spirn, S 2009, 'The Granite Garden: Urban Nature and Human Design', in S Wheeler and T. Beatley (eds), *The Sustainable Urban Development Reader*, Routledge, Abingdon.
Steinberg, T 1995, *Slide Mountain, or The Folly of Owning Nature*, University of California Press, Berkeley, CA.
Turner, B 2012, *Elemental: Central Otago Poems*, Godwit Books, Auckland.
Wheeler, S 2013, *Planning for Sustainability: Creating Livable, Equitable and Ecological Communities*, Routledge, Abingdon.

Chapter 6

Obligation and property monism

6.1 Introduction

To 'see' property patterns in human landscapes is to invoke a duality of perspective. One view is atomistic, an image of individual land parcels, and the distinct property lines that divide and fragment ownerships.[1] The other is holistic, the collective 'warp and woof' of property type that weaves a pluralistic fabric across place (Leopold 1999, p.168). The atomistic view is premised on a private paradigm where 'standardized, universal and measurable space' (Graham 2010, p.66) de-physicalizes place from context, and primacy is accorded to rights between persons about things (Banner 2011, pp.101–6).

By contrast, the holistic vision is intimately contextual and diverse, where rights, uses and claims to property inter-connect person to place. Into this conflicted 'seeing', where presently the private half-truth prevails, land obligation is an ideal adrift. Yet, as James Karp explains, developing a land ethic is critical, since 'land is fundamentally different from other forms of property', distinctive because it is 'essential to our right to survival' (Karp 1993, p.748). For this reason alone, Karp argues, rights of ownership must be 'limited by a duty of land stewardship' (ibid.).

This chapter argues that Karp's call for a duty of land stewardship will go largely unheeded where property in land is seen through the atomized private lens, a paradigm inherently ill-suited to generating concepts of obligation alongside right. It does not argue *why* we must change from the hegemonic view, but it does describe its failings. It also sets the stage for Chapter 7, which describes how *property diversity* offers new ways to rethink this seeming closed loop.

Section 2 commences by observing that definitions of stewardship or land obligation are inevitably instrumental where property is monistic. The vexed place of obligation in modern property is then canvassed in section 3, whether in terms of property traditions, theories, or hierarchies. In section 4, three institutional factors of modern property are identified that singly and cumulatively impede stewardship; *abstraction, commoditization and individualism*. These factors put substantive obstacles in our way of fostering an ownership 'suffused with moral content' (Penalver 2009).

Eric Freyfogle says that property patterns matter because they create a 'framework for managing and using nature ... they explain who gets to do what and where' (Freyfogle 2007b, p.107). Ultimately, which patterns we 'see', and their implications for 'who gets to do what and where', depend on which side of the dialectic prevails. Chapter 6 depicts the atomistic, mostly seen, half.

6.2 Defining stewardship through the (private) property lens

Stewardship is a nebulous, ill-fitting concept in modern property. Richard Barnes describes it as having 'a long theoretical heritage, albeit an ambiguous and marginal one, which has struggled in the shadow of the stronger, pro-dominion approach to the control of resources' (2009, pp.155–56). While often asserted as a duty, its place in property's structure is unsettled, an issue explored in section 3. Many scholars aspire to a property right imbued with an environmental ethic (Flournoy 2003). But defining stewardship through the private lens illustrates the unbridged gulf between aspiration and implementation. The result is that stewardship is articulated as practical and outcomes measured, an essentially extra-property construct.

Joseph Sax calls stewardship the law's 'awkward little secret' (Sax 1999, p.59), an inconvenient truth about property's problematic relationship with place. Margaret Davies explains the orthodoxy, and its counterpoint.

> Property is not an object at all, but rather a legally defined relationship between persons with respect to an object. 'Property' is only an effect, a construction, of relationships between people, meaning that its objective character is contestable. Alternative constructions of property, such as the notion of stewardship, may challenge the subject-object and person-property distinctions.
>
> (Davies 2007, pp.13–14)

Its 'awkwardness' is also explicable when various property law rules allude to, or have a passing resonance of, ownership obligation. These chimeric 'sightings' encourage optimistic claims, like Freyfogle's assertion that property law and ecology are kindred disciplines,[2] or Alyson Flournoy's comment that the 'clearest lens on society's environmental ethic is the common law of property... a logical starting point' (Flournoy 2003, p.98).

But what are these steward-like doctrines that constitute the likes of Flournoy's 'logical starting point'? Property rules have long accommodated fragmented beneficial ownership, the idea that land ownership is a 'trust with attendant obligations' (Caldwell 1974, p.766). However, legal history tends to attribute the evolution of the *use* to selfish rather than altruistic aims, the avoidance of feudal dues, or the preservation of dynastic privilege. Less typical was land use employed for 'some greater scheme ... religious, ethical, or ecological' (Brewer 2003, p.115). Likewise, rules such as waste, or the rule against perpetuities, purport to protect the interests of future unborn owners, thus suggesting a concern for inter-generational consequence. Yet, waste is not a generalized mandate to 'live lightly off the land' (Freyfogle 2006, p.149) but a blunt safeguard against deliberate damage to a remainderman's capital improvements.[3] In section 3, other examples are given, such as the prohibition on implied profits *a prendre*, or the good husbandry rules of agricultural tenancy. Yet, collectively these principles lack any overarching guiding principle, more ad hoc than doctrinally consistent. Property obligation seems to stall amidst a paucity of corroboration.

At the conceptual level, Joseph Singer's description of the 'castle' model of land ownership is one that makes adverse externalities 'magically vanish' (Singer 2010, p.79). The 'castle' reinforces the boundaries of dominion, and the illusion that trans-boundary spillovers are hermetically contained. Its dominance obviates the urgency of any need for right to be tempered by obligation. Its effect is seen in the historical record. 'Private owners are ... not good stewards: their perspectives are too short, they ignore ecological ripple effects, and their isolated decisions can produce chaotic land-use patterns' (Freyfogle 2007b, p.99).[4]

Ultimately, stewardship literature is compelled to jettison property's unfulfilled beginnings, and define stewardship in purely instrumental terms, self-evident truths about why 'land remains productive, fertile, and biologically diverse'.

> Is the soil kept fertile and in place? Are waterways clean and full of life? Are tracts of land devoted to uses for which they are ecologically well suited? Are landscapes sensibly laid out and pleasing to the eye and the ear? And are the modes of living and working on land likely to endure for centuries, without nature lashing back?
>
> (Freyfogle 2007b, p.18)

William Lucy and Catherine Mitchell concur: '[s]tewardship is not a substantive moral doctrine in itself but an instrumental concept ... a practical mechanism' (Lucy and Mitchell 1996, pp.596, 599). Despite its intuitive potential, stewardship remains property's awkward and ill-defined secret because, by and large, our dominant seeing of the private ownership modality keeps it so.

6.3 Locating stewardship in property traditions, theories and structure

Laura Underkuffler reasons that 'property is a zero-sum game in the context of finite resources' (Underkuffler 2006, p.1247). Win–lose becomes self-perpetuating, pitting property against the environment in an inexorable contest of futility. Re-calibrating this game requires either finding a viable place for obligation in property, or a fundamental re-conceptualization of property in land. This section pursues the former. First, it seeks out the available evidence of stewardship within existing property traditions. Second, it canvasses those legal theories that are sympathetic to property obligation. Third, it engages directly with institutional issues of structure. Despite some limited scope for developing stewardship within existing frameworks, this part concludes that in the main, Underkuffler is depressingly right.

6.3.1 Stewardship and property traditions

Common law ideas of property obligation subsist largely on the 'edge of the field' (Singer 2000a), peripheral to its mainstream concerns.[5] 'Limits on property rights are the exception, not the rule, the periphery rather than the core' (Alexander 2009). By contrast, caring for country is an elemental tenet of indigenous laws and customs. In settler societies, cultural perspective strongly influences the importance and role of obligation within property discourse.

The feudal nature of the Anglo common law and its attendant doctrines of tenure and estates, speak faintly of obligation as an historic consequence of ownership (Bosselmann 1994). Although the *Statute of Tenures* rationalized feudal incidents, the 'ghost' of feudalism (Buck 2006) was not fully exorcised, and principles that reinforced estate holder obligation to the Crown, such as escheat or quit rents, persist to limited extents, or are imitated by like ideas. Other property rules concerned with obligation also remain as isolated exemplars. The doctrine of waste precludes harmful activities by life tenants that permanently alter land for future reversioners or remaindermen, riparian right is premised on obligations owed to downstream owners, profits *a prendre* cannot be implied or prescribed because of their extractive nature (Bederman 1996, pp.1406–7), and agricultural tenancy laws are fashioned on concepts of good husbandry. Yet, collating these principles into the one sentence is confected, falsely conflating the common law's concern for future consequence. Nearly all are 'marginal outliers' (Raff 1998). As Karp notes, any comfort that legally trained persons draw from tying 'any new idea or perspective neatly to the past or to existing rules' is passing only. 'Stewardship means more' (Karp 1993, p.749).

By contrast, indigenous laws and customs are intimately attentive to the relationship between humans and the land. Bonds between people and place are familial, physical, cultural and spiritual, indicating a 'different construction of the idea of property and ownership' (Graham 2011, p.263), a construct where 'the role of humans [is] part of an interrelated living whole' (Thomas 2011, p.220). Nin Thomas asserts that Maori land values 'provide a bedrock of duties owed to the environment', while western law 'effectively dispenses with one of the Maori's three essential worlds, ultimate reality ... or at least marginalize it into being irrelevant to legal reasoning' (ibid., p.226). Inherent to this worldview is continuity, oral traditions that place responsibility to protect and preserve, in the case of the North American Haudenosauness nation 'for seven generations to come' (Engel 2011, p.75).

Hugh Brody's anthropological study of the Inuit peoples of northern Canada in the 1970s observes the settled nature of their relationship with land, and concludes that contrary to the stereotype, Western attitudes to land are more nomadic than the simple hunter-gatherer's. Westerners experience 'the lure of opportunity ... moving on, making progress, wondering if we might prosper there rather than here,' our mobility being 'the source of energetic colonial power' (Brody 2000, p.101). By contrast, the Inuit's worldview did not extend beyond their home; they had to manage the 'complicated business of maintaining the world around them to ensure that its produce is bountiful.' Central to this imperative was the maintenance of the natural world. 'The assumption held deep within this point of view is the place where a people lives is ideal: therefore change is for the worse' (ibid., p.117). Brody's thesis places stewardship at the heart of the indigenous relationship with land, an imperative to conserve the only earthly Eden known.

Indigenous land laws are also knowledge-based and localized, informed by the capacities and limits of the lands over which they apply.[6] Conversely, as Nicole Graham observes, modern property rights exist independently of their location. 'Modern property law conceptualizes and articulates limits to its application in terms of jurisdiction and authority. Yet this authority and jurisdiction derives not from the specific physical conditions of local places, but from itself in a circuitous and irrational fashion' (Graham 2010, p.267). Ownership, responsibility and knowledge are all inter-connected in the indigenous mindset, a self-correcting propensity to sustain land usage within geographic, climatic and temporal limits.

The risk in idealizing indigenous land law's contribution to land stewardship is one of hyperbolic over-reach. Carol Rose argues that indigenous people's management of natural resources is extensive, leading to both prehistoric and modern species' extinctions (Rose 1994, p.15). Tellingly, Rose argues that indigenous perspectives have less to offer a modern property ethic than superficially appears. Her reasoning is twofold: first they are premised on environmental bounty rather than scarcity; and second, their norms focus on human humility, rather than the immediate task of addressing destructive human behaviour (ibid., pp.14–19).[7] Despite Rose's cautionary note, indigenous perspectives underline the significance of property pluralism, and the broadening effects such diversity has on the meagre offerings of the common law.

6.3.2 Stewardship and property theory

If property doctrine (outside indigenous law) is a barren place for stewardship, to what extent can it flourish in more fertile theoretical soil? Again, the answer falls mainly to the edges, restricted to theories concerned with personal identity, or social or communitarian values, and is less applicable to mainstream law and economics analyses of property.

Margaret Radin's personhood theory is a 'long-ignored' intuitive property theory that 'focuses on personal embodiment or self-constitution in terms of things' (Radin 1992, p.958). Identity or embodiment of self becomes bound up with certain types of property. Radin distinguishes between *personal* and *fungible property*, and uses loss as a means to define each (ibid., p.960). Radin's personhood theory is useful in explaining the motives of stewardship. For example, Courtney White's study of the environmental ethics of ranchers in the American West identifies personal fulfilment as a key driver in a changing paradigm. White quotes one rancher:

> Ranchers have become applied ecologists ... nowadays it's all about stewardship, not food and fiber. But it's also having a passion about what you are doing ... like many, I'm grateful for the privilege of being allowed to take care of a little piece of the planet for whatever short amount of time we have.
>
> (White 2008, p.48)

Such relationships surpass purely commercial or economic rationales. Rather, the property becomes in Radin's words 'affirmatively part of oneself ... a scene of one's history and future, one's life and growth, an embodiment of personal autonomy' (Radin 1982, p.992). The difficulty with personhood theory lies in drawing the line between personal and fungible property.[8] Radin acknowledges that the dichotomy is in truth a continuum, one where stewardship values are closer to the personal end of the spectrum. Personhood also inspired a related theory of 'peoplehood' to explain group ownership of cultural property. Peoplehood 'draws upon ... themes of custody, care, and trusteeship, rather than comparably more fungible conceptions of property', a principle that includes both rights and obligations independent of traditional title that 'lies at the heart of cultural stewardship' (Carpenter, Katyal and Riley 2009, p.1067).

The links between property and stewardship are explicitly articulated in progressive property theory (Alexander et al. 2009). Progressive scholars challenge the near hegemony of law and economics analyses of property and seek to 'distinguish between dominant conceptions of property, and [their] underlying realities' (Blomley 2013). Progressive theorists say the orthodoxy is inadequate. Rather one must look to 'the underlying human values that property serves and the social relationships it shapes and protects' (Alexander et al. 2009, p.743). Such values are pluralistic, and include environmental stewardship, the impact of property externalities on future generations and the natural environment (ibid., p.744).

Amongst progressive property theorists, Eduardo Penalver is prominent for his advocacy of the virtues of land ownership. Penalver sees human flourishing enhanced by a long neglected virtue theory of property, specifically the virtues of *industry, justice,* and *humility.*[9] Humility is especially significant to land ethics; it requires a landowner, uncertain of the future consequences of their actions, to be guided by precaution and an intergenerational view of ownership. Humility is integral given the finitude of land, the inertia of land memory, and the adverse path dependence this engenders (ibid., p.831). In other words, human changes made to land have long-lasting, often irreversible effects that compound and mutually reinforce each other.

> The notion that land has a memory that stretches the impact of our current choices far into the future suggests an enormous responsibility on the part of those who make decisions about how to use it.
>
> (ibid., p.884)

Within dominant law and economics analyses of property, stewardship may be justified if it is sufficiently efficient or welfare maximizing. Harold Demsetz's seminal analysis that property rights arise 'when it becomes economic for those affected by externalities to internalize benefits and costs' (Demsetz 1967, p.354), may explain why it is economic in some circumstances for a private landowner to efficiently use scarce resources in a steward-like way. Moreover, law and economics theories invest heavily in the primacy of the *private* owner being best placed to 'take into account ... competing claims of the present and the future' (ibid., p.355). Private ownership creates incentives to use land wisely in response to market signals about the scarcity or value of the land's resources. But such perspectives fail to explain why land may equally 'facilitate the direct enjoyment of non-fungible and often social human goods [that] overshadow the motivating force of its investment value' (ibid., p.832). It also does not counter the alternative and equally logical conclusion that it may be more efficient in some circumstances for a private landowner to adopt the most destructive land use available.

The capacity of modern property to generate obligation as well as right is not a mainstream concern of liberal property theory or doctrine. Its outlier status is symptomatic of a wider systemic issue; is it possible to coherently locate stewardship within the structure of property, and if so, where? At a threshold level, the question posed is one of inherency; is land obligation inherent or autonomous to property? And if the former, the question becomes one of type: is stewardship a duty, a right, a rule, a qualification, or something else?[10] The remainder of section 3 canvasses the many divergent responses to these questions.

6.3.3 Stewardship and property's structure: is stewardship internal to, or external of property?

The case for obligation to be a 'thing' internal to property is heavily reliant on the assumption that property as a human institution is inherently social and relational. For example, Joseph Singer prefers a socially situated concept of property, the variously termed 'good neighbour', 'environmental' or 'citizenship' model (Singer 2006, p.329), where rights and other-regarding obligations are 'deeply entwined' in ownership, a 'reality' that the dominant castle conception masks.

> The citizenship model starts from an assumption that obligations are inherent in ownership ... Obligation is inherent in liberalism, but the castle and market models marginalize it. They seek to suppress consciousness of the obligations inherent in ownership, to draw our attention away from them.
>
> (Singer 2000a, pp.329–30)

In a similar vein, Gregory Alexander identifies a social-obligation norm inherent to Anglo-American law that has 'never been explicitly recognized ... or systemically developed' (Alexander 2009, p.819). While the social-obligation norm is primarily *social*, with its concern for human flourishing, well-lived lives, and a civic culture, it also has environmental implications.[11]

> Because human flourishing depends on social structures, the communities to which property owners belong may legitimately make demands of them to contribute out of their resources or to share their property in order to sustain those social matrices. Similar arguments ... can justify that individuals' use of their property [is] made in ways that do not permanently harm the environment.
>
> (Alexander and Penalver 2012, pp.95–96)

Others draw inherency from comparative study. Murray Raff examines obligation in civilian traditions, particularly German property law, to assert that an environmental obligation in property is 'implicit and too frequently overlooked' (Raff 1998, p.658). It is 'an aspect of property itself ... at the deepest jurisprudential level' (ibid., p.691). Raff does not require any Hohfeldian correlative to offset the whereabouts or existence of duty, '[s]ocial and individual obligations ... lie within the very essence of property ... without judicial presupposition of a basic right to do anything with it' (ibid.).[12]

Yet despite such claims of inherent obviousness, obligation remains stubbornly peripheral to common law property discourse. Thus, Alexander calls his social-obligation norm 'grossly underrated', and Singer's citizenship model remains aspirational. Indeed, Blomley suggests that Singer would be better engaged asking why the *practice* of the castle model is so successful, rather than fruitlessly trying to impugn its clearly dominant values (Blomley 2013). The premise that individuals owe obligations to others because we live in social communities is lost on the mainstream rational actor.

The counterpoint position is that stewardship is an anathema to property, and must by definition stand outside of it. This autonomous view, articulated by William Lucy and Catherine Mitchell dismisses the norms and practices of private property as dysfunctional and normatively objectionable, a form of 'useless currency'. Conceptual incompatibility means that stewardship must be a replacement for private property, not simply an adjunct to it. The private owner's 'extensive trinity of rights' are not vested in a steward. 'It is not feasible to claim the most extensive rights of exclusion, control and alienation over a resource, and yet be subject to a vast range of duties' (Lucy and Mitchell 1996, p.586).[13]

Likewise, scholars who recognize that obligation is a self-imposed moral or ethical restraint, acknowledge that it is a duty outside the law.[14] As Rose simply observes, if we are to have 'environmental good things ... we need to exercise some self-restraint' (Rose 1994, p.100). Or if not outside of the law, then stewardship is the responsibility of a discipline outside property law. For Klaus Bosselmann, developing a property regime with inherent responsibilities is the purpose of *environmental law* (Bosselmann 2008).[15]

If obligation is inside the institution of property, its case for inherency is either worn thin by its ceaseless circularity, or is simply over-reliant on assertion. This fragility is underscored when the unsettled place of obligation within property's formal structures is next explored.

6.3.4 Stewardship and property's structure: duty, right or rule?

At the taxonomic level, what form should stewardship take? Logically, a steward is a duty-bearer (Karp 1993, p.748). Aldo Leopold talks of 'a positive duty that society might rightly impose on landowners' (Leopold 1999, p.193). Richard Barnes similarly describes a steward as an owner subject to overriding duties, obligations that reflect the 'high degree of interest a community has in a particular resource' (Barnes 2009. p.52).

> Distilling the literature on stewardship reveals two key features; the duty to conserve and the duty to preserve. These duties have a profound effect on two particular incidents, the right to the capital (which includes the right to exclude) and the prohibition on harmful use.
>
> (ibid., p.157)

Barnes' linkage of duty to property's *incidents* reflects an analysis attributed to early twentieth-century American jurist Wesley Hohfeld. Hohfeld's 'main contribution to legal theory was to identify and name eight building blocks ... from which all legal relationships could be built' (Banner 2011, pp.102–3). The Hohfeldian analysis of right, duty, privilege, no-right, power, liability, immunity and disability, was designed to promote rigor in legal thinking. While it may be a 'hocus pocus [that] never caught on' (Banner 2011, p.104), Hohfeld helps in 'thinking straight' (Hohfeld 1913, p.18) about stewardship's place in property's structure. His linkage of right and duty affirms the capacity of property to generate duties, and exposes the fixation on property as merely a source of rights.

Hohfeld's building blocks work in two ways: as jural opposites and jural correlatives. *Duty* is the jural opposite of *privilege*, and the jural correlative of *right*. Importantly, the latter pairing requires that a duty will only subsist as a consequence of a strictly defined right. Hohfeld criticizes the indiscriminate use of the term 'right', arguing that it frequently mis-describes a multitude of contexts, including mere privilege. Hohfeldian right is properly ascribed to that which is solely a legally enforceable claim (Hohfeld 1913, p.32). Hence a duty of stewardship requires a parallel and strictly defined property right. Freyfogle implies that stewardship is a consequence of the right to use, where stewards enjoy 'clear rights to use but only limited rights to degrade and consume' (Freyfogle 2007a, p141).

Moreover, duty may be positive, 'an affirmative duty to preserve' (Sax 1999, pp.57–58); or negative, a duty to refrain from doing harm. Such duality reflects the preservation versus conservation tension in stewardship discourse. In practice, a steward's duty is invariably positive as well as negative, conforming to Hohfeld's explanation of duty as 'that which one ought or ought not to do' (Hohfeld 1913, p.32). To whom the duty is owed is likewise open-ended. It may be immediate: to neighbours, the local community; or more widely to society, future generations, the environment or the Earth itself (Karp 1993, p.752; Cribbet 1986, p.40).[16]

To others, stewardship is not articulated as a duty *per se*, but the result of a qualified right. Proponents of cultural property for example argue that stewardship arises as a limitation on the right to dispose.[17] In other words, rather than being a reciprocal consequence of a right, as Hohfeld presupposes, stewardship is the consequence of a diminished right. Sax explains that '[i]ndisputably, any such imposition takes something away from the owner, but it does not intrude markedly on the [owner's] core interests' (Sax 1999, p.68). The owner of a Rembrandt painting, much like the private owner of a biodiversity hotspot, is not denied rights to alienate, exclude, or reap economic benefit; yet there is no right to destroy, to 'throw darts at the masterpiece' that is implicit in the rights of ownership. This view is analogous to a conception of private ownership subject to the encumbrance of social or public interests (Yannacone 1978; Babcock and Feurer 1977).

Stewardship may also be articulated as a right, a *public* right to land health. Here the prism through which stewardship is viewed becomes a public, not a private one. As a result, esoteric debates about the parallel qualities of the private right, or the extent of its impairment, are subsumed by its wider focus. In this paradigm, rights are pluralistic and relative, however scholars concede that presently public rights can be untidy (Rose 1994, pp.19–25). Alison Rieser wistfully observes that 'a right to expect … lands and natural areas to retain their natural characteristics' is a public property right in search of a theory (Rieser 1991, p.393). David Farrier's ambition for a 'collective property right to biological diversity' is worthy (Farrier 1995, cited in Elmendorf 2003, p.457), but lacks practicality, with 'the scantest of toeholds in rural landowner communities' (Elmendorf 2003, p.456).

Finally, stewardship may be categorized as a *rule*. Christopher Rodgers' resource allocation model of property accounts for positive stewardship obligations as *property management rules* (Rodgers 2009, p.557). Property management rules 'prosecute a public interest objective – nature conservation' by 'controlling the terms on which access to the resource (land) is permitted' (ibid., p.570). Such positive management obligations, whether imposed by statute or contract, cannot be explained by 'extant property rights scholarship' (ibid., p.569). Rather, a fourth category of *rule* is needed to capture the substance of stewardship, an addition to Guido Calabresi and Douglas Melamed's rule hierarchy of property rules, liability rules and entitlements protected by inalienability rules (Calabresi and Melamed 1972).

The taxonomic smorgasbord that is duty, right, rule or qualification, fulfils Hohfeld's prophecy of imprecise terminology fostering a 'paucity and confusion as regards actual legal conceptions' (Hohfeld 1913, p.29). Such imprecision reflects a lack of vantage, the objective altitude necessary to gain perspective on stewardship's place and role in property. Presently, the climb to that vantage point is strewn with obstacles, the litter of recent iterations of property. Section 4 leaves structure aside, and inspects the content of that paradigmatic litter.

6.4 The impediments to stewardship

While stewardship may flourish in small, isolated outcrops, in the main it lies fallow on the unforgiving terrain of a liberal conception of property in land, a 'legal-economic ordering' where property is 'unitary, systemized and centralized' (Blomley 1994, pp.68–82). Sax says that this liberal paradigm embraces two basic ideas, neither of which accommodates stewardship. One is political, based on individual autonomy and privacy, the other economic, based on the right to the product of one's labour and effort (2011, p.4). Its ascendancy dates back to (at least) the enclosure period of the eighteenth and nineteenth centuries. Blomley traces its genesis to early seventeenth century jurist Edward Coke, and his project of transforming the common law from a 'variegated and diverse system of localized practices [into] a disembodied superstructure' (Blomley 1994, p.76).

In recent decades, its pre-eminence appears less assured, amidst a gathering sense that the paradigm is approaching a tipping point. Nicole Graham adopts Thomas Kuhn's theory of paradigm shift to situate our present predicament. Kuhn describes paradigms as 'the result of an accumulation of knowledge that works in its specific time and place ... [a] successful cultural adaptation to particular conditions' (Graham 2010, p.203). These social and ecological relationships are not universal truths about inexorable human progress, but simply 'true in a given time and place under a set of particular conditions' (ibid., p.2). Paradigms endure where 'on ideological and practical levels they continue to make sense of the world' (ibid., p.203). Paradigm *shifts* occur when the prevailing body of knowledge is no longer temporally or geographically appropriate. Institutional mal-adaption is a dawning realization that 'not only are other ideas or frameworks of meaning ... more plausible than the current paradigm, but also ... they seem more viable' (ibid.). Graham argues that in the case of property, the liberal paradigm is dysfunctional and approaching crisis. In settler societies especially, far from the historicized context of the English enclosure period, it lacks plausibility.[18]

This section argues that *abstraction, individualism* and a *land as commodity* mentality remain formidable impediments to the development of a land ethic. When viewed through the narrow private paradigm, they conceal the crisis that Graham foresees, and diminish the sense that we are at the cusp of a Kuhnian shift. Whether their hegemony remains so definitive when the perspective changes, is another question postponed to Chapter 7.

6.4.1 The primacy of individualism

Where property is universalized as a private and individual right, its relational attributes fade to near invisibility. Property becomes an individual entitlement in a contextual vacuum.[19] The private property rights movement, especially influential in the United States, exemplifies its one-sided excess (Cribbet 1986; Marzulla 2001).

However, such a skewed view represents a fundamental misreading of property. Scholars have written at length on the duality of property. Alexander describes it in terms of 'property as commodity, and property as propriety' (Alexander 1997). Underkuffler speaks of competing 'comprehensive' and 'absolute' approaches (Underkuffler 2006). Freyfogle identifies a cultural fault line, where abstract reasoning and individualism faces off 'particularity, context, and community' (Freyfogle 2007b, p.108). Freyfogle draws on history, identifying a watershed period after the Civil War in the USA, when a distinct public–private divide became prominent.

> The new public-private divide particularly influenced the ways people thought about private property ... an entitlement that people held in their private lives. It was something they exercised not as a springboard to virtue and public service as in the 18th century or as part of a larger community, but to protect their privacy and promote their personal economic welfare ... As an intellectual concept, private property had largely been freed from communal obligations.
>
> (Freyfogle 2003, p.81)

In a stewardship context, excessive individualism conceals the substantive truth of a landowner's communal responsibilities (Elmendorf 2003, p.437; Freyfogle 2011). Communitarian obligation is central to Aldo Leopold's land health,[20] where 'a conviction of individual responsibility' to land' (Leopold 1948, p.236) is proportionate to an understanding of wider community responsibilities. US Supreme Court Justice Blackmun adopted Leopold's refrain when he spoke of the context of private ownership. 'In this environmental context, I personally prefer the older and particularly pertinent observation and warning of John Donne ... no man is an island, entire of itself, every man is a piece of the Continent, a part of the main.'[21]

The decoupling of private ownership and communal obligation is prominent in disputes where landowners perceive that environmental restrictions represent a loss of property rights. In Australia, the implementation of native vegetation laws or water buy-back schemes is frequently countered by claims that property rights are being stripped away (Martin et al. 2013).[22] Until there is a cultural change about the communitarian context of private ownership, Lynton Caldwell says it is futile to expect stewardship to arise organically. 'Society itself must shift its focus of attention from the rights of the current landholder to the communal rights of all present and future society members' (Caldwell 1974, p.323).

Moreover, excessive individualism has perverse consequences. Karp observes that 'individuals have won ... excessive autonomy' and a consequential 'sheer irresponsibility' (Karp 1993, p.742). The collective result of such excess is 'a disassociation of humans from their environment on which they rely for survival' (ibid.), and an isolationist artificial view of the non-context of property rights in land.

6.4.2 *Land as commodity*

Alexander's property as commodity has been the dominant half of his dialectic. Particularly in settler societies, mobility has been dependent on a commodity view of land. Andrew Buck's explanation of the development of a distinctively Australian property law emphasizes the centrality of egalitarianism, an equal opportunity for all to acquire wealth through land as the original commodity (Buck 2006). In the United States, Caldwell observes a similar historical transition in 'the status of man-land relationships from vestiges of feudal land tenure to the treatment of land as a marketable commodity' (Caldwell 1974, p.761).

Viewing land as a purely fungible commodity has consequences for place, and the responsibilities owners have for its land health. Curt Meine's study of the US survey grid is illuminating in terms of the links it draws between commodity and abstraction. To Meine, the survey abstracts reality. Its standardized treatment of land 'overwhelmed the particularities of place, and for generations, encouraged the adoption of a hard utilitarian view of land as commodity.' (Meine 2004).[23] Moreover, commodification has moral consequences, because it 'focuses ... on the instrumental value of the good for sale, leading us to undervalue or disregard its inherent worth' (Hamilton and Bankes 2010, p.33).[24]

Theodore Steinberg's satire of the ownership of nature has a similar theme: landscapes such as Arizona's Sonoran desert suffer when 'the impulse to turn everything into [private] ownership ... imposes the 'logic of capitalism' on the 'nonideological matter-in-motion we call nature' (Steinberg 1995, p.10). To see land as simply its monetary value is symptomatic of 'a culture so single-minded in its pursuit of ... private property, [that it] may sacrifice what one anthropologist has called its "evolutionary flexibility" and thereby foreclose on other ways of relating to the earth' (ibid.).

6.4.3 *Abstraction*

Modern property also lacks connection to place, lost at some indeterminate tipping point when its focus shifted from the relationship between person and thing, to the relationship between person and person. The consequence of this de-contextualisation is abstraction,[25] a *fait accompli* so complete that jurists debate whether property is illusory 'thin air' (Gray 1991).[26] Abstraction has cast stewardship haplessly adrift, the artifice of person-to-person relationship denying it physical nexus. Michael Metzger observes its ecological risk.

> The source of our malaise may ... be rooted in our capacity for dealing in abstractions. The invention of language ... has enabled us to create separate realities, and to remove ourselves from the natural world in which we live to a cerebral world of our own creation.
>
> (Metzger 1975, p.796)

The entrenchment of abstraction in the Anglo common law has been an incremental yet unswerving process that began in earnest in the eighteenth century enclosure period. Enclosure marked a displacement of communitarian and social ideas of property diversity, with liberal notions suited to a more universal private property. In its rush to 'improve', it swept away ancient place-based rights, making idiosyncratic 'somewheres' ubiquitous 'anywheres'.[27] Nicole Graham cited landscape historian John Barrell to lament this loss.

> To enclose an open field parish means in the first place to think of the details of its topography as quite erased from the map. The hostile and mysterious road system was tamed and made un-mysterious by being destroyed; the minute and intricate divisions between lands, strips, furlongs, and fields simply ceased to exist.
>
> (Graham 2010, p.66)

Such radical change meant more than a mere readjustment of property right. Jeanette Neeson observes that common rights – what she termed 'ownership without possession' – conferred on commoners a sense of who they were and where they belonged. The 1788 case of *Steel v. Houghton* illustrates dispossession from place.[28] In *Steel*, rights to glean enjoyed by the indigent parishioners of Timworth were swamped by new ideas of property. Common property rights became a 'mere practice' condemned by their 'universal promiscuity' and perceptions of vagrancy. Where once property rights enforced links to place, they now policed exclusion through trespass.

This estrangement of right from place was further entrenched by the rise of a new property metaphor, the relative, divisible bundle of rights. The metaphor suited the changing times because its parts, especially the right to exclude, enabled the intensive exploitation of land and its resources free from interference. Land could be exploited without consequence to place. As Michael Heller notes,

> While the modern bundle-of-legal relations metaphor reflects well the possibility of complex relational fragmentation, it gives a weak sense of the "thingness" of private property.
>
> (Heller 1999, p.1193)

For diverse reasons, the bundle percolated into property discourse, and in 1888, two influential articles solidified its dominance (Goldstein 1998, p.367).[29] By the early twentieth century, the influential analysis of Wesley Hohfeld (canvassed in Chapter 1) entrenched the removal of legal relations from physical facts, such that 'land is not property, but the subject of property' (Hohfeld 1913, p.22).[30] Another contemporary abstraction was the hypothetical *Blackacre*. If landowner rights were essentially identical, then *Blackacre* was a useful contrivance to symbolize a universalized property in land. Freyfogle traces the rise of *Blackacre* to Harvard Law School in 1870, where the pedagogical practice of 'scientific case method' instilled rigor, the law library became a laboratory and law reports evolved into data. To learn law, 'a student need not and should not engage with the messy outside world. There was no need to pay attention to actual people, to struggle with ethical enigmas, or know anything about nature' (Freyfogle 2007b, p.109). This approach fostered high abstraction. 'In the case of property law, land was land and a parcel's physical features and context were legally irrelevant. So irrelevant was context that law students did not talk of real places, but hypothetical tracts such as Blackacre' (ibid., p.110).

Abstraction in property advanced by stealth. Stuart Banner blames property academics in part for its subtle entrenchment.

> There were no newspaper editorials or popular magazine articles insisting that property was or was not a relationship between people. Only lawyers thought about the issue, and even then only a probably very small fraction of the most philosophically inclined ... And of course law schools were the entry point for an increasingly large percentage of the broad policymaking community. All law students took a course in Property, and more and more of them would learn that property was not about things; it was about power over people.
>
> (Banner 2011, p.106)

Its incremental effect, whether by accident or design, is that property terminology fictionalizes the relationship between people and place and removes it to a plane where human actions, destructive or constructive, have no relevance or consequence. When Mary Houghton was legally displaced from ex-common lands of eighteenth-century Timworth, a connection with her local place was irrevocably severed. By the early twentieth century, 'relationship to place [was] irrelevant' and any thought to the contrary, Hohfeld argued, was 'fallacious' (Freyfogle 2011, p.719).

The implications of this fallacy are seen in Brody's transient mobility, or Kunstler's 'geography of nowhere', the 'weakening symbolic qualities of modern place' (Relph, cited in Garbutt 2011, p.55). Property's abstraction cannot speak to or describe an individual parcel of land's ecological limits. Nor can it remedy deepening estrangement from place. Hence, stewardship is left stranded by a property dialogue that speaks solely of artifice. Writ large, abstraction blinds us to the 'one terrible fact ... that civilization is just russeting on the skin of the biosphere' (Alexander and Penalver 2012, p.50).

6.4.4 Land memory

The cumulative effects of abstraction, individualism, and a land as commodity mentality are harmful property patterns, seared into human landscapes through Eduardo Penalver's *land memory* (2009). More consequential than causative, land memory has two lasting effects.

First, human changes to landscapes tend to an enduring physical permanence, either because the change is irreversible, or because it is too costly to remedy. And the finitude of land means that particular choices made about land use or property type necessarily preclude alternatives. Thus, the conversion of prime agricultural land into housing lots is a decision that has lasting land memory implications for both the stock of residential land and the corresponding quantity of food producing land. The same dynamic works for urban private property and public open space.

Second, this tenacity produces landscape inertia, an interplay of individual factors – physical, psychological and social – that 'pre-suppose and yield a pervasive path-dependence in land use' (Penalver 2009, p.831). Accordingly, the blunt knife used to carve out singular property patterns gives rise to a whole of landscape mentality that is 'exponentially' more durable than the individual memory of one land parcel (ibid.).

Together, these seeming inevitabilities of physical permanence and landscape inertia fasten the land's memory. As traversed in Chapter 2, Freyfogle's bleak account of Champaign County, Illinois, where public property accounts for less than 1 per cent of the county (Freyfogle 2011, p.271), is a depressing vision of a landscape monotone locked into inertial stasis. Stephen Wheeler's generic description of private urban sprawl on metropolitan fringes echoes this self-perpetuating cycle, of 'a chaotic, low-density exurban world ... dominated by large-scale corporate activity, with little sense of place, sensitivity to the environment or social cohesion' (Wheeler 2013, p.3). Conversely, more diverse property patterns may enable positive path dependencies that enhance human flourishing. Kunstler's description of childhood visits to a New England town with its 'substantial and dignified' public spaces, are a stark counterpoint to the bland private suburbia of his later youth. Land memory thus, seems to cut both ways, depending on which side of the property duality prevails. Freyfogle and Wheeler observe the harm of its monistic side, while Kunstler yearns for its diverse other-half.

6.5 Conclusion

This chapter argues that seeing property through a narrow, one-sided private view impedes land stewardship, the generation of obligation as an incident of property right. It renders its definition problematic beyond instrumental terms, fosters structural imprecision and pushes stewardship to the doctrinal and theoretical fringes. And to complete the picture, individualism, abstraction, and commoditization close the loop and institute an endless circularity, a negative land memory.

By contrast, Chapter 7 explores an alternative, more optimistic vision: the links between property diversity and stewardship, the latent connections alluded to in the closing paragraph of section 4.4. above. Unlike this chapter, it looks to the other half of the property duality, the property patterns of 'warp and woof' that weave a pluralistic fabric across place.

Notes

1 'Land parcels are discrete things, managed separately, and connected to one another only at the edge' (Freyfogle 1998, p.17).
2 'Ecology explains how activities on one land parcel can affect landowners and land uses elsewhere, [while] property law then evaluates these spillover effects' (Freyfogle 1998, pp.107–8).
3 Purdy argues that the adaptation of English waste doctrine to the American landscape stressed progress and economic expansion, such that '[i]t would be an outrage on common sense to call enhancement (the clearance of native forests) waste' (Purdy 2010, p.61).
4 This ripple effect renders retreat into public land 'enclaves' futile.
5 The focus on common law jurisdictions overlooks other legal traditions, for example stewardship in Scottish law (McKenzie Skene et al. 1999).
6 An analogy is pre-enclosure English common rights, many of which were specific to locality (Graham 2010).
7 Stone likewise queries the 'vaunted harmony between American Plains Indians and Nature' (Stone 1972).
8 Penalver likewise explores the blurred distinction between fungible and personal in terms of the family home (Penalver 2009).
9 Human flourishing is 'the obligation to support and nurture the social structures necessary for development of human capabilities' (Alexander and Penalver 2012, pp.95–96).
10 'When we gather together to make rules for our shared landscapes, we exercise one of our most important, positive *liberties*' (Freyfogle 2006, p.193). Brewer sees stewardship as a modern extension of the discourse of improvement (Brewer 2003, pp.118–19).
11 Obligation may also be also owed to future generations in cases of life-traversing projects (Alexander 2013).
12 McHarg concludes it is axiomatic that 'property rights ... are regarded as necessarily carrying with them obligations of a social nature', arguing that property's relational nature is the *source* of external legislative regulation (McHarg 2009, pp.361–62).
13 Lucy and Mitchell scrutinize common property as an alternative model for land custodianship, but find it wanting, chiefly on tragedy grounds (Lucy and

Mitchell 1996, p.600). Indigenous claims to cultural property are likewise 'better explained and justified through a stewardship model' rather than an ownership model. 'Stewardship tends to fall outside the paradigms of individuality and alienability upon which classic property law is premised' (Carpenter, Katyal and Riley 2009, pp.1028–29).

14 'The stewardship tradition is obviously powerful and deeply rooted, and impressively it grows out of self-imposed restraint, not as a duty imposed by law or even the strictures of public opinion' (Sax 1999, p.72).

15 Cf. Environmental law that has 'not adequately penetrated the content of property law' (Thomas 2011, p.12).

16 Stewardship is 'a duty that we all bear toward creation [that] has shaped our environmental law since the first Earth Day' (Byrne 2004, p.688).

17 Underkuffler 2003, p.110; Merryman 1976, p.1041; Mousstakis 1989, p.179; Merryman 1989, p.339.

18 'The dispossession and diaspora of the English regime of private property extended across the globe via colonization.' (Graham 2010, p.204)

19 Aldo Leopold warned of a 'bogus individualism' rather than responsible citizenship (Meine 2004).

20 Land health is the capacity of land for self-renewal.

21 *Sierra Club v. Morton* (cited in Stone 1988, p.94).

22 *Spencer v. Commonwealth of Australia* [2010] HCA 28.

23 Corner attributes the National Land Survey to Thomas Jefferson's concern to make land available for purchase. Its unintended consequence 'is a ubiquitous and standardized built environment ... [where] every place, regardless of special characteristics, begins to look and feel alike – neutral, flat and bland' (Corner 1996, p.32).

24 In the 1930s Leopold observed a phenomenon of farmers setting aside small areas for the restoration of prairie grasses. Leopold saw the first stirrings of a 'capital R Revolt – a revolt against the constricted tedium of a merely economic attitude towards land'. (Leopold 1966)

25 Steinberg argues that property law serves to reduce the complexity and mobility of nature into a 'giant legal abstraction.' Property law is 'the voice of reason that we use to tidy up the messy and dynamic world of nature' (Steinberg 1995).

26 Stuart Banner calls it 'the disappearing right' (Banner 2011, pp.106–8).

27 'Standardized, universal and measurable space [was] grafted over place so that the physicality and particularity of places became irrelevant' (Graham 2010, p.66).

28 *Steel v. Houghton et Uxor* (1788) 126 ER 32 (cited in Buck 2006).

29 Fairfax sees the bundle as a weakening of the Lockean ideal of property. Banner explains its rise in terms of a judicial willingness to widen the US constitutional takings clause. Goldstein links its ascension to the burgeoning worth of corporate and intellectual property, 'from things to rights reflected the rise of corporations and commercial and intangible property'.

30 Banner observes that Hohfeld's lasting legacy was his emphasis on property as relations between people (Banner 2011, pp.103–4).

References

Alexander, G 1997, *Commodity and Propriety: Competing Visions of Property in American Thought 1776–1970*, University of Chicago Press, Chicago.

Alexander, G 2009, 'The Social-Obligation Norm in American Property Law', *Cornell Law Rev.*, vol. 94, 745–819.

Alexander, G 2013, 'Unborn Communities' Cornell Law School research paper No. 13–83.

Alexander, G and Penalver, E 2012, *An Introduction to Property Theory*, Cambridge University Press, New York.

Alexander, G, Penalver, E, Singer, J and Underkuffler, L 2009, 'A Statement of Progressive Property', *Cornell LR*, vol. 49, 743–44.

Babcock, R and Feurer, D 1977, 'Land as a Commodity Affected with a Public Interest', *Wash. L. Rev.*, vol. 52, 289–334.

Banner, S 2011, *American Property, A History of Who, Why and What We Own*, Harvard University Press, Cambridge, MA.

Barnes, R 2009, *Property Rights and Natural Resources*, Hart Publishing, Oxford.

Bederman, D 1996, 'The Curious Resurrection of Custom: Beach Access and Judicial Takings', *Columbia Law Review*, vol. 96, no.6, 1375–1455.

Blomley, N 1994, *Law, Space, and the Geographies of Power*, The Guildford Press, New York.

Blomley, N 2013, 'Performing Property: Making the World', *Canadian Journal of Law and Jurisprudence*, vol. 26, no. 1, 23–48.

Bosselman, F 1994, 'Four Land Ethics: Order, Reform, Responsibility; Opportunity', *Envtl. Law*, vol. 24, 1439–511.

Bosselmann, K 2008, *The Principle of Sustainability: Transforming Law and Governance*, Ashgate, Aldershot.

Brewer, R 2003, *Conservancy: The Land Trust Movement in America*, University Press of New England, Hanover, NH.

Brody, H 2000, *The Other Side of Eden*, Faber and Faber, London.

Buck, A 2006, *The Making of Australian Property Law*, Federation Press, Sydney.

Byrne, J P 2004, 'Property and Environment: Thoughts on an Evolving Relationship', *Harv. J.L. & Pub. Pol'y*, vol. 28, 679–89.

Calabresi, G and Melamed, A D 1972, 'Property Rules, Liability Rules, and Inalienability: One View of the Cathedral', *Harv. L. Rev.*, vol. 85, 1089–128.

Caldwell, L 1974, 'Rights of Ownership or Rights of Use? The Need for a New Conceptual Basis for Land Use Policy', *Wm. & Mary LR*, vol.15, 759–75.

Carpenter, K, Katyal, S and Riley, A 2009, 'In Defense of Property', *Yale LJ*, vol. 118, 1022–125.

Carter, P 2009, *Dark Writing: Geography, Performance, Design*, University of Hawai'i Press, Honolulu, HI.

Corner, J 1996, *Taking Measures Across the American Landscape*, Yale University Press, New Haven, CT.

Cribbet, J 1986, 'Concepts in Transition: The Search for a New Definition of Property', *U. Ill. L. Rev.*, 1–42.

Davies, M 2007, *Property Meanings, Histories, Theories*, Routledge, Abingdon.

Demsetz, H 1967, 'Toward a Theory of Property Rights', *Am. Econ. Rev.*, vol.57, 347–59.

Elmendorf, C 2003, 'Ideas, Incentives, Gifts, and Governance: Toward Conservation Stewardship of Private Land, in Cultural and Psychological Perspective', *U. Ill. L. Rev.*, vol. 2003, no. 2, 423–505.

Engel, J R 2011 'Property: Faustian Pact or New Covenant with Earth?', in D Grinlinton and P Taylor (eds), *Property Rights and Sustainability: The Evolution of Property Rights to Meet Ecological Challenges*, Martinus Nijhoff, Leiden.

Farrier, D 1995, 'Conserving Biodiversity on Private Land: Incentives for Management or Compensation for Lost Expectations?', *Harv. Envtl. L. Rev.*, vol. 19, 303–408.

Flournoy, A 2003, 'In Search of an Environmental Ethic', *Colum. J. Envtl. Law*, vol. 28, 63–118.

Freyfogle, E 1988, 'Context and Accommodation in Modern Property Law', *Stanford L. Rev.*, vol. 41, 1529–1556.

Freyfogle, E 2003, *The Land We Share: Private Property and the Common Good*, Island Press, Washington, DC.

Freyfogle, E 2006, *Why Conservation is Failing and How it Can Regain Ground*, Yale University Press, New Haven, CT.

Freyfogle, E 2007a, *On Private Property: Finding Common Ground on the Ownership of Land*, Beacon Press, Boston.

Freyfogle, E 2007b, *Agrarianism and the Good Society: Land, Culture, Conflict and Hope*, University of Kentucky Press, Lexington.

Freyfogle, E, 2011, 'Private Rights in Nature: Two Paradigms', in P. Burdon (ed.) *Wild Law: The Philosophy of Earth Jurisprudence*, Wakefield Press, Kent Town, Australia.

Garbutt, R 2011, *The Locals: Identity, Place and Belonging in Australia and Beyond*, Peter Lang, Bern.

Goldstein, R 1998, 'Green Wood in the Bundle of Sticks: Fitting Environmental Ethics and Ecology into Real Property Law', *B.C. Envtl. Aff. L. Rev.*, vol. 25, 347–430.

Graham, N 2010, *Lawscape: Property, Environment, Law*, Routledge, Abingdon.

Graham, N 2011, 'Owning the Earth', in P Burdon (ed.), *Exploring Wild Law: The Philosophy of Earth Jurisprudence*, Wakefield Press, Kent Town, Australia.

Gray, K 1991, 'Property in Thin Air', *Cambridge LJ*, vol. 50, 252–307.

Hamilton, J W and Bankes, N 2010, 'Different Views of the Cathedral: The Literature on Property Law Theory', in A. McHarg et al. (eds), *Property and the Law in Energy and Natural Resources*, Oxford University Press, Oxford.

Heller, M. 1998, 'The Boundaries of Private Property', *Yale L.J.*, vol. 108, 1163–225.

Hohfeld, W 1913, 'Some Fundamental Legal Conceptions as Applied in Legal Reasoning', *Yale Law Journal*, vol. 23, 16–59.

Karp, J 1993, 'A Private Property Duty of Stewardship: Changing our Land Ethic', *Envtl. Law*, vol. 23, 735–62.

Leopold, A 1948, *A Sand County Almanac*, Oxford University Press, New York.

Leopold, A 1966, *A Sand County Almanac with other Essays on Conservation from Round River*, Oxford University Press, New York.

Leopold, A 1999, *For the Health of the Land: Previously Unpublished Essays and Other Writings*, Island Press, Washington, DC.

Lucy, W and Mitchell, C 1996, 'Replacing Private Property: The Case for Stewardship', *Cambridge Law J.*, vol. 55, no. 3, 566–600.

McKenzie Skene, D, Rowan-Robinson, J, Paisley, R and Cusine, D J 1999, 'Stewardship: From Rhetoric to Reality', *Edinburgh LR*, vol. 3, no. 2, 151–75.

McHarg, A 2009, 'The Social Obligations of Ownership and the Regulation of Energy Utilities in the UK and the EU', in A. McHarg et al. (eds), *Property and the Law in Energy and Natural Resources*, Oxford University Press, Oxford.

Martin, P, Kennedy, A, Page, J and Williams, J 2013, 'Environmental Property Rights in Australia: Constructing a New Tower of Babel', *Environmental and Planning Law Journal*, vol. 30, no. 6, 531–52.

Marzulla, N 2001, 'Property Rights Movement: How it Began and Where it is Headed', in N Blomley, D Delaney and R T Ford (eds), *The Legal Geographies Reader*, Blackwell, Oxford.

Meine, C 2004, *Correction Lines Essays on Land, Leopold, and Conservation*, Island Press, Washington, DC.

Merryman, J 1976 'The Refrigerator of Bernard Buffet', *Hastings LJ*, vol. 27, 1023–49.

Merryman, J 1989, 'The Public Interest in Cultural Property', *California Law Review*, vol.7, 339–364.

Metzger, M 1975, 'Private Property and Environmental Sanity', *Ecology LQ*, vol. 5, 793–819.

Mousstakis, J 1989, 'Group Rights in Cultural Property', *Cornell LR*, vol. 74, 1179–227.

Neeson, J M 1993, *Commoners: Common Right, Enclosure and Social Change in England, 1700–1820*, Cambridge University Press, Cambridge.

Penalver, E 2009, 'Land Virtues', *Cornell Law Rev.*, vol. 94, 821–88.

Purdy, J 2010, *The Meaning of Property: Freedom, Community, and the Legal Imagination*, Yale.

Radin, M 1982, 'Property and Personhood', *Stanford Law Rev.*, vol. 34, 957–1015.

Raff, M 1998, 'Environmental Obligations and the Western Liberal Property Concept', *Melb. Univ. Law Rev.*, vol. 22, 657–692.

Rieser, A 1991 'Ecological Preservation as a Public Property Right: An Emerging Doctrine in Search of a Theory', *Harv. Envtl. L. Rev.*, vol. 15, 393

Rodgers, C 2009, 'Nature's Place? Property Rights, Property Rules and Environmental Stewardship', *Cambridge Law Journal*, vol. 68, no. 3, 550–74.

Rose, C M 1994, 'Given-ness and Gift: Property and the Quest for Environmental Ethics', *Envtl. Law*, vol. 24, 1–31.

Sax, J 1999, *Playing Darts with a Rembrandt: Public and Private Rights in Cultural Treasures*, University of Michigan Press, Ann Arbor.

Sax, J 2011, *Ownership, Property and Sustainability*, University of Utah Press, Salt Lake City.

Singer, J 2000a, *The Edges of the Field Lessons on the Obligations of Ownership*, Beacon Press, Boston.

Singer, J 2000b, *Entitlement: The Paradoxes of Property*, Yale University Press, New Haven, CT.

Singer, J 2006, 'The Ownership Society and Takings of Property: Castles, Investments, and Just Obligations', *Harv. Envtl. L. Rev.*, vol. 30, 309–38.

Singer, J 2009, 'Democratic Estates: Property Law in a Free and Democratic Society', *Cornell Law Rev.*, vol. 94, 1009–62.

Singer, J 2010, 'Property Norms Construct the Externalities of Ownership', in G Alexander and E Penalver (eds), *Property and Community*, Oxford University Press, New York.

Steinberg, T 1995, *Slide Mountain, or The Folly of Owning Nature*, University of California Press, Berkeley, CA.

Stone, C 1972, 'Should Trees Have Standing? Toward Legal Rights for Natural Objects', *S. Cal. L. Rev.*, vol. 45, 450–501.

Thomas, N 2011, 'Maori Concepts of Ranga tiratanga, Kaitiakitanga, the Environment, and Property Rights', in D Grinlinton and P Taylor (eds), *Property Rights and Sustainability: The Evolution of Property Rights to Meet Ecological Challenges*, Brill-Nijhoff, Leiden.

Underkuffler, L 2003, *The Idea of Property: Its Meaning and Power*, Oxford University Press, Oxford.

Underkuffler, L 2006, 'Property as Constitutional Myth: Utilities and Dangers', *Cornell LR*, vol. 92, 1239–54.

Wheeler, S 2013, *Planning for Sustainability: Creating Liveable, Equitable and Ecological Communities*, Routledge, Abingdon.

White, C 2008, *Revolution on the Range: The Rise of the New Ranch in the American West*, Island Press, Washington, DC.

Yannacone, V 1978, 'Property and Stewardship: Private Property Plus Public Interest Equals Social Property', *South Dakota L. Rev.*, vol. 23, 71–148.

Chapter 7

Obligation and property diversity

7.1 Introduction

Stewardship is more likely to emerge where land use externalities have consequence. Contrast this to an individualized view of property – abstract and divorced from place – where externalities, harmful or otherwise, have no, or negligible, impact. To realize the former, property must bridge a conceptual impasse, between detached 'atom-counting' on the one hand, and making the pieces fit together on the other (Smith 2012, p.1709). Property diversity is a theory, that amongst its other possibilities describes how the pieces can and may fit together, one truthful of property on the ground. As such, cause and effect can be traced, its inter-connective structure less likely to make externalities 'magically vanish'.

This chapter leaves behind the frustrations and roadblocks of property monism, and considers the optimistic implications of property diversity for generating obligation as an incident of right. In section 2, it describes the architecture of property diversity, and its hopeful similarities to both environmental conceptions of property, and post-bundle property metaphors. Section 3 considers the inter-connective impacts of diversity's 'normative mosaic', the mix of property values that the private, public and common estates add to human landscapes. Last, section 4 analyses property diversity though performance theory, the imaginative idea that *doing* creates reality. It observes that acts of stewardship often involve cross-boundary partnerships of private, public and community landowners, and asks whether a greater seeing of good land use performances across diverse fora may help to unfreeze an otherwise intransigent paradigm. The chapter concludes by exploring two 'world-ed' micro-examples of good land use performance (Braverman et al., 2014).

7.2 The architecture of property diversity

Property diversity is important because it provides an institutional structure for the detection and measurement of harmful land use externalities. By contrast, as Henry Smith infers, if we see private property as an atom-counting exercise, then we are blind to any overarching structure. Its legacy is to perpetuate the piecemeal; a belief that good land use can be achieved through the novel application or recalibration of individual property tools.

The downside to atom counting is that it is *ad hoc*. It applies micro-solutions to macro-landscape problems, such that atomistic perspectives yield atomistic solutions. Paul Babie thus imagines urban landscapes re-shaped by an evolved easement for light that enables 'green roofs and green spaces', or easements of 'solar access' or 'wind power' that secure renewable energies (Babie 2012, pp.16–23). It also leaves the 'heavy lifting' to incorporeal hereditaments, while widespread interests, such as leases, lay unused or under-utilized in the property toolbox. Last, it raises issues of enforceability. Rights of amenity or aesthetics, like prospect or *jus spatiandi*, are traditionally unenforceable as easement rights, raising doubts as to the easement's environmental efficacy.[1] Similarly, covenants have long struggled to achieve proprietorial credibility; positive covenants require legislative intervention to overcome common law prohibitions,[2] while restrictive covenants must satisfy onerous tests as to the running of their benefit and burden in equity to have teeth.[3] Susan French sees 'problems of the future' frustrating conservation covenants, especially those granted in perpetuity (French 2006).[4] Another problem is a mal-adaptation of traditional common law interests to suit contemporary environmental ends. Samantha Hepburn criticizes the misuse of profits *a prendre* for the storage of sequestered carbon, noting that profits are conceptually concerned with extraction, yet the sequestration of carbon on forested land is primarily directed at long-term storage (Hepburn 2009, p.244).

An alternative solution is to craft new statutory *sui generis* rights in the place of inapt common law ones. To start from a blank slate overcomes an institutional problem: 'structural change in established property systems is not a prevailing theme. Property systems are inherently conservative, seeking continuity in their basic internal framework' (Hepburn 2009, p.240). Adrian Bradbrook agrees that it is up to the legislature to take the lead in creating new property rights,[5] citing statutory solar access rights in New Mexico as a template for developing analogous rights for on-shore wind turbines (Bradbrook 2009, p.403). He says that the pace of change required and the need for harmonization is beyond the common law's incrementalism (ibid., pp.410–11). While insightful, this debate is nonetheless stuck in the mindset of the individual property interest, be it existing or novel, common law or statutory. The emphasis remains as to how *private* property rights shape landscapes.

By contrast, Douglas Fisher looks to a bigger picture of how the law protects landscape values. Fisher concludes that 'for most purposes, the general principles of common law have proved not very effective – largely because they are linked to issues of property and land in individual ownership' (Fisher 2005, p.23). Despite property's natural predilection, the 'perception of landscape [being] inextricably linked to a range of notions of property' (ibid., p.5) results in property law proving ineffectual in protecting landscape values. Fisher attributes this to property's preoccupation with individual rights, and the disconnect this paradigm has with community values. Significantly, Fisher hints (in closing) that embracing a wider concept of property may be advantageous, citing native title or common property as emerging exemplars of property pluralism.

Fisher anticipates the potential of property diversity. As already traversed in Chapter 4, context, inter-connectivity and a faithful representation of real-life propertied landscapes are its hallmarks. This architecture of property diversity is also fundamentally the framework of an ecological view of property.[6] In 1992, Joseph Sax recognized an emerging economy of nature required different attitudes about land and its ownership (Sax 1992, pp.1445–46). In this economy, land's ultimate worth is measured by its provision of environmental services, not the artifice of its boundaries (ibid., p.1442).

Sax identifies four features of a re-defined property that serves both the needs of a transformative economy and nature's economy. First, there is less focus on individual dominion; second, more public decision-making about private land uses; third, increased ecological planning; and fourth, positive obligations to protect natural systems (ibid., p.1451). Sax also sees the usufruct as the closest model to capture an owner's revised property rights in an economy of nature, a right that does not confer exclusive dominion, but reflects the balance between an individual's right to exploit, and the community's countervailing dependence on the resource (ibid., p.1452). Sax's use-centric, inter-connected economy of nature bears a design (absent external regulation) with strong similarities to the architecture of property diversity.

The structure of property diversity also has its analogies in alternative property metaphors. While modern property is famously described as a bundle of (private) sticks, the rise of environmentalism in the 1960s and the basic ecological tenet that everything is connected to everything else (Metzger 1975, p.797), has weakened its hegemony. Its slow unravelling is symbolized by ideas such as Robert Goldstein's minimalist 'green sticks' inserted into the bundle (Goldstein 1998, p.374). Myrl Duncan likewise re-engineers the bundle with an emphasis on context and public rights in land, adding a 'public cord' to complete the bundle, symbolic of the ecological and communal bonds that connect and bind disparate private sticks (Duncan 2002, pp.804–5). By contrast, alternative metaphors reject the disaggregated bundle in favour of holistic, inter-connected conceptualizations analogous to diverse property, such as 'property puzzles' (Lehavi 2008). Tony Arnold's 'web of interests' is oft cited, featuring 'interconnections among persons, groups, and entities with an ... identifiable object at the center of the web' (Arnold 2002, p.333).[7] Water is another powerful metaphor suited to the diversity model, symbolic of 'context and relativity, accommodation and community' (Freyfogle 1988).

Henry Smith's 'modular' or 'architectural' theory is a recent and insightful addition to the catalogue of property metaphors. Smith sees property as a series of inter-connected modules, a basic architecture where the detachability of each stick-right is not the given that the bundle automatically assumes (Smith 2012, p.1700). As semi-autonomous and mostly self-contained modules, their level of interaction is less obvious. What is often seen is the intense level of interaction *within* the module, while intermodular connections are minimized in number, or concealed through interfaces that are 'information hiding and limited' (ibid., p.1703). Smith draws the analogy to a car, where independently functioning modules (such as braking systems or air-conditioning units) operate as part of an overarching architecture, but for reasons of information cost, most users need not know their level of integration. Smith says that a modular theory of property is information cost-effective in managing property's complexity. Property owners need only know the relationship of how their property rights interact with related rights, and not the full architecture, much like knowing that hitting the brake pedal will stop the car. In explaining the popularity of the bundle, Smith notes that it only provides a 'partial outlook' of the whole property structure. Modularity by contrast 'explains the structures we do not find' (ibid., p.1702).

Smith's modular theory has implications for property diversity, in depicting not only modules of 'lumpy' private property rights, but also their near-opaque links to public and common modules, structures we do not find. It also manages diversity's inherent complexity, by largely quarantining the critical need to know information within the relevant module, thereby saving information costs. But his theory is of most interest in explaining the effects, or non-effects, of externalities. It may explain why the adverse impacts of harmful land use escape notice, since the impact is absorbed or hidden within the largely self-contained module, while any extra-modular ripples almost disappear in the latent 'relatively sparse' interfaces that exist in between (ibid., p.1701).

Externalities hidden in the module are nothing compared to the atomized, universally detachable bundle of sticks that deem harmful land uses irrelevant. Joseph Singer identifies property norms arising from the 'ownership' or 'castle' models of property as responsible for making externalities disappear. Singer argues that the exercise of property rights always has impacts on others, externalities imposed 'on [those] not directly involved in a transaction or act' (Singer 2010, p.61). Where no 'legally relevant harm' is caused, such externalities are 'self-regarding' (ibid., p.63). Conversely, where the effect is adverse, it is a *harmful* externality. Importantly, a society's property norms interact with externalities by determining which acts are harmful, and which are benign. In making this judgment, they then operate to 'reveal or obscure the presence of externalities' (ibid., p.79). In castle or ownership models, property norms frequently hide harmful impacts on others, including the environment, such effects dismissed as *self-regarding* because property norms deem them so. In this way, adverse externalities 'magically vanish' (ibid.), since the prevailing property norm does not value the affected other's property rights. As traversed earlier, Singer's preference is a relational or socially situated concept of property; his 'environmental' or 'good neighbour' model, where property norms expose rather than conceal harmful externalities.

However, as we have seen in Chapter 6, the 'good neighbour' model struggles in the property monotone. Described by Thomas Merrill as the 'property strategy' (Merrill 2012), property's propensity is to divide landscapes into discrete parcels of individual ownerships. This strategy is a double-edged sword when it comes to acknowledging and measuring the impacts of externalities.

> By dividing the world into units of autonomous owner control, the property strategy creates a built-in incentive for owners to ignore aspects of their management that affect other units of autonomous owner control.
>
> (Merrill 2012, p.2089)

By contrast, the architecture of property diversity ensures that any 'built-in incentive' to ignore harmful land use is obviated. Indeed, Merrill predicts the potential of property diversity to act in this way, noting 'paradoxically, private property must be interlaced with networks of open-access or public property if it is to work effectively as a strategy for managing resources' (ibid., p.2091).

If seeing property as a bundle of sticks is only a partial outlook as Smith supposes, then seeing property as slightly connected modules of lumpy private rights is but a further extension of the vista. The architecture of property diversity is the long-range, perhaps fullest, picture, one where the inter-connections of public, private and common modules are more clearly in focus, and the implications of adverse land uses can both be seen and measured, as is appropriate in this post-bundle 'age of ecological consequence' (White 2008b, p.1).

7.3 Normative diversity

The optimal conditions for land obligation are also enhanced when a visible property mosaic yields a 'normative mosaic' commensurate to the diverse mix on the ground. As outlined in Chapter 4, property diversity inculcates multiple values across landscapes. To see the totality of the private, public and common estates is to enliven a values mosaic unique to each landscape.

This part suggests that normative diversity may be desirable for a number of reasons: first, it reflects the *truthfulness* of property patterns, 'the heterogeneity of property's real-life manifestations' (Grinlinton and Taylor 2009, p.xii). Second, it dilutes the values of property monism. Third, it has the potential to re-balance the collective values of land ownership. Discussion of the first and third rationales (essentially the architecture of *community* and how different communities manifest) is postponed to Chapter 8. This discussion will concentrate on the second rationale.

Exclusively private landscapes act in two ways: they distort the values of private property, and they marginalize or discredit any non-private value alternatives. As discussed in Chapter 1, an unrestrained private estate falsely conflates exclusivity, and as noted in Chapter 6, it promotes hard, utilitarian views of 'land as commodity', where land is seen in purely instrumental rather than ethical or personhood terms. Hanoch Dagan is critical of the values of a monistic view of property. Dagan says they fail to describe the 'lived' experience of property, the truth of people's relationships with the various institutions of property and the variable nature of the resource. His pluralistic view of property by contrast enables rights and responsibilities and promotes human values.

> Some property institutions are structured along the lines of the Blackstonian ... 'sole despotic dominion'. These institutions are atomistic and competitive. Other property institutions... are dominated by a much more communitarian view of property, in which ownership is a locus of sharing. Many other property institutions ... lie somewhere along this spectrum between atomistic and communitarian norms.
>
> (Dagan 2011, p.29)

What type of values mosaic is produced in the wake of the diverse property mosaic? Or to put the question another way, what values do different property types contribute to a whole of landscape perspective? Chapter 2 has canvassed sociability (Rose 1986) and 'pedestrian democracy' (Gray 2010) as enduring values of public property. In Chapter 3, Rose describes the norms of common property as proportionality and responsible shared use (Rose 1994). And private property has been shown to be far more multivalent than supposed: 'it is a mistake to view private property as one-dimensional, that its values embrace more than simple commodity' (Dagan 2011, pp.37–55). The end yield is a values polyglot, a hybrid mosaic where private-centric impediments to land obligation are less dominant, and overlooked communitarian and social values provide balance.

> [F]orms of property matter ... because these configurations of property rights constitute property institutions that facilitate various categories of human interaction, and thus promote important human values ... As human institutions, the forms of property should be crafted through bundling in a way that fortifies their normative desirability.
>
> (Dagan 2011, p.35)

Nor are property values static. For Dagan, pluralism means ongoing evaluation of the institutions of property in terms of their values and 'continued validity and desirability' (ibid.). Such a fluid approach 'is ... an exercise in legal optimism, an attempt to explain and develop the existing property forms in a way that accentuates their normative desirability while remaining attuned to their social context' (ibid., p.31). Like the reiterative effect of varied stewardship performances (to be discussed next), normative diversity has the potential to unfreeze the dominant values of the ownership model, and to allow others in.

7.4 A performance theory of stewardship

As outlined in Chapter 4, performance theory requires *doing* to create the related effect of reality. Hence, the 'reality' of stewardship depends on its repeated acts and representations. In other words, stewardship is not a pre-existing concept, but an effect constructed through constant practice. This deceptively simple idea is powerful because it is the antithesis of abstraction.

Performance theory applied to property diversity provides real world examples of public, private and community acts of stewardship across a plurality of fora. It intensifies the quantum of stewardship performance, and widens the class of steward-actors. Optimistically, it shifts stewardship from isolated one-off acts of altruism, to collective acts of land use that are universalizing and normalizing by their frequency and spread. Its most critical effect may lie in its unfreezing of property abstraction. Blomley's use of performance theory to describe the private ownership model of property, is arguably analogous to using performativity to describe stewardship.

To misquote Blomley,[8]

> If [stewardship] is a form of 'frozen politics', an emphasis upon the *performance* of [stewardship] perhaps begins to offer us some tools for an unfreezing to the extent that it alerts us that [stewardship] is iteratively produced in concrete social contexts, not found.
>
> (Blomley 2004, p.31)

Doing acts of good land use in concrete social contexts may be the simple tool that shifts focus. It may unfreeze our thinking about land stewardship, away from intellectual dilemmas such as linking duty with right, the discourse of subject–object, or other imponderables. Stewardship simply *is* because it is *done*. When performed in diverse property settings, its doing is multiplied and accentuated by its differences.

Performance theory also requires successful repetition. Similar acts build, precedent-like, on what has been performed before, providing templates for future acts. This *stare decisis* effect of performance is called *citational*. The past acts that a present act must cite to demonstrate validity, and thereby compel future performances, have to be 'more or less successful'. By contrast, citational failures are 'less likely to have performative effect' (Blomley 2013, p.36). In stewardship literature, piecemeal accounts of failure are numerous. There may be insufficient public ownership of critical conservation lands (Karkkaninen 1997), over-reliance on financial carrots such as incentives or grants (Elmendorf 2003; Gunningham and Young 1997), unsustainable retreats into national park ghettos (Farrier 1995), or dysfunction outside small homogenous groups (Caldwell 1974). Narratives of anecdotal failure are intended as lessons to avoid past mistakes, but their unintended consequence may be a debilitating precedent of citational failure, a concretized relational effect where stewardship is not a reality.

Nor is citation enough. Performances must also be *reiterative* to make property, 'sustained, repetitive ... often complicated work' (Blomley 2013, p.37). Endlessly repeated performances are its precondition and means for continuance. Reiteration means that stewardship must be mundane and engrained, not exceptional. Reiteration is a concept familiar to the common law of property. The truism that landowners cannot sleep on their rights is a warning that owners must continuously signal explicit indicia of possession, asserting their dominion through tangible acts, lest the law reward adverse trespassers with title. Indeed, sufficient *doing* may be emblematic of property doctrine, as Oliver Wendell Holmes remarked '[t]he life of the common law has not been logic; it has been experience' (cited in Goldstein 1998; also Frazier 1995). Like Carol Rose's constant yelling of 'this is mine' (Rose 1985), stewardship requires consistent, unequivocal performance.

Last, effective citation and constant reiteration requires context, what Blomley terms *assemblage*; the physical and human entities that actualize the performance and connect it to the world (Blomley 2013, p.39).[9] Importantly, stewardship performance cannot occur in the abstract, go-anywhere 'assemblages' we unthinkingly call Blackacre.

7.4.1 Performative diversity: two micro-examples of stewardship performance

Performances of stewardship frequently involve public, community and private actors collaborating across property boundaries. Similar to the happy coincidence of sustainable communities and property diversity depicted in Chapter 5, 'connective conservation' efforts speak of an intuitive link between property diversity and stewardship.[10] Sue Farran notes this serendipitous convergence with her observations of a contemporary phenomenon in England she calls an 'extraordinary return to the land' (Farran 2013). She writes of people 'coming together to cultivate land and grow things' (ibid., p.173) amidst a growing momentum of urban land stewardship. These performances occur in diverse spaces; community gardens and orchards, resurgent allotments, city farms and guerrilla gardening plots. Farran asks what this movement means for contemporary property, and concludes that many of these ventures occur outside traditional frameworks, novel arrangements such as 'crop shares and tree leases in community orchards, raised-bed leasing in the community backyards of tenement buildings, land sharing, community farm shares and local food coalitions' (ibid., p.188). These diverse tenures, in turn, are located across a diversity of property type, involving 'hybrid public/private relationships' and engagements 'distinct from and not dependent on ownership' (ibid., pp.175, 189).

This extraordinary return to the land can be measured by performance theory. If, as Blomley argues, real property is enacted by performances such as building fences, trimming hedges, writing law review articles or registering titles (Blomley 2013, p.33), equally, stewardship is enacted by Farran's guerrilla gardening, community orchard planting, or allotment farming. Performance theory across the diversity of property is best articulated by concrete examples of sustained and citational labour. This section concludes by examining two place-based micro-studies of good land use. The first typifies conservation efforts in the rangelands of America's West and is the subject of scholarly scrutiny. The other is a simpler, local landcare narrative set in regional Australia. Each enacts cross-boundary stewardship.

Recent land use conflicts in the American West have centred on the clash between commodity and non-commodity uses of publicly owned rangelands, specifically grazing and recreation (White 2008b, pp.1–3). Over-grazing has been blamed for land degradation, soil erosion and damage to riparian systems since the 1880s (Dana and Fairfax 1980). Environmentalists want cattle removed from the public domain (Ferguson and Ferguson 1983; Wald et al. 1991). Cattle advocates respond that recreation is itself a form of consumptive use. On surrounding private lands, urban growth has fed sprawl and the loss of open space. A collaborative model of land use management has been one response to the polarities of this land use debate.

> [P]eople from varied backgrounds have been seeking ways to depolarize environmental issues, reintegrate conservation, and build a

> new consensus for action. The common denominator is a commitment to land health on the part of individuals, neighborhoods, organizations, tribes, agencies and businesses, and a desire to achieve tangible results, whether on private, public, or community lands. These trends suggest the possibility of an emerging 'cross-landscape' constituency that can address the harmful feedback loops that encourage continued degradation of urban, suburban, exurban, rural, and wild lands alike.
>
> (Meine 2004, p.61)

The Malpai Borderlands Group in New Mexico and Arizona is representative of this trend: a cross landscape partnership of private owners that act in concert with public agencies to sustainably co-manage the Malpai natural resource region (Rose 1998, p.178; Keiter 2005, p.1175). The Malpai comprises 'more than a million acres of desert grasslands and broken mountains' (Elmendorf 2003, p.482); a mix of private and public lands, the latter including wildlife refuges and public domain leased under grazing permits. The Malpai Borderlands Group (MPG) is a not-for-profit community organization formed in 1994, consisting primarily of local ranchers. The region's centrepiece is Gray Ranch, a 'biologically rich 322,000 acre' property, considered 'one of the most significant ecological landscapes ... in private ownership' (White 2008a, p.121). Because of its unique ecological values, The Nature Conservancy purchased the ranch in 1990 (Brewer 2003, pp.185–215). Its aim was to transfer the holding to federal ownership as a wildlife refuge, but protests at the loss of a 'tax-paying, cowboy hiring' ranch (White 2008a, p.121) forced a change in strategy. A charitable foundation was formed to purchase the ranch as conservation buyer and working ranch operator.[11] Under new ownership, the Gray Ranch pioneered the concept of 'grassbanks', where rights to graze on its rich grasslands were sold to neighbouring ranchers in return for open space conservation easements,[12] the remediation of exhausted grazing lands and publicly funded conservation programs.[13] The MPG owns the conservation easements in its capacity as a land trust.[14] The easements protect 75,000 acres of private land as 'natural wildlife habitat and productive ranch land by preventing subdivision and development'.[15] What had once been a contentious landscape 'transformed quickly into a model of collaboration and conservation' (White 2008a, p.122), 'a land of intersecting groups' (Elmendorf 2003, p.483).

The second example is a micro-urban one in the ecological tradition of localism, historicized by Gilbert White and Henry David Thoreau.[16] Indeed, Nicole Graham describes adaptation to a new property paradigm as a 'process of becoming local' (Graham 2010, p.205). For over 20 years, the Wilson River Landcare Group (WRLG) rehabilitated the riparian zone adjoining the Wilson River in Lismore, Australia, turning a degraded area of debris from 'past floods, car tyres, old fridges, plastic bags, and cow carcasses' into a riverbank gallery rainforest on both sides of the river. The volunteer WLRG was formed in 1993 and initially commenced reforestation works on private lands to the north and south of urban areas. The group's heartland is now a series of re-vegetated public parklands adjoining the river and private flood prone land. WRLG's networks extend to Aboriginal, community and private landowners, as well as councils and schools. Apart from restoration of the native rainforest, the group has removed weeds, stabilized eroded riverbanks and improved water quality. Ultimately, the group 'plant[s] out of love for our amazing river', hoping their performative example in urban Lismore, is replicated by landholders upstream (Dell 2012).[17]

These vignettes affirm Joseph Sax's prediction that an economy of nature reduces the significance of property lines (1992). Stewards tend to look less at the artifice of demarcation, and more at the land in between and across the lines. They see nature as an unfragmented whole – in WRLG's case 'a globally significant biodiversity hotspot' (Dell 2012) – not 'distinct parcels of land and discrete natural resources valued piece by piece' (Freyfogle 2007, p.13). And it matters less whether the 'landowners' are private entities, public agencies, or a community group. From the steward's perspective, Joseph Singer's castle is less plausible. This is an insight into a 'different way of thinking about what ownership entails' (Sax 2011, p.9).

The performances of stewardship gleaned from these two examples are as diverse as Blomley's various acts of real property: re-planting rainforest trees, cleaning flood debris, swimming in clear rivers, lighting cool fires, negotiating conservation easements, preserving rural ways of life, or trading grassbank-grazing offsets. Blomley's notion of performativity directs us to the important question: what sort of property in land do we wish to see performed? Is it one fixated on individual property rights absent context, or one where many diverse rights and obligation sit together? These performances, by diverse owners across the boundaries of property type, suggest by their repetitive and successful doing that stewardship is a vibrant concept intimately connected to the diversity of our many relationships with land.

7.5 Conclusion

Chapter 6 argues that the private ownership model impedes the generation of obligation as a corollary of property right in land. By contrast, this chapter describes how property diversity yields a vista where private, public and community performances of good land use occur *in situ*, where a conceptual framework measures the impact of land uses, and an array of property values dilute one-sided norms that otherwise make harmful externalities 'magically vanish'.

Atomistic conceptions of property in land make it 'hard to spot and appreciate the connections when all we see are the pieces' (Freyfogle 2007, pp.30–31). In contrast to this singular vision, property diversity shifts landed patterns away from compartmentalized artifice to holistic interconnectedness; a re-sighting of property in land where generating obligation alongside right somehow seems less 'awkward.'

Notes

1 An easement will not be propertized if it does not accommodate the dominant tenement or form the subject matter of a grant.
2 Rule in *Austerberry v. Oldham Corporation* (1885) 29 Ch D 750.
3 In Queensland, covenants cannot be registered in the Torrens register, and are effectively unenforceable, s 98A Land Title Act 1994 (Qld).
4 These include that the conservation goals that covenants protect may become obsolete, useless or even harmful, or that development pressures will become too intense for private land trusts to resist (French 2006).
5 The role of the common law is a 'subsidiary' only (Bradbrook 2009, p.411).
6 Smith says that the architectural approach can do better than the bundle (Smith 2012, p.1692).
7 The 'web' metaphor aligns with two environmental principles, the interconnectedness of people and their physical environment, and the importance of the unique characteristics of each object (Arnold 2002). Kristen Carpenter et al. concur that the bundle is inapt in its depiction of stewardship (Carpenter, Katyal and Riley 2009).
8 The 'misquote' substitutes 'stewardship' for the words 'the ownership model of property'.
9 During enclosure, hedges used to divide and enclose were the 'assemblage' that created a new property discourse around law and space (Blomley 2008).
10 The term 'connective conservation' is used in the Gondwana Link project that aims to create a corridor of 1000km in Western Australia's southwest. Administered by not-for-profit company (Gondwana Link Ltd), the project links public agencies with private landowners and community organizations, such as Greening Australia, Bush Heritage and local friends groups. It uses combinations of outright purchase and conservation covenants in conjunction with public reserves and national parks to secure the corridor. See www.gondwanalink.org/index.aspx
11 The charitable trust established to purchase Gray Ranch is also a member of the Malpai Borderlands Group Inc.
12 The conservation easements are vested in the not-for-profit Malpai Borderlands Group, and preclude subdivision and urban development.
13 Such as 'cool fire' burning that encourages native vegetative cover, or restoration of native grassland and savanna habitat. See www.malpaiborderlandsgroup.org/about.asp
14 Land trusts are often described in a physicalized way. 'Land trust projects are place-based, connected to a piece of the Earth rather than being abstract or abstruse ... If we set up a new preserve, we can hike it, bird it, hug the trees, and wade in the water' (Brewer 2003, p.12).
15 www.malpaiborderlandsgroup.org/about.asp.
16 Worster attributes much of the intellectual force of modern ecological thinking to White who lived in the eighteenth-century village of Selborne,

Hampshire, and to Thoreau, who lived in nineteenth-century Concord village, Massachusetts (Worster 1994).

17 Early explorers chronicled that 'the river was narrower before they took the trees away and the water was clear, they could see to the bottom.' Vines and treetops crowded out the sky (Dell 2012, pp.6–7).

References

Arnold, C A 2002, 'The Reconstitution of Property: Property as a Web of Interests', *Harvard Environmental Law Rev.*, vol. 26, 281–364.

Babie, P 2012, 'How Property Law Shapes Our Landscapes', *Monash University Law Rev.*, vol. 38, 1–24.

Blomley, N 2004, *Unsettling the City: Urban Land and the Politics of Property*, Routledge, New York.

Blomley, N 2008, 'Enclosure, Common Right and the Property of the Poor', *Social and Legal Studies*, vol. 17, 311–331.

Blomley, N 2013, 'Performing Property: Making the World', *Canadian Journal of Law and Jurisprudence*, vol. 26, no. 1, 23–48.

Bradbrook, A 2009, 'The Role of the Common Law in Promoting Sustainable Energy Development in the Property Sector', in A McHarg, B Barton, A Bradbrook and L Godden (eds), *Property and the Law in Energy and Natural Resources*, Oxford University Press, Oxford.

Braverman, I, Blomley, N, Delaney, D and Kedar, A 2014, 'Expanding the Spaces of Law' in I Braverman, N Blomley, D Delaney and A Kedar (eds), *The Expanding Spaces of Law: A Timely Legal Geography*, Stanford University Press, Stanford, CA.

Brewer, R 2003, *Conservancy: The Land Trust Movement in America*, University Press of New England, Hanover, NH.

Caldwell, L 1974, 'Rights of Ownership or Rights of Use? The Need for a New Conceptual Basis for Land Use Policy', *Wm. & Mary LR*, vol.15, 759–75.

Carpenter, K, Katyal, S and Riley, A 2009, 'In Defense of Property', *Yale LJ*, vol. 118, 1022–125.

Dagan, H 2011, *Property, Values and Institutions*, Oxford University Press, New York.

Dana, S T and Fairfax, S 1980, *Forest and Range Policy: Its Development in the United States*, McGraw Hill, New York.

Dell, J 2012, 'Planting Seeds of Regeneration' *Northern Rivers Echo* (Lismore) 24 May.

Duncan, M 2002, 'Reconceiving the Bundle of Sticks: Land as a Community-Based Resource', *Envtl. Law*, vol. 32, 773–807.

Elmendorf, C 2003, 'Ideas, Incentives, Gifts, and Governance: Toward Conservation Stewardship of Private Land, in Cultural and Psychological Perspective', *U. Ill. L. Rev.*, vol. 2003, no. 2, 423–505.

Farran, S 2013, 'Earth Under the Nails: The Extraordinary Return to the Land', in N Hopkins (ed.), *Modern Studies in Property Law*, Hart Publishing, Oxford.

Farrier, D 1995, 'Conserving Biodiversity on Private Land: Incentives for Management or Compensation for Lost Expectations?', *Harv. Envtl. L. Rev.*, vol. 19, 303–408.

Ferguson, D and Ferguson, N 1983, *Sacred Cows at the Public Trough*, Maverick Publications, Bend, OR.

Fisher, D 2005, 'Can the Law Protect Landscape Values?', *NZ. J. Envtl. Law*, vol. 9, 1–49.

Frazier, T 1995, 'The Green Alternative to Classical Liberal Property Theory', *Vt. L. Rev.*, vol. 20, 299–371.

French, S 2006, 'Perpetual Trusts, Conservation Servitudes, and the Problem of the Future', *Cardozo Law Rev.*, vol. 27, 2523–33.

Freyfogle, E 1988, 'Context and Accommodation in Modern Property Law', *Stanford L. Rev.*, vol. 41, 1529–1556.

Freyfogle, E 1998, 'Bounded People, Boundless Land', in R Knight and P Landres (eds), *Stewardship Across Boundaries*, Island Press, Washington, DC.

Freyfogle, E 2007, *Agrarianism and the Good Society: Land, Culture, Conflict and Hope*, University of Kentucky Press, Lexington.

Goldstein, R 1998, 'Green Wood in the Bundle of Sticks: Fitting Environmental Ethics and Ecology into Real Property Law', *B.C. Envtl. Aff. L. Rev.*, vol. 25, 347–430.

Graham, N 2010, *Lawscape: Property, Environment, Law*, Routledge, Abingdon.

Gray, K 2010, 'Pedestrian Democracy and the Geography of Hope', *Journal of Human Rights and the Environment*, vol. 1, 45–65.

Grinlinton, D 1996, 'Property Rights and the Environment', *Australian Property Law Journal*, vol. 4, 1–62.

Grinlinton, D and Taylor, P 2009, 'Property Rights and Sustainability: Toward a New Vision of Property', in *Property Rights and Sustainability: The Evolution of Property Rights to Meet Ecological Challenges*, Martinus Nijhoff, Leiden.

Gunningham, N and Young, M 1997, 'Toward Optimal Environmental Policy: The Case of Biodiversity Conservation', *Ecology LQ*, vol. 24, 243–98.

Hepburn, S 2009, 'Carbon Rights as New Property: The Benefits of Statutory Verification', *Sydney Law Review*, vol. 31, no. 2, 239–71.

Karkkainen, B 1997, 'Biodiversity and Land', *Cornell L. Rev.*, vol. 83, 1–104.

Keiter, R 2005, 'Public Lands and Law Reform: Putting Theory, Policy and Practice in Perspective', *Utah L. R.*, vol. 4, 1127–226.

Lehavi, A 2008, 'The Property Puzzle', *Georgetown Law Rev.*, vol. 96, 1987–2028.

Meine, C 2004, *Correction Lines Essays on Land, Leopold, and Conservation*, Island Press, Washington, DC.

Merrill, T W 2012, 'The Property Strategy', *Uni. Pa. Law Rev.*, vol. 160, 2061–95.

Metzger, M 1975, 'Private Property and Environmental Sanity', *Ecology LQ*, vol. 5, 793–819.

Rose, C M 1985, 'Possession as the Origin of Property', *Univ. Chicago Law Rev.*, vol. 52, no. 1, 73–88.

Rose, C M 1986, 'The Comedy of the Commons: Custom, Commerce, and Inherently Public Property', *Univ. Chicago Law Rev.*, vol. 53, no. 3, 711–81.

Rose, C M 1994, 'Given-ness and Gift: Property and the Quest for Environmental Ethics', *Envtl. Law*, vol. 24, 1–31.

Rose, C M 1998, 'The Several Futures of Property: Of Cyberspace and Folk Tales, Emission Trades and Ecosystems', *Minn. L. Rev.*, vol. 83, 129–182.

Sax, J 1992, 'Property Rights and the Economy of Nature: Understanding *Lucas v. South Carolina Coastal Council*', *Stan. L. Rev.*, vol. 45, 1433–55.

Sax, J 2011, *Ownership, Property and Sustainability*, University of Utah Press, Salt Lake City.

Singer, J 2009, 'Democratic Estates: Property Law in a Free and Democratic Society', *Cornell Law Rev.*, vol. 94, 1009–62.

Singer, J 2010, 'Property Norms Construct the Externalities of Ownership', in G Alexander and E Penalver (eds), *Property and Community*, Oxford University Press, New York.

Smith, H 2012, 'Property as the Law of Things', *Harvard Law Rev.*, vol. 125, 1691–726.

Thomas, N 2011, 'Maori Concepts of Ranga tiratanga, Kaitiakitanga, the Environment, and Property Rights', in D Grinlinton and P Taylor (eds), *Property Rights and Sustainability: The Evolution of Property Rights to Meet Ecological Challenges*, Brill-Nijhoff, Leiden.

Wald, J et al. 1991, *How Not to be Cowed*, Natural Resources Defense Council, Washington, DC.

White, C 2008a, *Revolution on the Range: The Rise of the New Ranch in the American West*, Island Press, Washington, DC.

White, C 2008b, 'Conservation in the Age of Consequences', *Nat. Res. J.*, vol. 48, 1–13.

Worster, D 1994, *Nature's Economy: A History of Ecological Ideas*, Cambridge University Press, Cambridge.

Chapter 8

Community and the implications of property diversity

8.1 Introduction

In 1984, Joseph Sax identified community as the missing blank in American law. 'The notion of community entitlement is virtually empty space in the legal constellation ... there isn't even an accepted or commonplace legal definition of community' (Sax 1984b, p.1). Twenty-six years later, despite intermittent filling of that space, Sax sees little change, noting that 'almost every conception of land in modern times has ignored community values' (Sax 2011, p.13). Sax's observations highlight the dilemma of reconciling community and property in land, a challenge with existential and normative implications.[1] This chapter examines the marginalized links between property and community, a subject matter 'left unexplored' within property scholarship (Alexander and Penalver 2010, p.xxxiii), and asks whether property diversity may present some answers to that dilemma. For, as Sax also says '[d]iversity is a good thing, in human settlements as well as nature. Or, to put it another way, eclecticism is not a bad thing' (Sax 1984a, p.509).

Section 2 commences by exploring definitions of the term 'community' within property and geography scholarship. Section 3 then outlines legal theories that variously 'explain and evaluate the interaction between property and community' (Alexander and Penalver 2010, p.xxxiii). Other disciplinary insights into this relationship, principally the work of legal geographer Nicholas Blomley, form the basis of section 4. Section 5 is the concluding cornerstone of this chapter; it analyzes the reasons why property, in particular property diversity, is relevant to community. It argues that property and community are closely linked, however much their intimacy is obscured by a liberal polarity focused on either the state or the private individual. Curiously, this binary paradigm does not reflect the propertied truth of our human landscapes. By contrast, property diversity better approximates the communities in which we live. It 'unsettles' dominant assumptions of private uniformity (Blomley 2004), enlivens Joseph Sax's eclectic, and connects people to community. It fulfills the promise envisaged by Eduardo Penalver, whereby property becomes an *entrance* to, rather than *exit* from, community (Penalver 2005).

8.2 What is 'community'?

'Community' is a contested term that is 'maddeningly ambiguous' (Alexander and Penalver 2010, p.xxix), a 'fluid, often elusive concept' (Lehavi 2004, p.45). While it is no longer as empty a legal space as Sax described in 1984, it remains uncomfortable territory for property scholars. This section is a chronological and inter-disciplinary journey, examining in turn property and geography scholarship to describe the complex meanings of community.

8.2.1 Community in property scholarship

Sax's innovative study of the fate of several farming villages in an Arkansas national park was a 'provocative point of beginning for thinking about the substance of community interests' (Sax 1984a, p.503). Sax chose to define community as an aggregate of attributes. Using these villages as exemplars, Sax identifies 'distinctiveness, stability, a strong association of people with the landscape, [and the] maintenance of traditions' (ibid., p.503) to inform the meaning of community. Sax in particular emphasizes two factors, *distinctiveness* and *authenticity*. *Distinctiveness* is shaped by a community's idiosyncratic attributes, aspects of the local economy, its architecture, residents' lifestyles, links to the land, and so on. (ibid., p.509). *Authenticity* is an innate and subjectively intuitive quality, the 'genius of a place' that gives locations vitality. Humanist geographers such as Edward Relph write of the importance and increasing disappearance of authenticity of place (cited in Cresswell 2004). Authenticity is an organic measure, an amorphous quality generated from within, as contrasted to the confected indicia of 'community' imposed from without.[2]

Few directly took up Sax's provocative invitation. In the ensuing years, there was a widespread perception that 'scholarly attempts to define and conceptualize "community"' was futile' (Lehavi 2004, p.46). Certain scholarship focused on the dynamics of community norms, thereby defining community obliquely in terms of its normative effects. Robert Ellickson (1991) viewed community through the prism of a small, homogeneous group of ranchers in rural Shasta County, California, and the powerful effect of their insider norms maintaining a communal 'order without law'. Ellickson observes that norms lose potency when strangers intervene, or the community becomes diffuse or heterogeneous (also Engel 1994, pp.51–52). Implicit in this oblique perspective on community is an 'us and them' logic, what Alexander and Penalver call the 'insider/outsider dilemma', the necessity by implication to exclude outsiders in the process of constituting and defining a community (Alexander and Penalver 2010, pp.xxix–xxx). Hanoch Dagan similarly recognizes that 'some measure of practical or symbolic exclusion' is necessary to define communities, their 'demarcation from the broader society' (Dagan 2013, p.286). Such logic has positive and negative impacts, inclusive for those within the group, but alienating for those without. The negative consequences of exclusion are discussed later.

For the remainder of the twentieth century, property scholars continued to struggle with community. In 1992, Stephen Gardbaum's study of law, politics, and the claims of community, studiously avoided property (Gardbaum 1992). Two years later, Richard Ford claimed that defining community was an exercise in tautology, that there was 'no self-conscious legal conception of political space' (Ford 1994, pp.1857–60). Ford attributed the irrelevance of the 'development, population and demarcation' of decentralized space to a binary liberal worldview that analogized community as either 'the product of aggregated individual choices or the administratively necessary segmentation of centralized governmental power' (ibid., p.1857).

In the twenty-first century, a shift occurred, particularly with the emergence of progressive property theorists who argued that this binary view failed to account for property's truth. In 2009, Gregory Alexander, Eduardo Penalver, Laura Underkuffler and Joseph Singer summarized this evolving approach in a five-point 'Statement of Progressive Property'. In a significant departure from orthodoxy, this 'pluralistic and incommensurable' conception of property places community as a key pillar. Their fifth point states in part:

> Property enables and shapes community life. Property law can render relationships within communities either exploitative and humiliating or liberating and ennobling.
>
> (Alexander et al. 2009, p.744)

Progressive theorists reject the view that community is simply an agglomeration of individuals (Alexander and Penalver 2012, p.129). Rather, it is a discrete and 'intentionally capacious' concept. Alexander sees community as primarily social, a 'mediating vehicle' through which humans become socialized (Alexander 2009, p.766). Community has multiple forms that shatter the binary view. It is rarely unitary, but a complex network of communities so inter-twined that they 'cannot be fully separated' (ibid., p.767). Progressive theorists are also insistent in their rejection of the liberal view that individuals are free to voluntarily exit community. While communities are groups we may join, usually membership is involuntary; they are groups we find ourselves in. Involuntariness is important to progressive theory, individual property owners rarely exit community effortlessly either because of coercive communal norms, or high exit costs. Property binds people to community irrespective of individual choice (Penalver 2005, p.1972). Liberal exit without consequence is its antithesis.

Amnon Lehavi has advanced our recent understandings of property and community. While sympathetic to progressive theory, Lehavi rejects its broad understandings of community as 'vague, [and] over-inclusive' (Lehavi 2009, p.76). Instead, he devises three categories of community: intentional, planned and spontaneous. Intentional communities typically comprise groups with shared ideologies, values or beliefs distinctive from the mainstream.[3] Importantly, intentional communities do not arise because property structures make them easier or economically feasible. By contrast, planned communities are often greenfield residential communities, where there is little common interest between putative members, and property structures facilitate ease of incorporation and ongoing enforcement of community rules.[4] Spontaneous communities arise from existing established groupings, what Lehavi calls 'groups of physically-adjacent residents who live in "regular" neighborhoods [who] cooperate and coordinate over time, and in the process create a meaningful, enduring basis for localized communality' (ibid., p.59). Lehavi cites communities that arise to protect public spaces under threat ('friends of' groups) as an example of this third category. Lehavi's taxonomy is designed to better analyse the connections between community and property. For example, while property rules provide significant 'tailwind' for planned communities, they may be neutral for intentional communities, and offer disadvantageous 'headwinds' for spontaneous communities (ibid., pp.65–75). Property may ultimately create, maintain or undermine community (cf. Brown 2008, p.335).

8.2.2 Community in geography scholarship

The comparative insight of geographers into the question of what is 'place' is a useful counterpoint to property scholarship. But like community, place for geographers is a 'slippery concept' (Blomley 1994, p.112). Overwhelmingly, place is defined by its human meanings. It possesses two aspects, its material and visual forms, and its 'relationship to humans … the human capacity to produce and consume meaning' (Cresswell 2004, p.10). Place without human meaning is simply *space*, mere physical location subsidiary to intangible social investments. Relph gives examples of these human meanings: 'visuality, the sense of community that place engenders, the sense of time involved in establishing attachment to place, and the value of rootedness' (cited in Cresswell 2004, p.22). Penny English speaks of locales where 'people's life histories are threaded' (cited in Cresswell 2004, pp.465–66). Yi-Fu Tuan likens place to a 'calm center of established values', 'enclosed and humanized' compared to the freedom and openness of space (Tuan 1977, pp.54, 183–84).

Nicholas Blomley's *Law, Space, and the Geographies of Power* is a ground-breaking work in the emerging discipline of legal geography, the study of the links between law and geography.[5] Blomley unpacks place into *location, locales,* and *sense of place.*

> *Location* refers to the relative position of any place in relation to other places. *Locale* conversely treats the place from within as a specific site in which social relations are bounded and locally constituted. *Sense of place* refers to the experiential and representational map constructed of a specific place by its occupants.
>
> (Blomley 1994, p.112)

Location defines a community externally (vis-à-vis other communities), while *locale* defines it internally, as a physicalized, identifiable place invested with individual and collective meaning for its members. Its social aspects or *sense of place* describe the diverse relationships, connections, and norms that are necessarily intangible and aspatial. Sense of place is critical to understanding the fullness of community, that 'territorially based groups of people share some ... common denominator beyond mere proximity' (Lehavi 2004), 'shared values, participation in a shared way of life, identification with the group, mutual recognition' (Mason 2000, pp.19–25), or a strong connection to a particular locality that enables it to become a 'site of social solidarity' (Margalit 2009, p.223).[6]

Social commentator James Howard Kunstler sees community in similar spatial and aspatial terms. '[Community] is a living organism based on a web of interdependencies ... a local economy. It expresses itself physically as connectedness, as buildings actively relating to one another, and to whatever public space exists, be it the street, the courthouse square, or the village green' (Kunstler 1993, pp.185–86). Interestingly, Kunstler observes the significance of property to community, in particular the interaction of private and public lands.

8.2.3 Community is exclusionary

In defining community, it is cautionary not to overlook its negatives. Blomley warns that 'we should not over-romanticise or essentialise the local community. Small towns and villages can be stifling or oppressive places' (Blomley 2002, p.220). Similarly, Amnon Lehavi identifies 'animosity, xenophobia and intolerance' (Lehavi 2009, p.47) as adverse communitarian characteristics. This inherently exclusionary nature of community informs its brutal side, an unpleasant consequence of an existential imperative to keep outsiders out. For Jeremy Waldron, the term 'Inclusive community' is an oxymoron.

> 'True community' in the sense of 'actually-existing community' – a real entity actually structured by a communitarian – is not always as nice as it looks. Actually existing communities are often exclusionary and inauthentic.
>
> (Waldron 2009, p.189)

This chapter restricts itself to territorial communities, physically bounded *locations* and *locales*. This interpretation ignores the phenomenon of non-territorial communities (Cresswell 2004, p.68). It does so because the interaction between property in land and community is its primary analytical focus.[7] Its analogizing of place and community is likewise a useful contrivance in drawing on the legitimate cross-disciplinary overlap of property and legal geography scholarship. Each shares in common a concept of community that is bounded spatially but boundless socially (Gibson-Graham 2005, p.16).

In sum, community is a capacious and complex concept that modern property struggles to define or explain. In seeking answers to this conundrum, section 3 examines property's theoretical treatment of community.

8.3 Legal theories of property and community

As section 2 intimates, the notion of community is not a mainstream concern of modern property scholarship. That it is largely 'unexplored' is chiefly attributed to a dominant paradigm at worst hostile, or at best indifferent, to the interposition of a decentralized entity between the autonomous individual and the centralized state. Recent scholarship that links community and property reflects a fraying of that central logic (for example, Davies 2007 pp.115–38).

The consequences of community's marginalization are existential and normative. Community's existential dilemma has negative implications for its self-definition as a legal concept. It also has implications for its rights status and legal standing, whether interpreted narrowly as the discrete rights of a specific community, or more broadly as collective rights asserted by individuals who group-identify as community. Community's normative dilemma is in part a corollary of its existential one. Yet, as Alexander and Penalver observe, irrespective of legal status, 'community has a moral status that is distinct from those of neighboring owners or nonowning individuals' (Penalver 2010, p.xviii).

This part examines those legal theories and theorists that seek to explain (or not) the interaction of community and property. It situates them on a continuum, represented at one extreme by a view that community does not exist, rendering any interaction with property impossible, and at the other, by a view that community and property are intimately intertwined. At some indeterminate point on this spectrum, community also shifts from being an entity external to property, to an entity so immersed within the institution that it is no longer extricable. Identifying that moment of crossover is difficult given its opacity and deep implication.

8.3.1 The liberal perspective

For some neo-liberals, community as an entity does not exist. As Robert Nozick argues, '[t]here are only individual people, different individual people, with their own individual lives ... nothing more' (cited in Waldron 2009, p.168). This ideological hostility to community reflects its failure to fit 'neatly into liberal theory which sought to allocate all aspects of social life [including property] to one of the poles of its dualities ... either to the sphere of the state or to ... the free interaction of individuals within civil society' (Frug 1980, p.1076). To the extent that community is seen at all, it is viewed with deep suspicion in its capacity as an outlier agency of the regulatory state.

Yet the liberal paradigm is not a monolith. Some liberal theories acknowledge a conception of community, albeit as a mere or inadvertent consequence of individual choice, personal preference, or welfare maximization. This pale version of community is both a by-product and backdrop to rational actors voluntarily entering into, or exiting out of, associations of individuals. Importantly under this view, community is not an end in itself, but has value 'only to the extent that [it] conform[s] to the individual-state dualism' (Blomley 2004, p.77).

Alexander and Penalver identify *utilitarianism* and *contractarianism* as liberal theories with limited community resonance. Under utilitarian theory, the satisfaction of individual preference is the ultimate end. Any '[u]tilitarian analysis of community is refracted through this maximizing lens' (Alexander and Penalver 2010, p.xviii). The result is that community is instrumental; its value lies only in the extent to which it contributes to the satisfaction of an individual's preferences. Critical is a freedom to enter and exit communities at will, since individuals know best what satisfies their individual preferences, and as such, must be free to choose the communities into which they will enter or leave (Ellickson 1982). Such freedom transforms the individual-community relationship into a competitive one, where individuals move between communities, 'voting with their feet' (Alexander and Penalver 2010, pp.xix–xx).[8] Utilitarian community is thus an unrestricted, market-driven exercise, where a few communities become desired winners, and many others, losers. Eduardo Penalver describes the relationship of property to community in this model as one of 'property as exit', an inalienable freedom of self-sufficient individuals to enter and exit community without constraint or consequence. Exit eviscerates community in that it weakens its ability to demand the carrying out of 'unpleasant tasks or [to] maintain internal disciple,' simply because individuals 'hold all the cards' (Penalver 2005, p.1955). Community under the exit paradigm is optional, and is viewed with constant suspicion as a lurking threat to individual liberty (ibid., p.1900).

The liberal contractarian conception of community is thicker in that it takes 'the idea of belonging in a community seriously' (Alexander 2009, p.758). Its 'thickness' derives from its longer-term mutual reciprocity, and a rejection of a monistic view of property. Under contractarianism, individuals agree to enter into communities, sometimes by overt choice, but more typically, as a matter of implicit bargain to 'pursue some shared end' (ibid., pp.759–60). In so choosing to associate as a community, there is often a happy overlap of common and individual goods, although the latter remains paramount.

This primacy is seen in the tenet that an individual is never expected to make an uncompensated sacrifice for the community, since to sacrifice is to controvert personal autonomy, to be self-effacing (Dagan 2003; Alexander and Dagan 2012). However, the compensation need not be immediate, it may be repaid over the longer term. Dagan views the social responsibility of property ownership as one of 'long-term reciprocity', not one of 'utopian noncommodification' (Dagan 2007, p.1266). 'Long term reciprocity urges us to adhere to our plural and ambivalent understandings of membership [of community] as both a source of mutual advantage and a locus of belonging' (Dagan 1999, p.773). Dagan believes that long-term reciprocity is most sustained in smaller local communities, where 'our status as landowners also defines our membership' (ibid., p.774). Dagan's 'socially responsible ownership' is further along the continuum because it recognizes the longer-term nature of individual 'investments' in community, and because it strives to socialize an erstwhile liberal preoccupation with autonomous individualism. Importantly, it also sees the links between land ownership and community, and that a monistic view of property yields an incomplete and unsatisfactory account of community.

> Essentializing property as an exclusive right expresses and reinforces a culture of alienation that underplays the significance of belonging to a community, and perceives our membership therein in purely instrumental terms ... This approach defines our obligations qua citizens and qua community members as 'exchanges for monetizable gains', and thus commodifies both our citizenship and our membership in local communities.
>
> (Dagan 2011, p.45)

8.3.2 The interface of property norms and community

Another perspective on property and community is provided by the study of the implications of community norms on property. This scholarship sees community as a dynamic force, a tectonic-like plate that ceaselessly impacts on the content and boundaries of property rights. The intimacy inherent to this constant interaction pushes ever closer to the crossover point where community and property converge, where the colliding plates become an undifferentiated amalgam. This can be seen when the values of community become the values of property. For example, Dagan citing the heterogeneous reality of property identifies a number of property values, including autonomy, personhood, utility and *community* (Dagan 2011, pp.46–47).[9] Joseph Singer and Kevin Gray, among others,[10] have written widely on the relationship between community norms and property. Their scholarship reveals a fleeting snapshot of community; seen in the imprint it leaves on the contours of an owner's property rights. Their theoretical perspective is formative; community norms define the parameters of property rights; they presume the rightful owners of property entitlements, the legitimacy of their entitlements, and the effects of any externalities, harmful or self-regarding.

Kevin Gray's community of queuers is a micro-example of this interface, a 'self-help community' with two overarching aims, progress 'toward(s) a common goal, and in a shared commitment to make the [waiting line] environment ... more bearable' (Gray 2010, p.192). Social norms regulate the practice of queuing; such as entitlements of order, sanctions against pushing in, excusing temporary time-out absences or permitting the trading of places. An individual queuer's proprietary entitlement is based on time and place – a 'mobile estate' in land – which derives its coherency and enforceability through time's effluxion. While Gray's observations are consistent with *external* norms influencing the content of property rights, they also go further, speaking to a coalescence of (private) property and community arising from the generation of insider duties each queuer owes to others in the line, where 'the private property of each queuer mutates, subtly and indistinguishably, into a community of peace, order and good government' (ibid., p.192).

Singer and Gray are largely optimistic about the beneficial values of community on property. This optimism aligns with other scholars who write of the aspirational effect of community on property. Margaret Davies' desire for a 'more modern relational understanding of property,' is one that 'concerns individuals *and* communities: how they are formed, how they live together, and how they use their resources' (Davies 2007, p.2). Eric Freyfogle's hope for property is a 'community, or ecological vision that ... protects lands and communities while encouraging lasting ties between people and places' (Freyfogle 2003, p.133). Elsewhere, Freyfogle advocates for context and connectivity across the disciplines of property, ecology, and ethics, under the banner of 'Back Toward Community' (Freyfogle 2007, p.108).

8.3.3 The progressive perspective

Progressive property theorists are located across the divide on the property and community spectrum. For progressive property, community is centre-stage. Indeed, property and community are so intertwined that they cannot be separated. Gregory Alexander's 'sorely under-theorized' social-obligation norm (Alexander 2009, p.745) depends on a commitment to human flourishing within viable communities, places where an individual's capacity to become fully socialized and live well-lived lives is enabled. Community is an ontological concept that 'views the individual and community as mutually dependent' (Alexander and Penalver 2009a, p.129).

The connections between human flourishing, community and property are (like progressive property) pluralistic and incommensurable. Their inter-connectivity is such that each constitutive element becomes inextricably dependent on, and bound to the other. Hence 'to do well and to fare well', we need to situate ourselves within some form of 'communal infrastructure', since 'however much we value our personal interdependence, it is quite literally impossible for a person to flourish without others' (Alexander and Penalver 2012, p.87).

> [A]s free, rational persons, we never cease to operate within and depend upon the matrix of the many communities in which we find ourselves in association. Each of our identities is inextricably connected in some sense with others with whom we are bound as members of one or typically more communities. Each of our identities is literally constituted by the communities of which we are members. Asked who we are, we inevitably talk about the communities where we were born and raised.
>
> (Alexander and Penalver 2012, p.140)

The centrality of obligation to *property* is the final interlocking piece in this incommensurable jigsaw. Property owners are obliged 'to contribute ... resources, or to share ... property in order to sustain th[e] social matrices' (ibid., p.95) that make human flourishing possible. In small communities, the contribution may be voluntary or co-operative, but in larger communities, some redistributive mechanism is required to fund adequate social infrastructure.[11] In sum, the 'essential obligations [of property] ... are to belong, to participate, and to contribute' to community (Alexander and Penalver 2009a, p.144). Alexander suggests a number of bases for obligation to others in community, including a human need as social animals, long-term self-interest, the dependence to support social networks that arises from membership of a community, or a rational acknowledgement of the universality or mutuality of a community of rights, along the lines of 'if I value my own flourishing, then I must value the flourishing of others as well' (Alexander 2009, p.769).

Penalver's 'property as entrance' analysis (2005) is an insightful contribution to property and community scholarship in the progressive tradition. In contradistinction to property as exit, property as entrance sees individuals as inherently social. Property ties people into social groups (Penalver

2005, p.1892), and by giving owners 'a stake in their communities ... reducing their mobility, and inducing them to engage more fully in community life' (ibid., p.1940). In the entrance paradigm, community provides a stability and sociability that is 'given not chosen'. To leave is to often pay a high exit cost (ibid., p.1894), incurred because individuals over time increasingly identify with, and invest in their community. The dividend of higher exit costs is however 'more robust and deeply satisfying communities' (ibid., p.1955).[12]

Robert Ellickson accepts the logic of property binding people to their community. In writing of US housing co-operatives where rights of re-sale are pre-emptively restricted to below-market rates, he observes that 'reduced owner-occupant turnover may enhance solidarity among the co-operative's households' (Ellickson 2008, p.58). Elsewhere, he foreshadows the progressive tenet that communities are essentially involuntary (Ellickson 1998). In Chapter 3, a shareholder in co-operative owned land in northern NSW echoes Ellickson's solidarity and links to community, noting that their share's inalienability means 'we don't waste time wondering if we would be better off living somewhere else ... we have a commitment to place and community' (Metcalf 1995, p.52).

The progressive interlocking of property and community through human flourishing is crucible-like in its mutual self-reinforcement. It yields a composite characterized by the indivisibility of its once separate parts, a circularity that Penalver speaks to (Penalver 2009, p.870). Conversely, the weakness of a theory that is pluralist and incommensurable is its indeterminacy. Proponents argue that progressive property represents a 'lived experience of moral choice', and rather than being a weakness, indeterminacy is its strength (Alexander and Penalver 2012, pp.98–9101). Critics such as Jane Baron counter that progressive property is simply a conversation about human flourishing, common decency and democratic governance, which fails to send strong enough signals about property rights (Baron 2010).[13] Dagan intimates that it is overly utopian, and fails to satisfactorily account for an individual's need to satisfy preferences. He is specifically critical of progressive theory's insistence on involuntary membership of community.

8.3.4 Conclusion

The continuum metaphor illustrates the expansive array of property and community interaction. At one end, a neo-liberal nihilist view rejects any conception of community. People are autonomous individuals and their property ownership involves nil consideration of community. Further along the spectrum, anaemic versions of community manifest only as an optional consequence of voluntary personal choice. Property is a unidirectional exit from community. More robust conceptions of community accept that investments in community may be longer-term, involve degrees of reciprocity, and that satisfaction of personal choices can also be measured by non-commodity values. Where community norms inform the contours of property rights, the relationship between the two is necessarily close, and their location on the spectrum adjacent. And furthest from the neo-liberal perspective, theories of progressive property inextricably meld community and property through the medium of human flourishing. Along this spectrum, community changes from incidental backdrop to intrinsic context, and the role of property spins on its axis from exit to entrance to community.

8.4 Alternative disciplinary perspectives on property in land and community

As section 3 observes, apart from progressive property, most property theories see community as instrumentalist. It exists to serve welfare-enhancing individuals, or to shape the contours of property rights. Section 4 considers other disciplinary insights into property's relationship with community, principally those of legal geographer Nicholas Blomley. The part is structured around three perspectives that challenge the 'totalizing and individualizing' private ownership model. The first *maps* distinct property patterns to place and rejects as inadequate, detached representations of space devoid of particularity and inter-connectivity. The second argues that communities are sites of property *contest*, historical and ongoing, that define a community through each conflict. The third sees property as a series of ceaseless *performances* that individually and collectively constitute community by their reiterative *doing*. Mapping, contest, and performance are very different ways of seeing property in community. Each sees property as contextual, each has an ontological view of community, and each is empathetic to the idea that property diversity may be an entrance to community in ways oppositional to property uniformity being its exit.

8.4.1 Communities are maps of property diversity

The truism that 'context is everything' (Holder and Harrison 2002) is not a universal one for property. Indeed, the reverse is more accurate; the nature of modern property in land is abstract and placeless, 'divorced from the specificities and bonds of place and community' (Blomley 1994, p.53). Blomley identifies at the heart of the Anglo common-law of property a conscious disembodiment of property from context, a 'project' crafted by common lawyer Edward Coke in the eighteenth century that silenced plurality and led to the 'creation of a unitary legal map in which diverse local knowledges of the law were immediately suspect' (Blomley 2002, p.25).

Blomley challenges this historical 'project', tracing the 'shared complicities' of real property and cartography that conjointly erased context and diversity from the geography of contemporary communities (Blomley 1994, pp.67–105; also Whatmore 2002, p.211). While the common law was systematically homogenizing property, Blomley identifies a simultaneous 'cartographic sea change' that caused a 'profound change in social scale' from the local to the national and supra national (Blomley 1994, p.83). The combined effect was to institutionalize a 'displacement of the locus of social identity', (ibid., p.80) such that maps came to represent space as 'an objectified and asocial entity to which only the cartographer ha[d] special access' (ibid., p.91). Maps lost their 'sensuous and tactile nature' (ibid.) and became 'emptied of all the complexities and particularities that give meaning on the ground' (ibid., p.68). For property, this complicity resulted in its *alienation*, in both its sense of estrangement from place, and its capacity for commoditized disposal.

Blomley contests the paradigmatic spatial–legal map by suggesting an alternative map that rejects the former's objectified form. Drawing such a map is dependent on different spatial representations, 'alternative accounts of law, space, and social life' as well as understanding the 'contingencies, fractures, and conflicts' by which the abstracted map came to dominate (ibid., p.105).

Blomley uses the modern global city to disrupt the ubiquitous private ownership model, and supplant it with an alternative that acknowledges that cities are *terra populi,* (Blomley 2004, p.55), populated by distinctive communities with unique local practices and 'local knowledge' (ibid., p.56).[14] He argues it is unnecessary to 'unsettle the city' by resorting to precedents from First Nation or Third World legal systems. 'The shock that the "world is a various place" is profound given that we need not look abroad to find legal difference ... Local legal cultures closer to "home" are doubly unsettling' (ibid., p.57). Blomley fleshes out his 'unsettling' city map with a case study of the Downtown Eastside precinct in Vancouver, British Columbia. He cites community claims to an abandoned department store, struggles against gentrification and over-development, community claims to ownership of a small neighbourhood park, and the spread of garden encroachments into urban blight, as exemplars of how competing and unorthodox property can be mapped to specific place. Blomley concludes that 'a closer examination of urban property reveals a greater diversity of possibilities than the map suggests ... The ownership model however invites us to overlook or ignore these other estates' (ibid., p.22), 'to gloss over the plurality of "legitimate" claims and interests in land' (ibid., p.18).

Blomley posits that ironically the true map of urban property is revealed by default, through gaps on conventional city maps. This is unsurprising, given that real property has a negative relation with place (Blomley 2002, p.17) that renders 'localization and heterogeneity' invisible (Blomley 2004, p.79). He reasons that the primary purpose of cartographic mapping is to arbitrate, not record, determining not so much 'what is property', but what to *count* as property (ibid., p.15). To accurately capture the social intricacies of city life, diverse property must be re-embedded into its fragmented locality. Blomley exhorts that maps of such multiple geographies should not be ignored. 'In large part these maps have not been documented in critical scholarship. This is not because they are absent but because no one has looked for them' (Blomley 1994, p.54).

Paul Carter is one scholar who has looked for such a 'map'. Carter questions why 'our representations of the world have become so hard and dry', and why we treat as authoritative, maps that contain 'no trace of the knower' (Carter 2009, pp.5, 8). Like Blomley, Carter blames Enlightenment geography, arguing that '[t]he rectilinear grid imposed on the earth's surface ... ha[s] no connection to the lie of the land- and in a sense, no interest in it' (ibid., p.80). Carter contrasts modern maps with the maps of Australian Aboriginal artists, especially those of the Western desert school, which first come to prominence in the early 1970s.

> The Western Desert painters ... felt no need to read a painting from right to left or from a standing position as presented upon a wall. A work was read from any direction, as if it were lying upon the earth, and able to be walked about ... The Papunya artists appear not to have had names for their paintings. Asked what they called them, they might reply simply ... 'mine' or 'my country'. The white reception of these paintings endowed them with an orientation.
>
> (Carter 2009, pp.127–28)

Carter concludes that lines on maps are simply 'narrow pencils of shadow ... dark mortar joining the parts of the world together.' Carter shifts the focus from what is seen to what is unseen. Radically re-orienting our perspective reveals what Carter calls 'dark writing', 'the swarm of possibilities that had to be left out when the line was taken' (ibid., p.1).

The act of *mapping* property diversity within variegated community is a direct challenge to the private ownership model, since the latter 'renders other modalities of ownership invisible. [It] leaves no space for property that is neither private nor public' (Blomley 1994, p.15). By finding that space, by entertaining the 'swarm of possibilities' left out, a fuller, and more robust picture of community appears.

8.4.2 Communities are places of property contest

The ability to see diverse property patterns in community, to notice the marginal (van der Walt 2010, pp.91–97), is heightened by an awareness of the contested nature of property in land. In the case of certain Israeli property scholars, it is the backdrop of Jewish settlements on disputed territory (Stolzenberg 2010). For South African property jurists, the contest is racial as well as conceptual, a conflict between pre- and post- apartheid articulations of property.[15] For Blomley it is the historical narrative of his childhood village in the English Home Counties, where 'enclosures in the 17th and 18th centuries swept away many traditional commoner's rights in the name of improvement and monetarization ... [and conflicts] were fought out in the [surrounding] woods, fields, and villages' (Blomley 1994, p.xxii). By contrast, the traditional, settled view of property in land as ordered and peaceful is a stable and uncontested monotone. Ongoing contest, Blomley's 'resistant re-mapping', seems an important sub-text to property diversity.

Blomley extends his eighteenth-century agrarian analogy to the modern city, comparing the contextualized plurality of pre-enclosure England with the heterogeneity of urban place (Blomley 2004, p.79). Yet the city is more than an analogue, it is a contemporary iteration of an ongoing contest, part of a continuum - the historical resistance against the loss of the commons. Eighteenth-century commoners are now the twenty-first's marginalized and poor, who struggle to 'carve out a right to [urban] place' (ibid., p.xix). Where private interests prevail over the collective, not only is community property displaced, it also 'appropriates and encloses. It turns a collective interest into an individualized one' (Blomley 2008, p.316). Further, it is a contest that seems destined to continue, at least in less affluent neighbourhoods like Vancouver's Downtown Eastside that contest the assumption that property is settled and peaceful (Blomley 1994, p.54).

Contest also occurs across different planes of understanding. Not only is it a conflict between private and collective forms of property; it is a more profound struggle over the meaning and ultimate form of modern property. Thus, at one level, planning disputes over gentrification conceal conflicts between individual property rights and localized community ownership: '[C]ontemporary development contentions often pit the developer-owner's private property against the community's common property' (Blomley 2008, p.317). At the macro level however, the contest thrown up by property diversity is a direct challenge to the hegemony of property's central logic. Private property must continue to police and sanction its own property relationships, and at the same time, discredit public and communitarian alternatives. To concede once is to condone the enactment of alternative claims in land, one lost battle that is a portent of a lost war, 'the possibility, perhaps even the inevitability, of rearticulations of property' (Blomley 1994, pp.18–19).

Seeing property as *contest* is to recognize that the dominant iteration of property is far from settled. Where there is a focus on dissent, the diversity of property, and its links to community, manifest.

8.4.3 Property in community is performed

The idea of property as *performance* has arisen through the influence of geographers, such as Yi-Fu Tuan, who define place as a metaphor for stopping, resting and becoming involved. 'Enclosed and humanized space is place. Compared to space, place is a calm center of established values' (Tuan 1977, p.54). Yet, despite the images of rest and contemplation, the idea of becoming involved encompasses connectivity and constant practice. 'Places need to be understood as sites that are connected to others around the world in constantly evolving networks which are social, cultural, and natural. Places need to be understood through the paths that lead in and out' (Cresswell 2004, p.43). And once aligned with such networks, place must be constantly affirmed through reiteration, quotidian social practices that make and re-make. The need for constant practice therefore means that place is never finished, it is a perpetual work in progress.

As discussed in chapters 4 and 7, performance theory challenges the notion that property is a prior state of affairs (Blomley 2013, p.36). *Doing* does not merely describe or represent property, but doing *enacts* it. Geographers use performance theory to constitute place. Tim Cresswell argues that 'places are never established. They only operate through constant and reiterative practice – place is made and remade on a daily basis' (Cresswell 2004, pp.38–39). Blomley says that where performance theory is applied to property, it challenges the modalities of the ownership model that legitimizes only two temporal moments, the initial creation of property, and any subsequent transfer(s) of title. Instead, time is always important, as performance belongs in the constant acts of doing. 'Property depends on a constant doing. The enactment of property ... entails various forms of continuing persuasive practice' (Blomley 1994, p.22). This constancy of performance also has a citational effect, as over time, one successful act compels another through the sheer incrementalism of precedent (Blomley 2013, p.40).

Performances of property are not always positive, or optimistic. They may constitute a new community that displaces or dispossesses an earlier one, such as Stolzenberg's Jewish settlements on disputed Palestinian territory. The performance of these altered facts on the ground 'transform[s] de facto possession into de jure reality' (Stolzenberg 2010, p.113), the goal to create new communities with such an entrenched land memory that they cannot be uprooted. Such non-innocent performances underscore the negative, exclusionary realities of community previously described.

Good or bad, if property is *doing*, it becomes intimately contextual, rooted to its places of performance, its sometimes flawed community. *Doing* is the antithesis of detached objectivity, 'grounded in its locally lived experience' (Blomley 1994, p.55). Whether mapped, contested or performed, what Blomley calls 'alternative landscapes of property' offer new ways of seeing and explaining property in community. Their effect is to unsettle the tension between abstraction and 'grounded materiality' (ibid., p.55) and the paradigmatic premise upon which property uniformity is built.

8.5 Why is property, and property diversity, important to community?

Property as exit from community exerts a powerful normative force. As section 2 illustrates, it obfuscates how community is defined. Section 3 argues that it relegates legal theories that explain property and community interaction to the spectral margins. And as section 4 exemplifies, it takes alternative, extra-legal perspectives on property in community to make sense of what occurs on the ground.

Jeremy Waldron epitomized the brutality of property as exit in his writing about America's homeless in the 1990s. Waldron was critical of decisions made by city authorities that restricted access by homeless people to public spaces such as parks, footpaths and public toilets. Such demonization of the homeless rendered them 'property-less', denying them space to undertake basic human functions such as sleeping, eating or urinating. Waldron argues a group in a community who bears all the restrictions of property, but none of its benefits, is 'less free' than others. His simple observation that 'everything that has to be done, has to be done somewhere' (Waldron 1991, p.296) reveals a profound truism about property and its delineations of community. Property polices, in bounded space, where people belong, and where they do not. Property and community seem forever exclusive of each other when the former is calibrated as the latter's exit.

Yet, despite this seeming inevitability, property's relationship to community does not go unremarked. Kevin Gray opines that '[t]here is no community on earth without some concept of property' (Gray 2010, p.192). To Alexander and Penalver, 'systems of property are always at the creation of some community. Whenever we discuss property, we are unavoidably discussing the architecture of community and the individual's place within it' (Alexander and Penalver 2009a, p.128).

This section agrees that property is central to community. But this centrality is overlooked when property is seen through the private ownership prism. By contrast, property diversity has the potential to re-set this default. Its potential lies in the fact that property diversity, and its balance of property values, not only reflects the ground-level 'truth' of community; it also shapes and determines its contours (Dagan, 2011).

The flaw with the ownership model's sketch of community is that it is simplistic and under-developed, revealed as incomplete by Blomley's multiple gaps. These absences include not only the inconvenient patchworks of public and common spaces scattered amidst the private estate, but also the unorthodox property claims of community, and the physicalized implications of private property's social and communitarian values. To see beyond the private model is to recognize the concealed property patterns that suddenly materialize, that reveal a pluralistic, inter-connected and proportionate landscape of community; private, public and communal. To see property in the diversity of its accepted and eclectic forms is to establish (and maintain) an infrastructure that is 'the medium [for] the material and metaphorical embodiment of community' (Brown 2008, p.335). To borrow a metaphor from Hanoch Dagan, property diversity is 'a complex piece of music with full orchestration'; its alternative is 'looking only at a melody line [that] risks missing most of the performance' (Dagan 2011, p.72).

Section 5 canvasses a number of implications of property diversity for community. The list is not exhaustive. First, it highlights that property diversity and community are complementary, that the architecture of community is moulded by the heterogeneity of property. Second, it observes the 'normative mosaics' that are a corollary to each re-drawn map of diverse property. Normative mosaics not only reflect a community's localized balance of property values, but they are also in turn constitutive of each community. Third, it creates a theoretical space for community in an otherwise barren liberal binary worldview. Fourth, it explains the relevance and reveals the unrealized potential of what Andreas van der Walt calls property's 'eclectic marginality'. And fifth, it gives physicalized context to a variety of performances that collectively constitute and give meaning to community. The import of these implications lie in their joint and several abilities to make clearer, and in the process, normalize, the links between property and community.

8.5.1 Facts on the ground: a community's architecture

A snapshot of any community in Blomley's 'intensely propertied' city, reveals the latent presence of property diversity (Blomley 2004, pp.15, 22). Communities comprise a patchwork of private, public and common lands that adjoin, interconnect, overlap and compete. As well as being its faithful representation, property diversity is community's embedded architecture. Property patterns create, maintain and enforce the structure of private, public and community spaces that make up a city or town, and the hybrid zones that exist at its margins.[16] Such patterns determine formally and informally 'who is allowed to be where', and who is not (Waldron 2009, p.296).[17]

This pluralistic image accords with 'the lived experience of property' (Dagan 2011), the mix of property institutions that reflect an infinite multiplicity of human relations and physical contexts. Indeed, Dagan suggests that it if we were to start afresh with a blank slate, it would be extraordinary if property were conceived as a formless, context-free bundle of rights. Rather, property rights should vary according to the 'categories of social settings' and the 'categories of resources' in which it is situated (Dagan 2010, p.48).

To deny the patency of such facts on the ground is in Blomley's words 'geographical nonsense, [an] anti-geography' that fails to contend with 'the complex spatiality and the "place-boundedness" of society' (Blomley 2004, p.53). He says that property should conform to its geographic and structural diversity. To do otherwise is to stubbornly persist with the counterfactual. It would also condone a taking. For if property is theft, as Proudhon suggests, then Blomley's riposte is:

> The larceny entails that of the diversity (and perhaps the radical potential) of property ... Cities are sites in which people live inside the ownership model, but also depart from it. Collective claims to land and space are made. And private property turns out to be a good deal more multivalent, both ethically and analytically, than is supposed.
>
> (Blomley 2004, p.15)

Amnon Lehavi likewise prefers the truthfulness of facts on the ground, where communities are given form and structure as a panoply of property type.

> The lives of communities necessarily involve the full range of property regimes, including private, public, common, open access, and mixtures of these forms, as well as informal modes of resource control and management. This richness is not only a matter of fact, but also has normative merit.
>
> (Lehavi 2013, pp.153–54)

8.5.2 Normative diversity: a plurality of property values

Lehavi's second observation of 'normative merit' speaks to another implication of property diversity and community, the richness of diverse social values that arises from heterogeneity. Private, public and common property is each grounded in different, often complementary, social values (Dagan 2013, p.262). And not only is property 'deeply involved in our social values, [it] reflects them, and at times even participates in their formation' (ibid., p.4). When mapped across community, each property type therefore contributes proportionately to an infused aggregate that is both reflective and constitutive of the community in question.

The values and ideals of common and public property have been traversed in earlier chapters, the likes of sociability, 'pedestrian democracy' (Gray 2010a), and shared moderation of resource use. By contrast, the values of private property are typically individualistic and exclusive (Balganesh 2012), the seeming antithesis of community. However, as discussed in chapter 4, private property also has overlooked social and communitarian dimensions, a vindication of individual independence (*personal autonomy*), a commitment to personal identity (*personhood*), and the aggregate welfare of *community* (Dagan 2006, pp.18, 29, 30). These values do not diminish private property, but rather enhance it, by playing a 'crucial role in supporting diverse forms of interpersonal interaction and thus diverse forms of human flourishing' (ibid., p.33).

For Freyfogle, the links between private property and its normative values are explained by historical context. He argues that private property only makes sense where it serves or promotes the *public good*. Thus, its legitimacy depends on the rules of private property reflecting prevailing societal values (Freyfogle 2007a, pp.20, 25–26). Until the late nineteenth century, private property conformed to *settled* agrarian values, where quiet enjoyment, a qualified freedom from unreasonable interference, was its core rationale. This then shifted to an aggressive, industrial view, 'a right to halt physical invasions of space' (ibid., p.56), that matched a new priority, maximizing the exploitation of land. Freyfogle yet again detects a shift in the early twenty-first century, where the public good may be served by private property reflecting emerging ecological and environmental values (Freyfogle 2003, p.133). Freyfogle inserts community into this new value paradigm. 'For private property to serve contemporary society it needs to move in … the direction of community, responsibility and social connection' (ibid., pp.279–80). The valorized *public good* of private property in this century may be its meaning for community.

A multivalent private estate, combined with the norms of public and common property, produces a rich and variable mosaic of property values. Its variability depends on the property mix in each community; the end composition being what Dagan terms a '*local balance* of property values' (Dagan 2010, p.48). 'Local' implies a bounded place that shares degrees of social commonality, while 'balance' refers to the *relative proportion* of one property value vis-à-vis others. In practice, the most likely balance is the ratio of private values to public and community ones.

One logical enquiry that flows from local balance is the implications of imbalance. To adapt another Dagan proposition,[18] the relative proportions or degree of the mix may influence how individual communities constitute (and thereby see) themselves. Kunstler's study of the decline of America's cities tangentially touches upon this issue of relative mix. Kunstler blames a multitude of factors for urban decay; the car, the rise of ubiquitous shopping malls, and so on. He also singles out the decline of public property, which he attributes to a post World War II phenomenon that is 'an extreme individualism of property ownership'. This perversity 'tends to degrade the idea of the public realm … the landscape tissue that ties together the thousands of pieces of private property' that constitute a community (Kunstler 1993, pp.26–27). Moreover, lack of public property leads to isolation, disconnection, and ennui (ibid., p.14). Re-introducing more public property however provides 'decent public spaces that bring people together into casual face-to-face contact' and overcomes the monotony of private values that are redolent of sameness and intolerant of diversity. Property diversity has the capability to make our communities more interesting, to provide 'odd little corners for people with odd little lives' (ibid., p.260). Sheryll Cashin likewise draws this link. In 1950, she cites that over 70 per cent of metropolitan Americans lived in central cities: 'As a consequence ... city residents used and competed for the same public institutions – city schools, parks, transportation, and city hall. Common public institutions were a unifying force for a heterogeneous urban polity' (Cashin 2000, pp.1991–92). But by 1990, over 60 per cent lived in suburbs dominated by private property. For Kunstler and Cashin, recalibrating the property mix to accentuate a viable public estate may mean that 'Americans can have a decent public life, [and] redress the extreme privatization of life in postwar suburbia' (Kunstler 1993, p.262).

Georgette Poindexter argues that one implication of property imbalance is an unhealthy idolatry of private property, seen in the suburban deification of the manicured front lawn.

> The maniacal attention to lawn along the 'fenceless state' of suburbia can be used as a metaphor for the tension between the individual right to private property and the social interconnectedness of all property. It begs the question: who owns your front lawn - you or your neighborhood?
>
> (Poindexter 2002, p.204)

The effective privatization of public road verges eviscerates the public interest in that land (ibid., p.205), and in its imbalanced place, private idolatry flourishes.

Disproportionate private imbalance tends to diminish community (Franzese 2002).[19] Practically, it impairs a community's self-image and discourages civic participation (Roseland 2009, p.141). Normatively, it elevates the individualistic values of private property (its commodity or exclusionary tendencies), and ignores its other less visible communitarian values. It relegates the public and common estates to the margins (Ellickson 2010),[20] and vigorously resists public encroachment.[21] Imbalance is by its nature a one-sided drawing of community, an incomplete map that empowers private insiders, and consigns non-private outsiders to Paul Carter's 'dark writing'. Private imbalance may explain why Jeremy Waldron cynically concludes that 'inclusive community' is an oxymoron.

8.5.3 Locating community in property theory

A third implication of property diversity is the theoretical space it creates for community. In so doing, property diversity potentializes a pre-liberal paradigm, where intermediate entities (such as community) may be conceivably interposed between the state and an individual. In this way, it addresses the existential dilemma that community confronts.

Property diversity achieves this because it countenances that there are more property types than the dominant liberal ownership model allows. Property diversity frays the hermetic tidiness of any owner/non-owner, or private–public divide, essential to the liberal paradigm.

Property diversity also better explains the nature and importance of community. Liberal views stress the primacy, autonomy, and isolation, of the individual, and by association, their private property. 'The self is ... innate, and is not even constituted partially, by relationships with community' (Blomley 1994, p.205). At best, community is seen as a voluntary association, an entity into which rational actors periodically choose to enter and/or exit to maximize their welfare, or enhance their personal choice. Community is thus instrumental and incidental. The only compellable relationship an individual has is with the state, and because of this compulsion, it is viewed with suspicion. But as Alexander and Penalver note, such a binary worldview is unsatisfactory since it impoverishes our understandings of community (Alexander and Penalver 2010, p.xxii).

Carol Rose understatedly observes that 'the common law tradition is not entirely friendly to group [property] rights' (Rose 2006, p.13), and like Blomley, she says this is despite the evidence. While intermediate collective property is 'all around us', it is 'relatively little noticed' (Rose 2000, p.484). Rose attributes this myopia to a convergence of many factors, including 'the powerful libertarian appeal of individual property', where the unrestrained individual is 'free from intrusion' (ibid.). In such a realm there is no constraint of community; indeed there is no community.

The squeezing out of community and the creation of a vacant theoretical space between the autonomous individual and the regulatory state is evidenced historically by the decline of the corporate city, and with it, its collective status and power. Blomley (2004) and Gerald Frug (1980) each offer an account as to why city power declined in their respective home countries. Their consistent theme is a liberal hostility towards decentralized power, those entities intermediate between the state and the individual. Blomley traces the decline of 'the localized and particularized privileges of the medieval city' to the quashing of trade and mercantile monopolies in the early seventeenth century (Blomey 2004, pp.100–1). Frug explains that early US cities lost their 'considerable autonomy and agency' when two categories of corporation were created in the eighteenth century, one public and the other private. The public corporation was seen as an entity identified with the power-wielding state, and therefore suspect, while the private corporation was a rights-holder. The separation of power and rights between public and private corporations was problematic for the city, Frug argues, because once the rights enjoyed exclusively by the private corporation were removed, there seemed nothing left to protect (Frug 1980, p.1108). The city shifted 'from an association promoted by a powerful sense of community and an identification with the defense of property, to a unit that threatens both' (ibid., p.1119). The city/community fell between the poles of the autonomous individual and the consolidating power of the nation-state, (Blomley 2004, p.108). As a result 'the legal universe [became] at once totalizing and individualizing' (ibid., p.102), emptied of community.

As discussed, recent property and community scholarship suggests that this liberal view may be unravelling. Property diversity is consistent with this trend, one where community re-discovers its synergies with older notions of property in land that are specific and local, rather than placeless and universal.

8.5.4 The eclecticism or marginality of property

A fourth implication of property diversity for community is its enabling of alternative conceptions of property in land beyond strictly enforceable right. To be open to *difference* is to reveal a prolific array of practices, norms and claims that define people's diverse and heterogeneous relationships with land. Such claims include collective property 'rights' being enforced by community, or the notion that a person's sense of belonging is somehow proprietorial. Recognizing the marginal or eclectic is a start to seeing property as something that 'potentially brings a community together, rather than that which separates it into exclusive units' (Davies 2007, p.127). Blomley sees the telltale signs of (an otherwise amorphous) community through its unorthodox claims to collective property. Locked out by the liberal paradigm, community nonetheless finds voice, and importantly form, when it asserts such alternative claims. Property diversity shifts focus from the all-consuming narrative of private property, and countenances the radical possibility of community, including its marginalized, having discernible interests in land.

Marginal property finds fertile ground in activist dissent, advocated by 'property outlaws' who 'offer a view of property law as a dynamic institution ... broadly reflective of evolving community values as opposed to a fixed set of natural entitlements' (Penalver and Katyal 2010, p.15). Blomley's property outlaws are the poor of Vancouver's Downtown Eastside, who collectively make claim to a disused department store, Woodwards, as community space. Their 'property' claims are framed in eclectic terms:

> This interest is a collective one – note the frequent invocation of 'us' – and also a clearly localized one. This property interest in Woodward's, moreover, is not one of alienation or transfer. It cannot be monetarized but is, rather, predicated on use, occupation, domicile and inherent need.
>
> (Blomley 2004, p.52)

Being open to the eclectic counters an unswerving tendency to be narrow and unreflective in our thinking about property. Margaret Davies says this is desirable. The post-enclosure 'dominant idea of private property' should be 'resisted, challenged or reconceptualized' wherever possible (Davies 2007, pp.115–16). One such strategy involves 'constructing different concepts of property and/or rediscovering non-private forms of ownership from Western legal history' (ibid., p.117). As this indicates, Davies sees alternative property in both ancient and modern forms. She cites the Countryside and Rights of Way Act 2000 as a statutory re-enactment of the former. A manifestation of the latter is a community's contemporary interest in heritage, a shift from erstwhile class-ridden ideas about stately homes, to 'community-based intangible heritage', (ibid., p.128), and a democratic and inclusive version of the collective interest in living streetscapes or communities (ibid., p.130). Davies draws the link between property diversity and community. She sees it as means to break down atomistic private ownerships into a wider network of property types that brings community together through connectivity.

Amnon Lehavi's 'local public commons' is an example of marginal property that facilitates community cohesion (Lehavi 2004). 'Local public commons' are 'modest' public lands ostensibly owned by local governments (parks, playgrounds, or swimming pools) that are claimed and controlled by residents in close proximity to the resource. Lehavi analyses the factors that make successful local public commons work, identifying a neighbourhood intimacy that allows frequent users to become acquainted, and develop 'a limited level of reciprocal norms of "contribution in return for use"' (Lehavi 2004, p.47). Those outside the immediate area rarely use such commons, either because of the cost of commuting, or the availability of similar local commons elsewhere. Similarly, Blomley attributes collective local ownership to two factors; a history of use and habitation, and a local landscape that is achieved through collective action or political struggle (Blomley 2001, p.124).

Avitil Margalit's concept of *property as belonging* is yet another example of the potential for property diversity to enhance community. Margalit describes the interest of a community of fans in a football club as a *social interest* in property, derived in part from the multiple meanings of 'belonging'.

> Something 'belongs' when it is an attribute or a part of a person or thing ... to belong means to be a member of a group or an organization. [B]elonging also denotes a property relationship.
>
> (Margalit 2009, p.223)

Davina Cooper likewise sees property in belonging to a community. Her study of property relations between students and teachers at an independent English school reflect a 'tension between the right to exclude and the norm of inclusion' (Cooper 2007, p.18). Exclusion 'depicts things and spaces as [conventional] property' while inclusion 'represents the space as property, in the sense of being constitutive of community life' (ibid.). Cooper surmises that this variegated school community only makes sense to outsiders such as herself if 'the black box of unofficial property' is opened up, and notions like belonging are placed alongside orthodox proprietorial understandings.

The marginal perspective on property is outside property's central logic. It lacks the imprimatur of formal legal standing or rights status. It is concerned with individualized context, not universal principle. But it is identifiable to those that seek it, enacted by diverse performances, and occasionally vindicated. It even possesses a certain doctrinal logic.

> It will tend to look for the paradox and the contradiction rather than for broad theory and grand narrative, for diversity rather than uniformity, for dissent rather than consensus, for conflict and chaos rather than consent and order.
>
> (van der Walt 2010, p.100)

Seeing the eclectic in property enables a creative bricolage with the dominant and 'oppositional ownership model' (Blomley 2004, p.23), an interaction that potentializes creativity and flexibility in our thinking about property. Diversity enables collective claims to property outside the ownership model, and as a consequence aggregates otherwise disconnected elements of community. As van der Walt counsels, 'we have to leave room for otherness, for difference' (van der Walt 2010, p.104).

8.5.5 A diversity of performance

A fifth implication of property diversity lies in the sheer variety of performances of property that occur across a community. The collective sum of this *doing* is Dagan's full orchestration of property in community, a complex harmony that correlates to the intricate patterns of property right, use and claim, ambitiously mapped by legal geographers.

Property diversity means that across community, there are many and varied enactments of property across many and varied venues. Private property has been previously traversed as created by performances as mundane as building fences, paying rates or keeping off someone else's lawn (Blomley 2013, p.33). Such performances enact and affirm the normative values of private property, privacy, commodity, and personal autonomy. On public lands, people likewise perform acts that affirm values such as sociability and inclusion, playing soccer on sports fields, hiking though national forests, or picnicking in city parks. And on common property, eligible owners assert common use rights that reinforce proportionality and shared moderation; tending community gardens, exercising membership rights in clubs or co-operatives, or using common property such as pools or tennis courts in strata schemes.

The collective narrative of property diversity is the narrative of community, a myriad of enactments that are physicalized to bounded location, and representational of sense of place. 'Owners' of diverse property, whether enforceable right, or valorized sense of belonging, perform a conception of property that is not by automatic default external to community.

8.6 Conclusion

This chapter argues that property in land and community shares a close relationship, albeit one that is not overtly recognized, defined or theorized. Property in land is both structural and constitutive of community. It reflects how community is made up. 'Maps' of property patterns in community can be detached cartographic outlines that reflect the simplicities of the private ownership model. Or, as Blomley argues, alternative maps can be drawn that capture the eclectic, inter-connected modalities of property beyond the orthodox. Property, and its range of diverse values, is also constitutive of community, its normative measure.

Yet, routinely property is seen as 'exit' from community. Property is the private realm of autonomous, welfare-maximizing individuals. At best, community is an instrumentalist (and optional) construct that exists to serve such individuals. At worst, narrow private values eviscerate community. The significance of property diversity lies in its potential to recalibrate this property as 'exit' default. As section 5 canvasses, property diversity has many implications for community. It tells its geographic truth and conforms to its structure, it yields commensurate mosaics of property values, it finds it theoretical space, and it makes possible alternative property paradigms grounded in the real-world context of community. Property diversity helps to fill Joseph Sax's 'missing blank'.

Notes

1 By existential, I mean formal legal status (see for example Sax 1984a, p.506). By normative, I mean the values of community.

2 Sax argues that authentic communities should not be viewed as museum pieces, and need to adapt to changing circumstances (1984b). Cf. 'totem objects designed to convince us that we live in a thing called *community*' (Kunstler 1993, p.123).

3 Lehavi uses the example of Israeli Kibbutzim (Lehavi 2013).

4 By covenants, rules, and restrictions (CRR), also known as by-laws, in condominium or strata schemes.

5 Blomley's scholarship is described as 'agenda-setting' in a 2014 historical review of legal geography (Braverman et al. 2014, p.5).

6 This interpretation is also problematic for geographers because it synonymizes 'place' with 'community' (Doreen Massey cited in Cresswell 2004).

7 Lehavi focuses on territorial communities because of the effects of physical proximity, closer ties, and repeat encounters (Lehavi 2009, p.49).

8 The idea of households 'moving with their feet' to more enticing communities is attributed to Charles Tiebout (Ellickson 1982, pp.1547–54).

9 Elsewhere Dagan writes that 'a responsible conception of property can and should appreciate ... virtues of the market norms, but should still avoid allowing these norms to override those of the other spheres of society' (Dagan 2007, p.1260).

10 Other communities where norms inform property rights include surfers (Nazer 2004), ranchers, (Ellickson 1993), or university campus food cart owners (Duhl 2006).

11 In the case of private property, 'special obligations accompany private ownership of those aspects of a society's infrastructure upon which the civic culture depends' (Alexander and Penalver 2012, p.182).

12 Blomley speaks similarly of people using property to 'anchor themselves to community' (Blomley 2004, p.156).

13 Baron's criticisms have wider implications, specifically the 'propertiness' of entitlements to 'well-lived lives', a concept central to progressive property theory. The extent to which such rights are more political than legal is moot, particularly where progressive proponents articulate such ideas through an American political prism.

14 Blomley says that property law is a form of local knowledge (Blomley 2004, p.56).

15 Van der Walt writes of a property law curriculum taught in law schools that was/is relevant to privileged white residential areas and business only, compared to the property law of much of the black majority.

16 'Property law is like a language that direct[s] the shapes of physical spaces' (Rose 2006, p.3).

17 'Property rights are based partly on formal documents of title ... and partly on expectations that grow from informal arrangements such as long-standing possession, a course of dealings, oral statements, informal understandings, personal relationships, social practices and customs of the trade' (Singer 2000, pp.45–46).

18 'Property, is deeply involved in our social values, reflects them, and at times even participates in their formation' (Dagan 2012, p.4).

19 'Post-industrial changes eviscerated many pre-determinants of community' and 'prior to the 20th century phenomena of industrialization and urbanization, sense of community was a natural part of life' (Franzese 2002, p.565).

20 Such 'marginality' is remarkable where 'open-access public streets and parks' represent up to one-third of an American city's landmass (Ellickson 2010, p.1026).

21 Opposition to public paths or rail trails amongst adjacent private owners is

common. Landholders neighboring the Otago rail trail in New Zealand were vocal in their opposition.

References

Alexander, G 2009, 'The Social-Obligation Norm in American Property Law', *Cornell Law Rev.*, vol. 94, 745–819.

Alexander, G and Dagan, H 2012, *Properties of Property*, Aspen Publishers, New York.

Alexander, G and Penalver, E 2009, 'Properties of Community', *Theoretical Inquiries in Law*, vol. 10, 127–60.

Alexander, G and Penalver, E 2010, 'Introduction', in G. Alexander and E. Penalver (eds), *Property and Community*, Oxford University Press, New York.

Alexander, G and Penalver, E 2012, *An Introduction to Property Theory*, Cambridge University Press, New York.

Alexander, G, Penalver, E, Singer, J and Underkuffler, L 2009, 'A Statement of Progressive Property', *Cornell LR*, vol. 49, 743–44.

Balganesh, S 2012, 'Quasi-Property, Like, But Not Quite Property', *U. Pa. L. Rev.*, vol. 160, 1889–925.

Baron, J 2010, 'The Contested Commitments of Property', *Hastings L.J.*, vol. 61, 917–67.

Blomley, N 1994, *Law, Space, and the Geographies of Power*, The Guildford Press, New York.

Blomley, N 2001, 'Landscapes of Property', in N Blomley, D Delaney and R Ford (eds), *The Legal Geographies Reader*, Blackwell, Oxford.

Blomley, N 2002, 'From "What?" To "So What?" Law and Geography in Retrospect', in C Harrison and J Holder (eds), *Law and Geography: Current Legal Issues*, Oxford University Press, Oxford.

Blomley, N 2004, *Unsettling the City: Urban Land and the Politics of Property*, Routledge, New York.

Blomley, N 2008, 'Enclosure, Common Right and the Property of the Poor', *Social and Legal Studies*, vol. 17, 311–331.

Blomley, N 2013, 'Performing Property: Making the World', *Canadian Journal of Law and Jurisprudence*, vol. 26, no. 1, 23–48.

Braverman, I, Blomley, N, Delaney, D and Kedar, A 2014, 'Expanding the Spaces of Law' in I Braverman, N Blomley, D Delaney and A Kedar (eds), *The Expanding Spaces of Law: A Timely Legal Geography*, Stanford University Press, Stanford, CA.

Brown, A 2008, 'Crofter Forestry, Land Reform and the Ideology of Community', *Social & Legal Studies*, vol. 17, no. 3, 333–49.

Carter, P 2009, *Dark Writing Geography, Performance, Design*, University of Hawai'i Press, Honolulu.

Cashin, S 2000, 'Localism, Self-Interest, and the Tyranny of the Favored Quarter: Addressing the Barriers to New Regionalism', *Geo. LJ*, vol. 88, 1985–2048.

Cooper, D 2007, 'Opening up Ownership: Community Belonging, Belongings, and the Productive Life of Property', *L. & Soc. Inq.*, vol. 32, 625–64.

Cresswell, T 2004, *Place A Short Introduction*, Blackwell, Malden, MA.

Dagan, H 1999, 'Takings and Distributive Justice', *Virginia Law Review*, vol. 85, 741–804.

Dagan, H 2003, 'The Craft of Property', *California Law Rev.*, vol. 91, 1517–71.

Dagan, H 2006, 'Property and the Public Domain' *Yale Journal of Law and the Humanities,* vol. 18, 84–93.
Dagan, H 2007, 'The Social Responsibility of Ownership', *Cornell Law Review,* vol. 92, 1255–73.
Dagan, H 2010, 'Reimagining Takings Law', in G Alexander and E Penalver (eds), *Property and Community,* Oxford University Press, New York.
Dagan, H 2011, *Property, Values and Institutions,* Oxford University Press, New York.
Dagan, H 2013, 'The Public Dimension of Private Property', *Kings Law Journal,* vol. 24, 260–88.
Davies, M 2007, *Property Meanings, Histories, Theories,* Routledge, Abingdon.
Duhl, G 2006, 'Property and Custom: Allocating Space in Public Spaces', *Temple L. Rev.,* vol. 79, 199–248.
Ellickson, R 1982, 'Cities and Homeowners Associations', *University of Pennsylvania Law Rev.,* vol. 130, 1519–80.
Ellickson, R 1991, *Order Without Law: How Neighbors Settle Disputes,* Harvard University Press, Cambridge, MA.
Ellickson, R 1998, 'New Institutions for Old Neighborhoods', *Duke Law Journal,* vol. 48, 75–110.
Ellickson, R 2008, *The Household: Informal Order Around the Hearth,* Princeton University Press, Princeton.
Ellickson, R 2010, 'The Inevitable Trend Toward Universally Recognizable Signals of Property Claims', *William & Mary Bill of Rights Journal,* vol. 19, 1015–32.
Engel, D 1994, 'The Oven Bird's Song: Insiders, Outsiders and Personal Injuries in an American Community' in C Greenhouse, B Yngvesson and D Engel (eds), *Law and Community in Three American Towns,* Cornell University Press, Ithaca.
Ford, R 1994, 'The Boundaries of Race: Political Geography in Legal Analysis', *Harvard Law Rev.,* vol. 107, 1841–921.
Franzese, P 2002, 'Does it Take a Village? Privatization, Patterns of Restrictiveness and the Demise of Community', *Villanova Law Rev.,* vol. 47, 553–93.
Freyfogle, E 2003, *The Land We Share: Private Property and the Common Good,* Island Press, Washington, DC.
Freyfogle, E 2007a, *On Private Property: Finding Common Ground on the Ownership of Land,* Beacon Press, Boston.
Freyfogle, E 2007b, *Agrarianism and the Good Society: Land, Culture, Conflict and Hope,* University of Kentucky Press, Lexington.
Frug, G 1980, 'The City as a Legal Concept', *Harvard Law Rev.,* vol. 93, 1057–154.
Gardbaum, S 1992, 'Law, Politics, and the Claims of Community', *Michigan Law Rev.,* vol. 90, 685–760.
Gibson-Graham, J K 2005, 'Surplus Possibilities: Postdevelopment and Community Economies', *Singapore Journal of Tropical Geography,* vol. 26, 4–26.
Gray, K 2010a, 'Pedestrian Democracy and the Geography of Hope', *Journal of Human Rights and the Environment,* vol. 1, 45–65.
Gray, K 2010b, 'Property in a Queue', in *Property and Community,* Oxford University Press, New York, NY.
Holder, J and Harrison, C 2003, 'Connecting Law and Geography' in J Holder and C Harrison (eds), *Law and Geography,* Oxford University Press, Oxford.
Kuntsler, J H 1993, *The Geography of Nowhere: The Rise and Decline of America's Man-Made Landscape,* Simon and Schuster, New York.

Lehavi, A 2004, 'Property Rights and Local Public Goods: Toward a Better Future for Urban Communities', *The Urban Lawyer*, vol. 36, 1–98.

Lehavi, A 2009, 'How Property Can Create, Maintain, or Destroy Community, *Intellectual Inquiries in Law*, vol. 10, 43–76.

Lehavi, A 2013, *The Construction of Property: Norms, Institutions, Challenges*, Cambridge University Press, Cambridge.

Margalit, A 2009, 'You'll Never Walk Alone: On Property, Community and Football Fans', *Intellectual Inquiries in Law*, vol. 10, 217–40.

Mason, A 2000, *Community, Solidarity and Belonging: Levels of Community and their Normative Significance*, Cambridge University Press, Cambridge.

Metcalf, B 1995, *Co-operative Lifestyles in Australia: From Utopian Dreaming to Communal Reality*, UNAW Press, Sydney.

Nazer, D 2004, 'The Tragicomedy of the Surfers' Commons', *Deakin Law Rev.*, vol. 9, 655–713.

Penalver, E 2005, 'Property as Entrance', *Virginia Law Rev.*, vol. 91, 1889–1972.

Penalver, E 2009, 'Land Virtues', *Cornell Law Rev.*, vol. 94, 821–88.

Penalver, E and Katyal, S 2010, *Property Outlaws: How Squatters, Pirates, and Protestors Improve the Law of Ownership*, Yale University Press, New Haven, CT.

Poindexter, G 2002, 'Idolatry of Land', in C Harrison and J Holder (eds), *Law and Geography: Current Legal Issues*, Oxford University Press, Oxford.

Rose, C M 2000, 'Left Brain Right Brain and History in the New Law and Economics of Property', *Oregon Law Rev.*, vol. 79, 479–92.

Rose, C M 2006, 'Property and Language, or the Ghost of the Fifth Panel', *Yale Journal of Law and the Humanities*, vol. 18, 1–28.

Roseland, M 2009, *Toward Sustainable Communities*, New Society Publishers, Gabriola Island, BC.

Sax, J 1984a, 'Do Communities Have Rights? The National Parks as Laboratories of New Ideas', *University of Pittsburgh Law Rev.*, vol. 45, 499–511.

Sax, J 1984b, 'The Rights of Communities: A Blank Space in American Law', lecture at Natural Resources Law Center, University of Colorado, School of Law, July 11.

Sax, J 2011, *Ownership, Property and Sustainability*, University of Utah Press, Salt Lake City.

Singer, J 2000, *Entitlement: The Paradoxes of Property*, Yale University Press, New Haven, CT.

Singer, J 2009, 'Democratic Estates: Property Law in a Free and Democratic Society', *Cornell Law Rev.*, vol. 94, 1009–62.

Singer, J 2010, 'Property Norms Construct the Externalities of Ownership', in G Alexander and E Penalver (eds), *Property and Community*, Oxford University Press, New York.

Stolzenberg, N 2010, 'Facts on the Ground', in G Alexander and E Penalver (eds), *Property and Community*, Oxford University Press, New York.

Tuan, Y 1977, *Space and Place The Perspective of Experience*, University of Minnesota Press, Minneapolis.

van der Walt, A J 2010, 'The Marginality of Property', in G Alexander and E Penalver (eds), *Property and Community*, Oxford University Press, New York.

Waldron, J 1992, 'Homelessness and The Issue of Freedom', *UCLA Law Rev.*, vol. 39, 295–324.

Waldron, J 2009, 'Community and Property – For Those Who Have Neither', *Theoretical Inquiries in Law*, vol. 10, 161–92.

Whatmore, S 2002, 'De/Re Territorializing Possession: The Shifting Spaces of Property Rights', in C Harrison and J Holder (eds), *Law and Geography: Current Legal Issues*, Oxford University Press, Oxford.

Conclusion

This book promised in its introduction 'not to take property for granted'. It also promised 'to be attentive as to how things are *not*'. In trying to keep to these commitments, it has explored two key questions: what comprises property diversity in land, and what are (at least) some of its implications for our propertied landscapes. Its call to action is to be conscious of the myopic constraints that limit our 'seeing' of property in land. Optimally, we should be enlivened to property's imaginative possibilities. If, as Carol Rose warns that what we see is what we get, then we must be prepared to be open to the possibilities, to the seeing of something paradigmatically new, and all the implications this 'new "envisioning" may bring' (Rose 1994).

In responding to these two enquiries, this book has canvassed the literature of the private, public and common estates, property and community scholarship, and stewardship discourse. It has also reached beyond legal property scholarship in its selective review of legal geography and sustainable urban design. Its novelty lies in not only collating this literature into one body of work, but in viewing it through the prism of landed property diversity. Some of this literature is extensive, in particular that of common property or stewardship. Other literature is emergent, such as property and community. And other areas are surprisingly threadbare, of which the standout is the near vacuum of public property jurisprudence.

The book also flagged numerous concepts worthy of further study. The theoretical underpinnings of public property in land, especially the relationship of propriety to inclusion, remain underdone. Likewise, there is much scope to expand on the coincidental convergence between discernible patterns of property diversity, and the design and functioning of livable communities. Another idea meriting wider investigation is the 'mapping' of the property mosaic to specific place, reducing the complexities of diversity and inter-connectedness to pictorial form. And yet another putative project lies in the implications of 'local balances of property values' (Dagan 2013, p.274). How constitutive of community are its relative patterns of property? Does too much private property inform a community markedly different to one with extensive public or community estates?

Each line of now future enquiry has proved to be beyond the scope of this book.

Another major item of unfinished business is this question: what if the private ownership model is not an inadvertent or accidental default, but a positive normative choice? What if the atomized, property as 'exit' iteration of property in land is a conscious, societal preference? Is property diversity then reduced to an esoteric and ultimately moot exercise that seeks out 'in Canutian fashion ... property forms that buck the trend' (Blomley 2013)?

A tentative answer to this particular unfinished business is to recognize that property is likewise, and perpetually, unfinished business. As chapter 1 outlines, the idea of private property has constantly evolved. Prior to the eighteenth century, there was 'no clear and unqualified definition' of private property in any 'legal dictionary or the works of any legal writer' (Blomley 2007, p.4).

Yet by the end of the twentieth century, private property seemed unassailable. Property's meanings and dimensions ebb and flow with the tide of societal imperative. What now appears settled and appropriate – arguably the result of our present normative choices – may not be so felicitous in the future.

Performance theory suggests likewise. If property is enacted by ongoing, infinitely variable performances, there is no inevitability that these performances are locked into a closed loop. Things change. Where different performances of property make better contextual sense, analogous performances are likely to recur, and incrementally a new pattern manifests that becomes citational in its reiteration. As recent property history shows, these shifts are imperceptible, since 'every morning, as we wake up, property is – more or less – as it was when we went to bed' (Blomley 2013, p.37).

It is rare to see the precise moment when different property performances begin, except perhaps in retrospect, or through the eyes of the prescient observer. In chapter 7, the closing discussion of 'earth under the nails' chronicles the extraordinary rise of ancient and new ways of engaging with the physicality of land. Sue Farran's communitarian phenomenon may be the forerunner of some paradigm shift, or it may be a false dawn. But either way, it is testament to property's dynamism, and the dynamic of change.

If property is a series of ceaseless performances, then Blomley's 'truth versus success' critique directs us to the most important question – what sorts of performances render alternative property paradigms less marginal and thus more successful? Chapter 5 points to the thoughtful design interaction of private, public and common space, and the observable outcomes this has for sustainable human landscapes. Chapter 7 sees cross-boundary collaborations of good land use. Chapter 8 identifies performances of diverse property that find legal space for community. Indeed, this book is one such act, a written performance of an envisioning of a different property in land that challenges how we describe the so-called dominant paradigm.

The private ownership model is (mostly) our propertied reality because that is what we practice, day in, day out. It is successful because it largely *is* (Blomley 2014, p.88).[1] The extent to which it purports to tell property's 'truth', (Banner 2011) or reflects majoritarian sentiment, or conscious normative choice, is secondary to its pragmatic reality.[2] In restricting ourselves to this narrow paradigm, we have got back what we see. But this paradigm has consequences. It is abstract. It views land as commodity. It divides the world into disconnected atomized parcels. It makes adverse land use externalities 'magically vanish'. It marginalizes the communities in which we live. Stuart Banner's remark (in chapter 6) that property academics bear a certain responsibility for the rise and entrenchment of property abstraction is equally cogent for property diversity. Perhaps it is incumbent on those of us who regularly teach property law to talk less of Blackacre, of less *anywhere*, and more *somewhere.*

What does this book mean for property law? As a body of work, it is a nuanced description of a re-conceptualized property right in land that (notwithstanding its explorations of diversity's outer limits) remains grounded in the common law, and the common law jurisdictions discussed herein. However, in extolling the descriptive virtues of a wider seeing, it has institutional consequence. At one level, it deliberately sets out to break the nexus between 'property', and the reactive assumption that 'property' is only the private right. At another level, it means that the *res* matters. The thing, in this case, the land, is not simply the object of the property relationship; rather it is an integral part of it. This implication is significant because it departs from the orthodoxy that property is a unified category. If context matters for *real* property, then what does this mean for other forms of property? What is the effect of one property type diverging from the core tenet that property is not dependent on the nature of the *res*?

From the outset, this book has explicitly restricted itself to land. It has (unwittingly) taken Henry Smith's modular approach by concerning itself only with the module called 'real property'. In so doing, it has ignored extra-modular impacts. Perhaps, like Smith's metaphor, where side effects are intensely felt within the module, but have negligible impact outside, any spillover from this reconceptualization may be self-absorbed and largely self-contained. As James Karp observes, maybe land *is* fundamentally different. Yet as logic dictates, this difference does impugn the integrity of the unified category of property. This book acknowledges the irony that in looking at the broad diversity of *real* property, it has itself been myopic to consequential effects outside the module. This paradox joins the ever-expanding list of spin-off topics worthy of later writing.

If one is to sum up the take-home lesson from this book, it is this: the private ownership model is a descriptively inadequate, incomplete account of what happens on the ground. Seeing this paucity for what it is is a first, yet necessary, step in beginning to imagine the 'swarm of possibilities' that a diverse reconceptualization of property in land offers. Such a profound, yet subtle shift has implications for not only the institution of property itself, but also the propertied world in which we live. Optimistically, that can only be a good thing.

Notes

1 'Existing systems persist not because of unalterable human nature ... but because of the inertia of established habit' (Blomley 2014, p.88).

2 Banner says that 'philosophers and law professors try to discern property's true nature' but usually without success. Banner concludes that property 'is a human institution that exists to serve a broad set of purposes. These purposes have changed over time, and as they have, so too has the conventional wisdom about what property is "really" like' (Banner 2011, pp.289–90).

References

Banner, S 2011, *American Property, A History of Who, Why and What We Own*, Harvard University Press, Cambridge, MA.

Blomley, N 2007, 'Making Private Property: Enclosure, Common Right and the Work of Hedges', *Rural History*, vol. 18, 1–21.

Blomley, N 2013, 'Performing Property: Making the World', *Canadian Journal of Law and Jurisprudence*, vol. 26, no. 1, 23–48.

Blomley, N 2014, 'Learning from Larry: Pragmatism and the Habits of Legal Space', in I Braverman, N Blomley, D Delaney and A Kedar (eds), *The Expanding Spaces of Law: A Timely Legal Geography*, Stanford University Press, Stanford, CA.

Dagan, H 2013, 'The Public Dimension of Private Property', *Kings Law Journal*, vol. 24, 260–288.

Rose, C M 1994, 'Seeing Property' in *Property and Persuasion Essays on the History, Theory, And Rhetoric of Ownership*, Westview Press, Boulder, CO.

Index